Motivation and Culture

California School
Of Professional Psychology
LIBRARY

6160 Cornerstone Court East
San Diego, CA 92121-3725

Motivation and Culture

Donald Munro

John F. Schumaker

Stuart C. Carr

Editors

ROUTLEDGE
New York and London

Published in 1997 by
Routledge
29 West 35th Street
New York, NY   10001

Published in Great Britain by
Routledge
11 New Fetter Lane
London EC4P   4EE

Copyright © 1997 by Routledge
Printed in the United States of America on acid-free paper.
Book design by Charles B. Hames

Library of Congress Cataloging-in-Publication Data
Motivation and culture / eds. D. Munro, J. F. Schumaker, & S. C. Carr.
     p. cm
Includes bibliographical references and index.
ISBN 0–415–91509–0 (hardcover : alk. paper).
ISBN 0–415–91510–4 (pbk. : alk. paper).
1. Culture.   2. Motivation (Psychology).   3. Ethnopsychology.
I. Munro, Donald.   1940–   .   II. Carr, Stuart C.
III. Schumaker, John F. 1949–   .
HM101.M82   1997
155.8—dc21   96–51882
                                            CIP

Contents

Personal Values and Motives

Intercultural Exchange in the Workplace

Intrapsychic Processes

The Biology and Culture Nexus

Introduction

DONALD MUNRO

This is the part of an edited volume that some say nobody reads but that would be conspicuous by its absence. If they are right, it probably indicates that there are two types of readers: those who like to have an overview of what a book has to offer and perhaps a quick introduction to the individual chapters normally provided in journal articles by the abstract, and those who like to go straight to what the individual authors have to say in their areas of expertise. The latter group may be already lost to us at this point, though there may be some who return after having read some of the chapters to find out what the editors have to say about the significance of the whole collection. We will try to satisfy both groups, first, by giving an account of the book's reason for existence in the beginning and our view of what it says at the end, and then by reviewing each of the individual chapters.

All three of us have spent some part of our careers working in countries where the dominant culture of the mass of the population is very different from that of the people from whom we have sprung, so even if a fascination with studying foreign cultures may not have been the initial motivation for going to such places, surviving the everyday concerns of making a living, getting along with colleagues from another culture, and making sense of the political and economic events happening around us were bound to create a need to find meaning in the situations we encountered. More specifically, all three of us had worked in central and southern Africa in the period 1965 to 1995, tumultuous years in that part of the world as the previously dominant "white" foreign culture gave way to the indigenous one. As with any cultural change, this one did not happen overnight as formal political and economic control shifted. Rather, the process had already started in the early years of colonialism as the discomfort on the part of indigenous people began to become evident and as the coping abilities of the colonialists began to be tested. It persists today and will do so well into the new century and millennium as the processes work through to produce a variant of human society that we can now only imagine. We ourselves were, and continue to be, emotionally and intellectually part of and affected by social changes that may be seen clearly (or just "through a glass darkly") only in retrospect by the collective of historians, sociologists, and other social scientists whose interpretations will be dominated by constructs still to emerge in that future society.

The relationship between the political and social level, and the personal and motivational one was brought out for me (the first editor) when I moved from Zambia, then five years post-independence as an African-governed nation, to Rhodesia in 1970, then five years into the period known as "the U.D.I. years" (Unilateral Declaration of Independence by the white government from British rule). I was told at the time by colleagues who were sociologists and political scientists that I was "going against the tide of history." This insight I found rather startling then, not because it was surprising for social scientists to believe that there would be political changes in Rhodesia that would be against the traditional interests of people like me who came from Europe, but because my (conscious) motives for making the move had to do with career and family and nothing whatever to do with historical, sociological, or political goals. What I later realized was that what may be going on at the level of countries and societies and what is going on in the hearts and minds of individual people have no necessary connection with each other, and may indeed be difficult to describe within the same conceptual system, much less reconcile. The reader will find that this is one of the themes that emerge in this book.

At a more formal level the reason for the book was a growing realization that the topic of motivation has been rather poorly developed within cross-cultural psychology, and consequently answers to questions about *why* people of different cultures behave as they do (differently or similarly) are difficult to find. Wondering what to recommend as reading for a possible new course of lectures that would link motivation theory with culture, we found little of substance. One reason for this is that the topic of motivation itself has gone through a period of decline over the past twenty-five years or so, reflecting the change in the dominant theoretical models in mainstream psychology. Another personal anecdote by the first editor illustrates what happened. Invited by Marshall Segall to attend a workshop at the New York City campus of Syracuse University in 1968 for cross-cultural researchers in developmental psychology, I presented a paper based on some work in Zambia that linked early childhood intellectual and social development with mothers' encouragement of independence. This used a dominant approach to motivation at the time, based on constructs such as anxiety and achievement motivation. There, too, I was startled by being taken to task by some of the other contributors for holding onto this outdated approach instead of one based on cognition. What I had been caught up in was one of the early currents of the cognitivist revolution that spread though psychology in the following ten years, sweeping away not only naive behaviorist accounts but those based on biological and psychoanalytic foundations (and in motivation the notions of innate and learned drives).

The cognitivist approach served cross-cultural psychology well, as is evident from a reading of the 1980 *Handbook of Cross-Cultural Psychology* (Triandis et al., 1980), a six-volume monument to the success of that movement in its heyday of the 1960s and 1970s. In particular, it enabled an understanding of cultural phenomena that was much more sympathetic to indigenous interpretations than those based on supposedly universal biological, behavioral, and psychodynamic processes. But the affective in human experience tended to be neglected or to be seen through the filter of cognitive and linguistic interpretation, and with affect theory goes much of motivation theory. Sociological work has effectively shifted in the same direction, though for a different reason: the equivalent of cognitivism in psychology has been the importance of interpretation, and latterly postmodernist thought has questioned the possibility of any unified interpretation of cultural phenomena or any valid comparison between cultures. Cultural anthropologists, who continue to find value in (universalistic) psychodynamic accounts that are also seen as redundant or obsolete by mainstream psychology, are therefore left to carry the argument that emotion is an important explanatory construct for studies relating culture to individual motivation.

Our aim, then, is to begin to show how an understanding of personal motivation has something to offer our approach to culture, and by the same token that culture affects individual motives. With the wisdom given by hindsight over about a century of largely separate attempts to understand motivation and culture, we believe that we should be able to put some of the resulting findings and interpretations together. Of course, we do not believe that we are providing the final picture, if such a picture is even conceivable. Nor are we unaware that we are dominated by the concerns of our own cultural backgrounds, and our own theoretical hobbyhorses, in choosing and displaying the wares that our authors have to offer. What we have attempted to do is to collect from eminent researchers and thinkers across the world a variety of elements that need to be fitted together, or allowed to interact with one another, so that a new chemistry of motivation can emerge that does justice to culture as well as to biological, cognitive, and social dynamics. We do this in an atmosphere of growing international recognition of what cultures can teach one another, not only for engendering economically productive motives in people but for aiding the eternal human quest to understand what life is about and how happiness can be found.

Did our projected volume have a theme or themes, then, or does one emerge from the chapters that lie ahead? The reader is best left to judge the outcome, but we can say what we did and what we tried to do. We originally conceptualized three levels of analysis at which motivation and culture could be seen to relate to each other and set out to obtain varied contributions for each. These levels were (moving from the most individualistic to the most social) intrapsychic processes, interpersonal relationships, and organizational and intergroup contexts. We also envisaged a fourth section, which would look at theoretical and historical perspectives generally. Although this seemed a good idea at the time, it turned out to be somewhat difficult to fulfill, because many of the contributions we received brought out unexpected aspects of the topics. This resulted in a different way of grouping the topics, which, although not at all incompatible with the original notion of levels, provides a fresh perspective on that approach.

We provided our contributors only with the nature of the overall task: to construct a volume that would bring culture and motivation together so that each illuminated the other, and the topic or domain in which they should write, which in all cases was nominated because of their previous contributions to the literature. We did not impose any particular theoretical viewpoint and, indeed, hoped that we would receive widely divergent kinds of arguments, as we did. It therefore is particularly interesting that several contributors do seem to be wrestling with the need to take two or more levels of analysis into consideration in formulating the work in their domain. This might be an example of the zeitgeist or it might indicate an eagerness on our part to find evidence for the validity of our point of view; the reader will judge. Of course, the idea of different levels of analysis is not new, and no claims are made as to its invention; rather, we wish simply to emphasize its particular importance for a comprehensive model of the relationship between motivation and culture.

Chapter Summaries

THE first section "Theory and Concepts" (an explicitly historical account has been lost from the original section), comprises two chapters that present two very different answers to the question of how motivation and culture can be related. The first answer, which includes the notion of levels, may be seen as the more traditional of the two, in that it takes an established philosophy and applies it to the particular issue at hand; the chapter therefore is more a reminder to the reader that a clear conceptualization of both motivation and culture is required for us to be able to relate them clearly to each other, and a further reminder of how this might be done without straying outside the normal boundaries of scientific discourse. The second chapter is much more modern in its concern with how we construct motivation socially and mentally, and perhaps points more to a method of observing the relationships between motivation and culture than it does to ways of constructing or reconstructing specific theories or reinterpreting existing data.

Don Munro's chapter, "Levels and Processes in Motivation and Culture," combines the notion of levels discussed above with another type of emphasis, on action or process as the main concern of psychology rather than on the static entities or structures that still preoccupy much of our scientific community. Although psychology recognizes molecules and neurones and brains, and mental structures of ability or personality, it should give primary importance to "what is going on" inside them and, by the same argument, what is going on in groups and societies. Furthermore, what is going on is *qualitatively* different at each of these levels so we should not expect to find the processes of social interaction at the level of culture *simply* reflected in brain processes. He then argues that our main task is to relate these processes at successive levels to one another in order to understand the whole (moving) picture of biological, psychological, and social actions that we observe as cultural behavior.

Yoshi Kashima's chapter, "Culture, Narrative, and Human Motivation," addresses the question not of what motivation is or of how motivational processes are organized but of how it is internalized, and proposes that the answer lies in the universal, everyday, "world-making" business of narrative. Narrative shapes our motives by shaping our goals and the way we attain these goals, as well as our perceptions, and our ways of remembering and thinking and feeling. The link between motivation and culture is thus formed by the transformation of the collective cultural narrative into the personal, self-narrative, the individual's account of the world and his or her place in it. And just as the formation of the narrative in the culture is something that goes on without reflection by those who are part of the process, so the internal version does its work without our person consciousness.

Applying the levels construct, the book then moves to the highest or most social level of analysis with two contributions in the section "Social and Interpersonal Processes." Russell Geen and John Shea, in chapter 3, "Social Motivation and Culture," trace the changing conceptions of how the social group impacts apparently directly on the behaviors of individuals in two opposite ways: social facilitation of action and social loafing. The first of these has been studied for much longer, and explanatory theories have gone through a succession of stages, from an early reliance on reductionistic concepts such as drive and habit to the realization that cognitive and social explanations have better explanatory power and also help to unite these apparently opposite human tendencies within one conceptual scheme. The authors propose that the need for social inclusion (or the anxiety of being excluded) provides a good account of these tendencies, and that possibly culture itself "provides a buffer against one's own vulnerability and mortality." But they also show how cultures of different kinds can engender outer motives and behaviors that are different, even opposite in nature.

Robin Goodwin, in chapter 4, "Cross-Cultural Personal Relationships," provides us with a comprehensive review of the ways people relate to one another at the intimate level in various cultures, particularly ways of handling friendship, romantic attachments, and marital relationships. He posits that such relationships have a critical role in cultural and political change. Beginning from the early attempts merely to extend findings about relationships in Western countries, and the inadequate account of the findings given by sociobiologists, he focuses on cultural differentials such as those provided by Geert Hofstede and Shalom Schwartz and the less-well-known Mary Douglas, which seem to provide promising ways of integrating findings at the level of culture and of the individual. However, his own work in Russia and elsewhere provides cautions about the ease of arriving at a complete account, which he sees as requiring much more systematic research.

The next section, "Personal Values and Motives," continues the attempt to provide links between cultures and individuals by looking at the ways that values and particularly pervasive motives are shaped by culture and help to shape the behavior of individuals within cultures. Shalom Schwartz's chapter, "Values and Culture," begins by reminding us of the explanatory range of the values concept, which is seen to transcend situations in providing our "mental programming" of beliefs, feelings, goals, and behavioral standards.

He reviews the well-known work of Hofstede, which provided a set of four cultural dimensions for values that has underpinned many subsequent studies of the relationships between culture and action since its publication in the early 1980s. However, the generality of Hofstede's findings have been questioned on several grounds, and Schwartz presents us with an alternative conceptualization based on his own systematic investigations around the globe. This new system is then shown to provide natural groupings of countries based on common historical and cultural developments.

Stephen Wilson looks at one of the most often cited master motives in Western societies, self-actualization, in chapter 6, "Self-Actualization and Culture." In particular, he raises the question of why there are no fully developed theories of sociocultural change to explain this phenomenon. He suggests that sociologists have downplayed the importance of self-actualization because of their critique of modern society, which assumes that people are motivated primarily by status, power, and wealth, and that modern people are self-absorbed and individualistic. He then reviews the work of four social scientists—John Hewitt, Anthony Giddens, Kenneth Gergen, and Stephen Marks—which has provided a more positive view: self-actualization is capable of providing commitment to the ever-shifting roles required by modern society and an openness to experience and zest for living, and this can provide the foundation for a comprehensive sociocultural theory of self-actualization. In this chapter, culture is defined in relation to historical development rather than geographical regions.

Chapter 7, "Conformity, Calculation, and Culture," is also contributed by a sociologist, James Valentine. His extensive studies of conformity in Japanese society yield the paradoxical finding that although the Japanese concur with Western observers in viewing themselves as conformist, with fear of exclusion and loss of face as the underlying motivation, this masks a profound and pervasive nonconformity, or conformity to a deviant group norm. Valentine's carefully worked analysis of this paradox relates the person's "strategic calculation" of his or her outer self-presentation in relation to inner feelings, and he then shows how a similar analysis might apply to findings from Britain and from other cultures normally considered quite different from Japan.

Another kind of linkage between the social/cultural and the interpersonal levels is provided in the next section, "Intercultural Exchange in the Workplace." Chapter 8, "Work Motivation and Culture," by Henry Kao and Ng Sek-Hong, takes issue with the assumption frequently made in the West, namely, that life at work is invariably motivated by concern with personal satisfactions and individualistically "making it." Focusing on Eastern perceptions of the centrality of a moral commitment to the group as the basis of work motivation, the authors elucidate for us how the modern East Asian economies like Japan, Hong Kong, and China have shown the capacity to develop different hybrid motivational systems that suit their unique situations and histories. They have embraced critical features of the capitalistic approach in combination with traditional values such as trust in the family or organization and the duty to persevere in the face of adversity. The authors suggest that Western countries that wish to emulate the economic successes of the East should not try to import these motivational systems across the cultural divide but build on their own traditional versions of similar values. Multinational companies, acting both as standard-bearers for one culture and guests of another, can provide the conduit for the exchange of valuable elements from both.

Kao and Ng's point is reinforced by Stuart Carr and Malcolm MacLachlan in chapter 9, "Motivational Gravity." Their social psychological model of how personal motivation for achievement actually works in the social context of the workplace demonstrates how little attention has been paid to the social cost of the self-promotion that is taken for granted as the basis for career progress. They argue that these costs are particularly heavy in multinational settings with a combination of collectivistic or egalitarian values among peers and job insecurity among managers. Carr and MacLachlan review a range of evidence, mainly from Third World countries, that supports their argument that individual achievement is likely to be held in check by "pull-down" from peers combined with "push-down" from superiors. Such "motivational gravity" not only thwarts the economic objectives of the organizations concerned but puts into question the presumed link between achievement motivation and satisfaction from productivity. Fresh theories of motivation at work thus have much to gain from consideration of how particular cultural situations affect the way that motives are worked out in practice.

"Intrapsychic Processes," the next section, has three chapters that look at aspects of motivation that are intensely private but nevertheless have very powerful effects on behavior and may be the most important motivational forces in life. William Wedenoja and Elisa Sobo, in chapter 10, "Unconscious Motivation and Culture," unite the ideas of the dynamic unconscious of repressed affective material with which Freud and Jung revolutionized psychology (and which anthropologists continue to apply to cultural differences and similarities in healing practices, religious experience, dreaming and symbolism, sexuality, and so on) and the modern and more prosaic cognitive unconscious, from mainstream psychology. They show this to be a powerful combination of ideas in understanding how collective cultural values, norms, beliefs, and models of how to live become transmitted to the individual without awareness as the "undeniably real" world that we inhabit.

Joan Miller, in "Cultural Conceptions of Duty," chapter 11, explores an aspect of motivation that is rarely featured in texts: the tension felt by Westerners between morality and duty to the social group on the one hand, and self-expression and satisfaction of personal desires on the other. She contrasts this with the situation in certain collectivistic societies such as the Hindu, in which individuals are seen as naturally social and performance of duty is therefore personally satisfying. She reviews evidence that in such societies endogenous motivation is associated with acting from a sense of social obligation and shows that whereas moral agency is universal, its expression is culturally variable.

John Schumaker's "Religious Motivation Across Cultures," chapter 12, makes the case that religion represents one of the few truly universal human traits: no culture is devoid of religious beliefs and practices. Even in apparently secular societies, such as in parts of modern Europe, or irreligious countries, such as those repressed by Marxism, there is evidence of alternative forms of secondary religious activity continuing in such form as cults, New Age beliefs, and invisible worship that come out into the open when circumstances allow. He proposes that this is because religion provides protection from our own fears, gives us the feeling of control, because there is an instinctual need for it or because (to quote one of his references), "people cannot tolerate an unrelenting diet of the rational."

"The Biology and Culture Nexus," which is the last section but not the least in its importance in the picture of motivation across cultures, has two chapters, both of which could be said to be concerned with the nature/nurture issue. Dona Lee Davis points out in "Sexual Motivation Across Cultures," that there has been little cross-cultural research on sexual motivation, as distinct from descriptions of behaviors. Partly as a consequence, medical and psychoanalytic interpretations of similarities and differences in sexuality between cultures have held sway. Davis reviews some of the evidence collected by anthropologists that shows that marriage and sexual behaviors have to be seen in the context of wider cultural concerns, for example, the New Guinea Sambian tribal males' preoccupation with aggression and with their physical strength and domination of women. She also discusses feminist critiques of medical assumptions about the healthiness of supposedly normal sexual desires and behaviors, citing the negative impacts of gender inequality and traditional views of the woman's sexual role on their greater need for intimate relationships.

In the final chapter, "Aggression, Violence, and Culture," John Paul Scott looks at the importance of the social dominance/subordination relationships on the control of aggression among animals such as wolves and humans. He takes the view that although the *capacity* for aggression may be in the genes, "it must be developed under a great variety of environmental and experiential processes," so that cultural traditions are critical and social institutions such as economic organization encourage peace. Regrettably, there is resistance to change in many societies and a reluctance to acknowledge that information supplied by research (playing "a role somewhat analogous to gene mutation") may be of the greatest importance in human societies.

Despite the fascinatingly different perspectives on the relationships between motivation and culture presented in this volume, the reader will find many common themes and echoes of common assumptions. For example, Kashima's idea of cultural transmission through narrative can be seen as an alternative version of Wedenoja and Sobo's unconscious transmission of cultural values; Munro's abstract theme of levels underlies Scott's argument about the place of experience in relation to genetic factors; and both Kao and Ng's paper and Miller's emphasize the moral dimension in motivation for quite different purposes. What all the authors share is a view that for motivation theory to make sense of the varieties of human behavior, we must take into account the cultural context in which the behavior occurs rather than simply the biological, cognitive, or affective forces within the individual or

the social forces between people in groups. But these other forces are not relegated as irrelevant. Even if it were easy to demonstrate that culture accounts for more of the variance than the other factors, any account that relies entirely on the culture explanation leaves out *how it works*. So at the end we expect the reader will repeat the call so often heard in the social sciences (for example, Schweder & Sullivan, 1993), and so little listened to: the call for more cooperative cross-disciplinary research and theorizing, to provide the precise equations required at various levels of analysis for us to utilize the knowledge so far gained about the ways our cultures affect our personal motives.

References

Schweder, R. A., & Sullivan, M. A. (1993). Cultural psychology: Who needs it? *Annual Review of Psychology, 44,* 497–523

Triandis, H. C., Berry, J. W., Lonner, W. J., Heron, A., Brislin, R. W. & Draguns, J. G. (Eds.). (1980). *Handbook of cross-cultural psychology,* Vols. 1–6. Boston: Allyn & Bacon.

Theory and Concepts

Chapter One

Levels and Processes
in Motivation and Culture

Donald Munro

Any consideration of the relationship of culture to motivation depends on a conception of motivation and a conception of culture that can be linked. Although definitions of *motivation* and *culture* may be suggested by other writers in this volume, and certainly have been supplied by numerous writers in the past (e.g., Rohner, 1984, or Jahoda, 1992, for culture in relation to psychology; Reeve, 1992, pp. 3–27, for motivation), to a large extent we rely on our implicit general understandings of the two terms when we discuss their relationships. Those of us who approach the relationship as psychologists, with our history of emphasis on the biological end of the scientific spectrum, tend to regard individual motivation as the main focus of attention and to have a more elaborated set of constructs for it, and perhaps a rather simplistic conception of culture as an agglomeration of individual behaviors, values, beliefs, and so on—especially those that are evident in cross-cultural encounters. Anthropologists, on the other end of the spectrum, tend to center on culture as the important domain and view individual motivation as a function of the larger society in which the individual is a member. Furthermore, and perhaps more important, the direction of causality is likely to be seen to flow from the area in which we are expert to the other; that is, psychologists "explain" culture in terms of individual motivation but anthropologists tend to do the reverse. Psychologists tend to be reductionistic in accounting for social and cultural phenomena by reference to cognition, learning, and biology; cultural theorists tend to be "upwardly reductionistic" by accounting for individual behavior in terms of group processes and history, and socially constructed meaning.

In this chapter an attempt is presented to get beyond the limitations of our perspectives by looking at individual psychology and the group culture within a single framework. This framework has previously been proposed (Munro, 1992) as a solution to a very similar problem within psychology itself, namely, the schism between those who espouse a neuropsychological reductionism and a positivist perspective as the solution to the unification of psychology, and those who regard a relativistic and socially constructed reality as the more ontologically valid perspective on the discipline. One might add in passing that there is a related tension between scientists and practitioners, between those who see themselves as seeking fundamental and universally generalizable truths and those who rely on working hypotheses about ever-changing practical realities.

The model proposed here is holistic in the sense that all aspects of human behavior are seen as interlocking systems but differentiated in terms of a number of levels of analysis. This feature enables us to realize that we are dealing with only one ultimate reality, so biology and culture are not regarded as incommensurable. A principal gain from this awareness is that it is no longer necessary to focus on one domain as the preeminent basis for explanations about human action. However, we can legitimately focus on particular levels of that reality for different purposes—indeed, we must do so, because it is humanly impossible to comprehend everything at once.

The second major feature of the model is that it is primarily focused on process rather than structure, on action rather than things, while recognizing that structures provide useful snapshots (or freeze-frames) of action at particular points in time. Although psychological theorists have long recognized the desirability of considering both structure and process (Marx & Hillix, 1979; Koch & Leary, 1985), there has been a strong tendency for them to adopt structuralist models and methodologies, and to investigate fixed entities such as intellectual capacity, personality factors, inherited or learned motives, enduring values and beliefs, established social relationships between people, and so on. Even the notion of change (as in the development of the child) is dealt with indirectly as the difference between a starting state and a finishing state rather than as something *happening*.

A problem with traditional psychologists' accounts is that we have a concept of ourselves as scientists investigating ontological truths rather than practitioners concerned with ongoing social action. Our journals are full of "findings" about what *is*. We have tended to think that knowledge is cumulative and that eventually we will know everything that is worth knowing about human behavior. But in this chapter we will regard most research findings as ephemeral, as mere snapshots of how things were at particular points in the human family story, and we will concentrate on how to understand and influence ongoing and future action at the level of the person, and how this is affected by (and affects) the set of dynamic processes called culture.

Processes and Levels of Analysis

ADOPTING a focus on process allows us to define *motivation* as *an explanation for coherent action*. In a sense, a truly comprehensive theory of motivation must be a theory of the whole of psychology, or even of social science in general, because every muscle twitch, every neuronal firing, every tiny gesture a person makes, at the micro level, and every human life, every family story, every culture's history, at the macro level, must be accountable—not just retrospectively but prospectively too. Although we may build a theory abstract enough to accomplish this, in practice we are concerned with particular sequences of identifiable events. How we isolate these sequences and focus on them is itself a function of psychological processes that complexly involve biological, cognitive, social, and ultimately cultural processes. Our theory, then, needs not only to be reasonable psychologically but to be capable of encompassing the various things that people in varied cultures will want to account for.

By the same token, culture is not earthenware and metal artifacts, or buildings and towns, or books and universities, or the structure of families and organizations, or the structure of beliefs and values per se but the collective *human action* that is determined by these things and structures (and that produces new things and structures that determine new actions in the next generation). This is what is meant by the perhaps tired but true expression that culture is alive. Furthermore, it is coherent human action, in the same sense as given above in defining motivation. Thus, to comprehend culture we have to understand the various forces that shape human motivation.

The basic idea of processes occurring at different levels may be explained through a diagram (see Munro, 1992, p. 113), but equally by asking the reader to bring to mind any event or action. An event in the purely physical world will do, for example, the explosion of a star or the collision of two subatomic particles, but a human behavior would be most appropriate in this case. That action is bound to be part of a chain of events leading up to it and then into the future: we normally construe that some other event or events *caused* it to happen, and others in turn will flow from it, if we allow our imaginations to play through a few successive "frames of the movie." But there are other things in the picture, too, some out of focus and some invisible altogether. Those that are out of focus are other parallel event chains, things that are going on at the same time though they have no discernible connection with our imaginary action. As the reader sits reading this chapter (itself an example of an action sequence) millions of other entirely unconnected things are going on in the world. We might also include things that are not actually happening, although the necessary components are available. We tend as scientists to relegate such hypothetical action to the realm of the fiction writer, ignoring the thought that what happened last time may not happen next time. That possibility is the very stuff of motivation.

Some event chains are unique and never recur. They are detectable because they are unusual, and attribution theorists (e.g., Heider, 1958) have pointed out that we have trouble accounting for them. Some events are recurrent; that is, they are in a circular chain of events, or are linked to other cyclical events so that they can be anticipated. Many biological events are of this kind, including motivated behaviors that are driven by diurnal phenomena in the outside world or cyclical needs in the organism, such as eating and sleeping. And some event chains "feed back" on themselves, thus providing control over their recurrence; the cybernetic loop involved is the basis for the study of all kinds of systems, whether biological or social, natural or engineered by humans (Miller, 1978; Weinberg, 1979). The turning on of a heater by a thermostat and satiation of biological needs are notable examples of such feedback, and also of the recurring processes just mentioned. Examples can also be found at the level of the social group and in the wider society, though they typically involve very much more extended and convoluted chains of events, so they are even more difficult to apprehend directly—in fact, they are often viewed as constructions of the human mind rather than "real" processes (e.g., Gergen, 1990).

Depending on how wide a purview we adopt, at any one level large numbers of such event chains are simultaneously activated, involving many singular events or actions. Some event chains are causally linked, though others may appear to be independent at a particular point in time. Perhaps the best way to imagine this is to think of it as a pattern of overlapping circles (or daisy chains), that represent not *things* but sequences of *events*. These events can be represented as a, b, c, and so on (or individual daisies), which are parts of event chains A, B, C, and so on. Where circles intersect is the point at which they affect one another because they have some part of their processes in common. For example, the series of events a, b, c, ... within A may depend on a particular condition being fulfilled at event c, which is also part of sequence B; until the series of events in B satisfies that condition, the sequence in A will be interrupted and suspended in time. In this way sequence B controls sequence A. Let us say A represents you reading the morning newspaper, involving turning pages, scanning, reading an item, as a, b, c, and B represents you having a simultaneous conversation with your spouse about the news, involving spoken phrases a, b, c. Then A may be suspended at point b while you listen to a question, d in B. In this way, the conversation B controls your newspaper reading A at this point of overlap.

The causality may also be bidirectional—possibly the sequence B is also dependent on sequence A's being "ready" to receive the information at the common node. Given that the number of event chains A, B, C, and so on is very large (and each has varying numbers of components a, b, c, and so on), it is clear that the number of ways that the overall set of overlapping events can go is immense.

Complexity

A FULL understanding of the behavior of such assemblages depends on knowing their structure, what the rules are at the common nodes (e.g., the social rules about listening to the other person), and what is going on in each component. Sometimes this knowledge is obtainable and can be comprehended, and we can therefore predict what will happen in the near future within this limited universe. But sometimes we cannot see what is going on, and the system appears to be behaving in a chaotic fashion. The outcome can be interesting or even beautiful in its effects if it is possible to observe it (Gleick, 1987), even though we cannot understand it easily or predict what will happen next. However, most life forms seem to have a strong tendency toward *self-organization* (Waldrop, 1992), such that particularly viable kinds of process tend to occur in nature more often than chaotic or random ones. Human behavior usually seems coherent to the observer, in that particular action sequences always follow each other, so we can learn to predict what will happen next. Brain processes and perhaps the behavior of cultures also show such self-organization.

The difficulty of obtaining a complete understanding of these complex processes and the beginnings of efforts to tackle the problems, are contained in a recent conference announcement carried by electronic mail on the Internet. In a call for papers for a conference on complexity in organizations,

Anderson (1996) summarizes the situation (quoted at length with the permission of the author; some punctuation added):

> "Complex organizations" have been an important arena in organizational studies for decades. Historically, organizational scholars have examined vertical complexity (the number of levels in a hierarchy), horizontal complexity (the number of differentiated departments), and spatial complexity (the geographic dispersion of organizational subunits). Organizational environments have also been characterized as more or less complex depending on how heterogeneous and dispersed resources are within them.
>
> However, a different view of complexity is emerging that may have important implications for organizational scholarship. Within the past decade, interest in the "sciences of complexity" has increased dramatically. The study of complex system dynamics has perhaps progressed farthest in the natural sciences, but it is also beginning to penetrate the social sciences. This interdisciplinary field of study is still pre-paradigmatic, and it embraces a wide variety of approaches. Although it is not yet clear whether a genuine science of complexity will emerge, it does seem clear that scholars in a variety of fields are viewing complexity in a different way than organizational scholars traditionally have.
>
> A number of findings now seem fairly well established, including the following:
>
> • Many dynamic systems do not reach an equilibrium (either a fixed point or a cyclical equilibrium).
>
> • Processes that appear to be random may actually be chaotic, in other words may revolve around identifiable types of "attractors." Tests exist that can detect whether apparently random processes are in fact chaotic.
>
> • Two entities with very similar initial states can follow radically divergent paths over time....
>
> • Very complex patterns can arise from the interaction of agents following relatively simple rules. These patterns are "emergent" in the sense that new properties appear at each level in a hierarchy.
>
> • Complex systems may resist reductionist analyses. In other words, it may not be possible to describe some systems simply by holding some of their subsystems constant in order to study other subsystems.
>
> • Time series that appear to be random walks may actually be fractals with self-reinforcing trends. In such cases we may observe a "hand of the past" in operation.
>
> • Complex systems may tend to exhibit "self-organizing" behavior. Starting in a random state, they may naturally evolve toward order instead of disorder.

Time and Causality

MOTIVATIONAL processes have been defined as coherent series of actions. When we identify a behavior as motivated, it is usually because we have noticed it before in the same person or in other people; it seems to have a beginning (a cause) and an end or terminating condition (which may lie in the future, and defines the objective that the person appears or persons appear to be pursuing). Similarly, cultures may be identified by coherent patterns of behavior that keep recurring in certain (groups of) people, and that seem to have some reason for them and some purpose as well. Thus, to understand both motivation and culture requires that we study the structure of the ongoing processes and the rules that seem to control the flow of action where processes intersect. It is clear from Anderson's (1996) summary that this will be no easy task.

A fundamentally important point is that events happen in time. This means that causes and effects are separated in time, and causality is therefore less obvious unless we can observe for extended periods. In general, events at the lower (more micro) levels of reality are faster. It is easier for the physicists, chemists, or biologists to understand what is going on at their levels of understanding than it is for the psychologist, and it is generally easier for the psychologist than for the sociologist or anthropologist because events recur at shorter intervals in time at the biological levels than at societal levels. Things happen within a society that can be understood only if our historians can provide accounts of events that are detailed enough for the various levels of analysis to be taken into account. This is one of the problems of the study of culture, and to a lesser extent in regard to an understanding of individual motivation.

The major task of the investigator and theorist is to link the action sequences at any level to those in adjacent levels, and so on until an exhaustive understanding has been achieved. As we move "down" one level, we encounter a similar picture in terms of event actions and chains but involving different kinds of actions. Thus, if our original action sequence concerns a social event involving two persons (embedded in a field of other social events), at the lower level, we have two sets of individual behavioral actions (which are independent from each other *at this level,* though they may share structural similarities). Moving down another level we would account for these behaviors in terms of the action sequences performed by the person, which may also be largely autonomous or unrelated to one another, and at yet another level down, we would begin to make use of internal "psychological" or "mental" action sequences. If we continue this, we arrive at the stuff of neuroscience and eventually physics; if we proceed upward, we arrive at processes of interest to sociologists and anthropologists, including those that are typically taken to characterize particular cultural groups.

Two important issues remain to be clarified. One is the number of such levels; the other is the relationship between them, particularly in respect to causality. The number of levels is not specified as part of the theory. There is a convenient division between levels reflected in professional and subprofessional disciplines: between psychology and anthropology and between neuroscience, cognitive psychology, social psychology, and so forth. To a large extent this is a practical matter of how clearly we are able to differentiate analytic levels conceptually and how specific our observational methods are. However, it should be pointed out that many of the theoretical problems in the social sciences can be attributed to a tendency to confuse levels of analysis and to jump between noncontiguous levels in providing "explanations" of phenomena (Munro, 1992). Thus, for example, body healing processes are accounted for by mental or social events without regard to the intervening levels; although the demonstration of a correlation in time between clearly separate processes is useful and suggestive, it does not provide an adequate explanation of causality.

Various suggestions have been made as to specific levels: clinical psychologists Sundberg, Tyler, and Taplin (1973, p. 101) suggested cell, organ, individual, group, organization, society, and supranational. Social psychologists Breakwell and Rowett (1982) used intrapsychic (cognition, affect, and basic personality), interpersonal, intragroup, and intergroup, and their scheme was largely adopted by Doise (1986), though with definitional changes. And last, three philosophers of the social sciences, Harré, Clarke, and de Carlo (1985), in *Motives and Mechanisms,* used three levels: neurological, psychological, and social. A number of natural-science writers and philosophers of science have used similar schemes (see Munro, 1992, p. 113); one of the most recent contributions stems from the ideas of James Miller, a major contributor to general systems theory for many years, proposing eight levels from cell to supranational system (Miller & Miller, 1995, p. 172). If we consider the levels that are represented in conventional motivation theories (see any text such as Reeve, 1992), at least eight to ten levels might be required to do justice to the range of possibilities, even if we ignore subcellular and suprahuman system levels such as viruses and the biosphere.

The main point to be emphasized here is that it is critical to understand that each level should provide a complete account of actions at that level in its own terms. When we talk about the social behavior of persons in a small group we can provide descriptions and observations of sequential (possibly causal) effects without reference to any other level; the social group in question is part of a larger society. But when we move to describing how the group interacts with other groups at that level, we are talking about the behavior of groups, not of individual persons. Similarly, cognitive processes such as remembering and problem solving should be related to one another at their level of analysis; apparently linked neural events are at a lower level of explanation and apparently consequential behavioral acts are at a higher level of explanation. Thus, we should not explain thinking as "just neural activity" or the behavior of a nation of peoples as merely aggregated individual actions. In particular, the patterns of social interactions that are sometimes taken to define a cultural group are not simply the combined effect of a number of individuals; they can be accounted for by social processes that might often appear abstract but that are just as real as the motor behavior of an individual or the electrochemical action of a neurone. Furthermore, by the same principle operating in the opposite direction, human behaviors are not simply due to persons' family roles or the cultural group to which they belong.

Further to the above, actions at any level should not be mapped simplistically onto those at adjacent levels. It is in this respect that the model is most different from the conventional hierarchical structural models relevant to atoms, molecules, cells, organs, and so on. A handshake between two people is not just a set of motor behaviors nor just a social action—it can be explained in terms of relationships and actions (including speech and other forms of communication) at its own level of analysis. Furthermore, there are some actions that are meaningful at this particular level but do not feature in the next level up. Neurones do many things that have no effect on thinking; people can do many things while in a social group that have no effect on the actions of the group that affect its relationship to other groups; and some aspects of the interaction between groups can be studied quite independently from the society or culture of which they are part. Nevertheless, the task of linking or "articulating" levels (Doise, 1986) in order to reveal correspondences and causal relationships is a central task of theoretical social science.

Finally, causality is of fundamental importance in the consideration of motivation because the basic motivational question is "Why did s/he really do that?", that is, there is a search for the locus of the ultimate cause of a particular behavior. As has already been mentioned, in looking at conventional theories of motivation, we find causes being postulated at all levels, from the cell to society (and in the case of sociobiological theory, the evolution of life itself). Also mentioned before, we search for causality within the particular level that interests us, by looking for the prior events or conditions that initiated action sequences that appear to be motivated or by looking for the conditions that will terminate them—the apparent goals of the person. Theoreticians tend to look for causality at other levels (reductionistically or contextually); lay people tend to look for antecedents and goals on the same level, leading to further confusion.

I take the view that any human behavior transcends all levels, so that attempts to determine a particular level to which causality can be traced are futile, except to the extent that we learn about the links between levels. *All* actions are represented at the cellular level, are neurally mediated, involve cognition, are behavioral, are part of what is going on interpersonally, and are functionally determined by society, *simultaneously*. Furthermore, all human behavior is embedded within ongoing processes at any of these levels, and the identification of prior conditions or final terminators for motivated behavior is arbitrary. Which particular theory we use to account for actions and bring them under control if we are helping professionals or managers of some sort is a matter of convenience and ease of understanding. To a large extent, choice of theories in any field is determined by technology, by what tools are available. This does not mean that alternative theories are invalid. To try to control a neurotic behavior in a particular person, or his or her coming late for work, or his or her antisocial behavior by changing society or the culture of the group to which that person belongs is not wrong in principle but very inefficient in practice.

In this chapter we do not concern ourselves with the practical matter of "motivating" people in the conventional sense but concentrate on understanding their motivations in the context of culture. In line with the foregoing explanation of causality in the model, we can adopt McGuire's (1983, p. 7) dictum "Because all hypotheses are true, all are false"; that is, in understanding motivation we can give consideration to a wide variety of explanations at different levels of analysis, each of which is able to provide a partial account of the behavior in focus.

Linking Motivation and Culture in the Common Framework

IT has become common in the social sciences to interpret motivation in terms of (more or less conscious) desires and strategies for attaining various goals (e.g., D'Andrade & Strauss, 1992), which may be seen as having been socially constructed and internalized through the social group and culture in which the person grows. The approach adopted here is not incompatible with that position, though we take the view there are (also) "real" events going on in the external world, only some of which are concerned with others' interpretations and evaluations. Thus, motivation cannot be interpreted, even from the standpoint of the anthropologist, simply as "the product between events and things in the social world and the interpretation of those events and things in people's psyches" (Strauss, 1992, p. 1).

Similarly, culture is not just "integrated, stable sets of meanings and practices unproblematically reproduced through socialized actors" (Strauss, 1992, p. 1), or "socially established structures of meaning" (Geertz, 1973, p. 12), or the "software of the mind" (Hofstede, 1991, title). Human cultures have multiple aspects, but clearly all of them are connected in some way with human action processes, whether they be artifacts (ranging from earthenware produced by our primitive ancestors to the contents of libraries), behaviors (ranging from motor habits to particular ways of thinking, communicating, and influencing the behaviors of others), or abstractions (beliefs and knowledge) about the world, about ourselves and other people, and about our products and about our own abstractions.

D'Andrade (1992) comes closer to a multilevel view of motivation in relation to culture in saying (p. 3, original italics), *"Cultural models ... can have motivational force* because these models not only label and describe the world but also set forth goals (both conscious and unconscious) and elicit or include desires." These models are transmitted, according to D'Andrade, as schemas, which are "conceptual structures" that tell the person how to react when certain situations arise (a better term for such structures might be script, after the artificial-intelligence theories of Abelson, 1981, and others). D'Andrade's conception also includes that "schemas are processes, not objects" (p. 29), and "instigate action" because they "can function as goals," so the similarity of his theory to that presented here can easily be seen.

It should be added that culture can also affect motivation at lower, physical levels, in that cultures produce artifacts and alter the environment in such a way that other mental processes that serve motivational states are also affected. To take a very simple example, the nature of the buildings in which we live and work (and that are, of course, products of our culture) imposes certain constraints on what we can do, and over time we learn to limit what we aspire to do, in order (sometimes literally) to avoid "hitting our heads against a brick wall." Much more important, information and the interpretations of it that are produced by culture similarly limit behaviors and are therefore part of the motivational environment.

Perceiving that there is culture is (the result of) a process, as is the perception that there are different cultures. Although modern social scientists are happy to use broadly accepted concepts of culture in talking about the groups and practices with which they are familiar, few would gainsay that the boundaries of cultures are fuzzy and arbitrary and depend largely on the purposes of the person (whether scientist or layperson) who is describing them. In terms of accounting for my motivation, I may have more in common with a Russian-speaking Eskimo who has trained as a psychologist than with my brother who practices another profession. What we are doing when we describe a particular human culture as different from others is to engage in an intuitive (that is, largely socially but unconsciously learned) process, akin to the statistical procedure of cluster analysis, in connection with things and behaviors that vary along a very large number of dimensions. This process is itself a product of the culture of the observers and is affected by their current motivational goals.

The promotion of such a holistic view may leave some readers distinctly uneasy that we may never be able to analyze culture and motivation problems. But the requirement to consider the larger model of human activity and to be aware of the limitations and the ephemeral nature of local linkages between particular cultures (or cultural differences) and particular motivational states does not make these exercises pointless. For everyday practical purposes, such as planning clinical interventions or managing people in work organizations, such local models are essential. Furthermore, such model making as is engaged in by other writers in this volume leads us toward the proper goal of the theorist: to map comprehensively the myriad linkages within and between levels of understanding of both motivational and cultural phenomena.

References

Abelson, R. (1981). Psychological status of the script concept. *American Psychologist, 36,* 715–729.

Anderson, P. C. (1996). *Call for abstracts: Applications of complexity theory to organizational science.* E-mail message from Philip.C.Anderson@Dartmouth.EDU, Wed. Feb. 21.

Breakwell, G. M., & Rowett, C. (1982). *Social work: A social psychological approach.* London: Routledge & Kegan Paul.

D'Andrade, R. G. (1992). Schemas and motivation. In R. G. D'Andrade & C. Strauss (Eds.), *Human motives and cultural models.* Cambridge: Cambridge University Press.

D'Andrade, R. G., & Strauss, C. (Eds.). (1992). *Human motives and cultural models.* Cambridge: Cambridge University Press.

Doise, W. (1986). *Levels of explanation in social psychology.* Cambridge: Cambridge University Press.

Geertz, C. (1973). *The interpretation of cultures.* New York: Basic Books.

Gergen, K. J. (1990). Social understanding and the inscription of self. In J. W. Stigler, R. A. Schweder, & G. Herdt (Eds.), *Cultural psychology: Essays on comparative human development* (pp. 569–606). Cambridge: Cambridge University Press.

Gleick, J. (1987). *Chaos.* London: Heinemann.

Harré, R., Clarke, D., & de Carlo, N. (1985). *Motives and mechanisms.* London: Methuen.

Heider, F. (1958). *The psychology of interpersonal relationships.* New York: Wiley.

Hofstede, G. (1991). *Cultures and organizations: Software of the mind.* New York: McGraw-Hill.

Jahoda, G. (1992). *Crossroads between culture and the mind: Continuities and change in theories of human nature.* London: Harvester.

Koch, S., & Leary, D. E. (1985). *A century of psychology as a science.* New York: McGraw-Hill.

Marx, M. H., & Hillix, W. A. (1979). *Systems and theories in psychology* (3rd ed.). New York: McGraw-Hill.

McGuire, W. J. (1983). A contextualist theory of knowledge: Its implications for innovation and reform in psychological research. In L. Berkowitz (Ed.), *Advances in experimental social psychology,* Vol. 16 (pp. 1–47). New York: Academic Press.

Miller, J. G. (1978). *Living systems.* New York: Wiley.

Miller, J. L., & Miller, J. G. (1995). Greater than the sum of its parts, III: Information processing subsystems. *Behavioral Science, 40,* 171–182.

Munro, D. (1992). Process vs. structure and levels of analysis in psychology: Towards an integration rather than reduction of theories. *Theory and Psychology, 2,* 109–127.

Reeve, J. M. (1992). *Understanding motivation and emotion.* New York: Harcourt Brace.

Rohner, R. (1984). Towards a conception of culture for cross-cultural psychology. *Journal of Cross-Cultural Psychology, 15,* 111–138.

Strauss, C. (1992). Models and motives. In R. G. D'Andrade & C. Strauss (Eds.), *Human motives and cultural models* (pp. 197–224). Cambridge: Cambridge University Press.

Sundberg, N. D., Tyler, L. E., & Taplin, J. R. (1973). *Clinical psychology.* Englewood Cliffs, NJ: Prentice-Hall.

Waldrop, M. M. (1992). *Complexity.* London: Penguin.

Weinberg, G. M. (1979). *On the design of stable systems.* New York: Wiley.

Chapter Two

Culture, Narrative, and Human Motivation

YOSHIHISA KASHIMA

Culture affects human motivation. Cross-cultural variability in motivation is well known (Kornadt, Eckensberger, & Emminghaus, 1980, for a review). What is problematic is just *how* culture influences human motivation. The process by which culture is internalized and exerts its directive force is a contentious issue because it touches on a central question of the social sciences, that is, the relation between the collective and the individual (Holland, 1992).

To assume that culture is unproblematically internalized is to "oversocialize" the individual (Wrong, 1961) and to oversimplify the process by which a person actively appropriates socially shared meaning (Valsiner, 1989). Yet, to assume that individuals are equipped with a set of needs and that a culture simply supplies specific contents to it commits a fallacy of abstract individualism (Lukes, 1973). The fallacy lies in the assumption that the individual is endowed with a fixed set of needs and that a social institution is there to satisfy them, when in fact human needs are shaped and perhaps even created by the social institution.[1]

The main aim of this chapter is to suggest that part of an answer to the question may be found in narrative. Although many researchers recently emphasized the importance of narrative in psychological research (e.g., Bruner, 1986, 1990; Polkinghorne, 1988; Sarbin, 1986), a possible link between culture and motivation is yet to be explored from this perspective to the best of my knowledge. In the following sections, I will develop and make a preliminary case for a hypothesis that narrative provides a cultural basis for human motivation. After a brief discussion about the nature of narrative, I will outline psychological functions of narrative by selectively drawing on the empirical literature and consider implications of this hypothesis for psychological research on culture and motivation.

Narrative

NARRATIVE has been variously defined by scholars in different disciplines. At one extreme, Labov (1972) defined a minimal narrative as two temporally ordered clauses in the past tense. At close to the other extreme, Burke (1945/1969) required a narrative to consist of an actor, an action, a goal or intention, a scene, and an instrument, which form his "Pentad," the structure of a narrative. To Burke, an imbalance among elements in the Pentad gives rise to a good story; the process of resolving the imbalance constitutes the main body of the story. Whether one takes Labov's minimalist approach or Burke's more structured approach, narrative's semiotic function is to provide a higher order structure, which gives coherence to a sequence of action.

As Ricoeur (1981, p. 277) put it,

> a story describes a sequence of actions and experiences of a certain number of characters, whether real or imaginary. These characters are represented in situations which change.... These changes, in turn, reveal hidden aspects of the situations and the characters, giving rise to a new predicament which calls for thought or action or both. The response to this predicament brings the story to its conclusion.

In short, a narrative picks out a coherent and meaningful unit from the continuous stream of human activities by giving the beginning and ending to the segment, thereby giving it a temporal closure.

There are at least two pieces of prima facie evidence for postulating narrative as a vehicle by which culture influences human motivation. First, narrative is universal. As Lonner (1980) pointed out, narrative is one of the human universals that appear to exist in every known human culture. Be it myths (e.g., a Chinese mythology of the production of the world from Chaos), folktales (e.g., Little Red Riding Hood), epics, novels, or motion pictures, every culture has some form of story. Second, narratives are prevalent in everyday discourse. When a person explains his or her action to another person, it often is by way of telling a story (Harvey, Weber, & Orbuch, 1990). Businessmen explain their success by telling a story (reported in Baumeister & Newman, 1994). Even social scientists tell stories in their academic writing (Greimas, 1990). To put it simply, people tell stories to one another in every human culture.

Obviously, this is not enough evidence. What is prevalent is not always influential. Moreover, cultures differ in the extent to which narratives are used in everyday discourse, and in the manner in which stories are told (e.g., Michaels, 1991). Nevertheless, one person's telling of a story to another person is part of the process in which conventional meanings are conveyed and new meanings are created. I submit that narrative is a significant part of everyday activities of ordinary people. It is a medium through which cultural meanings are produced and reproduced.

Properties of Narrative

One of the significant properties of narrative is its "worldmaking" function, to borrow Nelson Goodman's phrase (1978). Narratives construct a meaningful world of human experience. Further, the meaningfulness of a narrative is not exhausted by whether the events described in the story actually occurred in the world (Bruner, 1990; Ricoeur, 1981), though the currently popular perspective in cognitive science equates meaning with truth values, that is, whether a proposition is true or false.

This point requires further explanation. In discussions of meaning, two kinds of meaning have traditionally been recognized, that is, *sense* and *reference* (Gibbs, 1994). The following example illustrates the difference between sense and reference. Although the morning star and the evening star refer to the same object in the world (same reference), their senses are different. Whereas "the morning star is the evening star" is true and informative, "the morning star is the morning star" is true but silly. Two words with the same reference are not simply interchangeable in meaning because they may have different senses. Narratives make sense, but they do not necessarily have their references. The meaning of a narrative is not exhausted by whether there exist external events in the world to which the narrative refers. A significant part of the meaning of a narrative lies in its internal coherence constituted by its interlocking parts.[2]

The structure that gives a narrative coherence may be analyzed from various perspectives (Burke, 1945/1969; Greimas, 1966/1983). To examine the implication of narrative on motivation, however, Greimas's structuralist scheme, which was developed on the basis of Propp's (1968) analysis of Russian folktales, may be most informative. According to Greimas, a story may be analyzed in terms of three pairs of *actants*. Actants are clusters of actions that may be performed by various entities in a story. One pair, *subject* and *object,* constitutes the axis of desire. Subject pursues the goal, object of desire, in the story. Another pair, *helper* and *opponent* constitutes the axis of conflict. Helper facilitates and opponent hinders the subject's pursuit of the object. Finally, *sender* and *receiver* constitute the axis of communication. Sender gives information and objects to receiver. Frequently, it is the sender who gives the subject the object of desire. In this case, the same character turns out to act as both subject and receiver.

To illustrate how this works, take the following simple story. A beautiful princess is captured by a dragon. Her father, the king, declares that whoever saves the princess shall marry her. A handsome prince learns about this, overcomes many difficulties, slays the dragon with the help of his magic sword, and marries the princess. Greimas's scheme may analyze this story as follows:

> Subject = handsome prince
> Object = beautiful princess
> Helper = magic sword
> Opponent = dragon, many difficulties
> Sender = king
> Receiver = handsome prince

Greimas's analysis highlights two of the properties of narrative that are central to the examination of a cultural basis of human motivation. First, narratives describe an actor's goal-directed activities (also see Burke, 1945/1969). According to Greimas's analysis, in describing subject's pursuit of object, a narrative defines a goal and a corresponding desire, as well as the ways in which one may attain the goal (or fail to attain it), and a variety of factors that may facilitate or hinder the movement toward the goal (helpers and opponents). A story embodies a package of information about how to achieve what goal (or how not to achieve what goal).

Furthermore, many contemporary narratives have a significant cognitive or subjective dimension (Greimas & Courtés, 1976; Todorov, 1977). A story not only describes overt actions but also reveals the characters' covert thoughts, feelings, and desires. Bruner (1986) compared Joyce's *Clay* and an anthropologist's exposition about rituals, and found that the former had 202.4 instances of references to subjective expressions per 100 sentences, compared to the latter's 50.6. There is some historical variability in the prevalence of subjectivity in stories (Auerbach, 1953; Kahler, 1973), and it is likely that cross-cultural variability exists in this regard.

Second, narratives positively or negatively sanction certain goal-directed activities described in the stories. In the example above, sender (king) gave the object of desire (princess) to receiver/subject (prince). The story then positively sanctions the goal-directed activities, both the goal and the way the hero approached the goal.

Some narratives may dispense sanctions in a slightly more complex manner. Imagine a story in which a dishonest prince and an honest prince attempt to rescue a princess. The honest prince fails to rescue the princess because of the obstruction by the dishonest prince, who actually rescues her. Nevertheless, the princess falls in love with the honest prince, marries him, and lives happily ever after. This story positively sanctions the honest prince's deeds but negatively sanctions the dishonest prince's deeds. In general, to the extent that certain deeds (goals and manners of goal attainment) are positively sanctioned (or others are negatively sanctioned) in a story, the story moralizes positively sanctioned deeds relative to others (see White, 1980–1981, for a similar observation).

While highlighting the goal-directed nature and the moral implications of a story, as Ricoeur (1981) pointed out, Greimas's analysis plays down the fundamental temporality of narrative. At one level, Ricoeur's observation is trivially true. A certain order of events and actions is required in order for a story to make sense. After all, unless the dragon kidnaps the princess, the prince cannot rescue the princess. However, Ricoeur (1984, p. 52) suggested that narrative plays even more fundamental a role in configuring human experience of time: "[T]ime becomes human to the extent that it is articulated through a narrative mode, and narrative attains its full meaning when it becomes a condition of temporal existence."

The significance of temporality in understanding human social action has been emphasized by many social theorists. For example, as Bourdieu (1977) pointed out, the custom of gift exchange in some cultures can be understood only as a temporal event, that is, someone's giving of a gift to someone else, and the latter's returning of the gift to the former. One cannot reverse the order of these events. Moreover, the *tempo* of returning is also highly important. One cannot return a favor immediately, or ten years later.

In summary, four properties of narrative were highlighted in this section. The meaning of a narrative is not exhausted by "truth values" but is significantly framed by its plot and internal coherence. A narrative's coherence typically stems from the structure of goal-directed activities, which consist of goals, the description of how to attain the goals in what order, and often the description of covert experiences of the characters in the story. A narrative often involves a moral dimension by positively or negatively sanctioning some goal-directed activities relative to others. Finally, narrative is fundamentally temporal.

Social Psychological Processes Involving Narrative

The central role narrative plays in both intra- and interpersonal processes is best illustrated by Bartlett's (1932) seminal work on social psychology of narrative reproduction. In one of the experiments, Bartlett presented an American Indian folktale, "The War of Ghosts," to undergraduates at Cambridge University. Their task was called "serial reproduction": each student reproduced the story to another undergraduate, who in turn retold the story to another, and so on. In the repeated retelling, the story of ghosts gradually became more and more like a reasonable story of everyday activity in the early part of twentieth-century England.

The transformation of an alien story to a culturally familiar form suggests that storytelling is a fundamentally social *and* psychological process. In the process of reproduction, the ghost story was culturally appropriated, filtered through socially shared conceptions about objects and events in the world. Bartlett called such socially shared conceptions *schema*. Contemporary cognitive anthropologists would call them *cultural models* (Holland & Quinn, 1987). Although some theorists postulate a stable, template-like mental structure, others postulate more dynamic processes involving episode-based memories (Schank & Abelson, 1995; Smith, 1980–1981). Whatever the nature of a narrative representation may be, one social function of narrative is clearly to reproduce a canonical form, that is, socially shared representations of social events and actions.

However, narratives do not simply reproduce socially shared meanings; they also produce novel and yet socially *shareable* meanings. According to Bruner (1986), narratives help create new meanings by virtue of their capacity to *subjunctivize* human actions and social events. That is, the narrative form allows the storytellers to provide their own personal and subjective perspectives and to describe the character's mental processes at the same time that actions and events unfold in the world. Narratives make such new meanings comprehensible by supplying the context in which novel events and actions become part of a coherent plot.

This function to create new meanings in a culturally understandable way makes narrative an effective form with which to give explanations or accounts to others for actions and events that violated social expectations and norms (that is, a culturally canonical pattern). Bruner (1990) argued most strongly that narratives are most often generated when expectations are violated (see Lucariello, 1990, for some evidence). Likewise, Harvey, Weber, and Orbuch (1990) suggested that storied accounts are often provided when expectations in close relationships are breached.

To put it succinctly, narrative can serve two functions in cultural processes. The act of telling stories helps reproduce socially shared conceptions and meanings, and produce socially shareable conceptions and meanings. By framing actions and events in a way that is relevant to other narrativized actions and events, narrative storytelling makes it possible to relate the new to the old, to make the unfamiliar familiar. In so doing, narrative adds new meanings to the actions and events by going beyond the information given.

Affective and Cognitive Process. Provided that humans have a strong need to belong and to communicate with conspecifics, and that narratives play an important role in the construction of socially shared meanings, it is no surprise that the individual psychological process is also influenced by narratives. First of all, narrative is an *encoding* device that gives a structure to human experience. That is, people use narratives to interpret everyday social events and actions. For instance, Pennington and Hastie (1986, 1988, 1992) proposed the Story Model of jury decision making. They proposed that jurors construct a story from various evidence in a trial, and the story mediates their evaluation of evidence and judgments of guilt. In their program of research, Pennington and Itastic used multiple methods (think-aloud protocol, memory measures, and judgment) to gain impressive support for their model. Other legal scholars also suggested the importance of stories in legal decision making (Ewick & Silbey, 1995).

Once encoded, narratives aid *recall* of information and thereby facilitate the reproduction of cultural beliefs and knowledge. People tend to recall events that are expected in a story better than those that are irrelevant or unrelated to it (see Hastie, Park, & Weber, 1984, for a review). Although there is some interpretive ambiguity regarding the recall of unexpected events (Bower, Black, & Turner, 1979, versus Graesser, Woll, Kowalski, & Smith, 1980), overall, the literature generally suggests that events that are difficult to integrate into a narrative structure are likely to be forgotten.

Narratives may help regulate *affect* (Bruner, 1990). Baumeister, Wotman, and Stillwell (1993) suggested that stories make a difference to emotional experience. When a negative event happens, it may be reinterpreted by constructing a narrative to make one feel more positive about it. For instance, Murray and Holmes (1994) suggested that North American university students used narratives to reinterpret negative attributes of their romantic partners, so that their sense of confidence in their relationships can be maintained. More generally, people tell stories to construct confidence in close relationships.

Finally, narratives may facilitate *problem solving and planning.* Gick and Holyoak (1980, 1983) showed that reading a story about a situation analogous to a problem facilitated people's problem-solving activity. Participants in this study were told that a malignant tumor needs to be treated by rays, but that a single, powerful ray directed at the tumor will destroy the surrounding healthy tissue as well. In one condition, participants were told about a military general who captured an enemy fortress by dividing his army and having small units attack the fortress from many directions. The telling of the military story increased the probability of solving the tumor problem; the solution was to use multiple rays from many directions converging on the tumor, just like small military units converging on the fortress. The military story that captures the causal structure of the tumor problem enabled people to solve problems and make plans for action.

Narrative and Self. All these cognitive activities influenced by narratives may be employed to construct one of the most significant narratives of all, that is, *self-narrative* (Bruner, 1990; Gergen & Gergen, 1988; Polkinghorne, 1988). As Gergen and Gergen (1988) put it, self-narrative is "the individual's account of the relationship among self-relevant events across time" (p. 19). Polkinghorne (1988, p. 150) summarized the position:

> [W]e achieve our personal identities and self concept through the use of the narrative configuration, and make our existence into a whole by understanding it as an expression of a single unfolding and developing story. We are in the middle of our stories and cannot be sure how they will end; we are constantly having to revise the plot as new events are added to our lives. Self, then, is not a static thing nor a substance, but a configuring of personal events into a historical unity which includes not only what one has been but also anticipations of what one will be.

Put simply, an individual constructs a narrative such that he or she is the main protagonist, or subject in Greimas's terminology (1966/1983), in the self-narrative.

However, the construction of a self-narrative is not a solitary, private activity. As Miller, Potts, Fung, and Hoogstra (1990) suggested, children's self-narrative may be socially constructed by their caregivers telling stories about the children, the caregivers intervening in the children's storytelling, and the children appropriating others' stories as their own (also see Nelson's discussion about autobiographical memory, 1993). Adults' self-narrative, too, may rely on similar processes of social construction. The act of storytelling about oneself is fundamentally a social and psychological process.

Toward a Narrative Conception of Human Motivation

MY argument that narrative provides a cultural basis for human motivation is built on the following propositions:

1. People tell stories to one another.
2. Stories typically contain desired goal states and ways of attaining them in terms of sequence of actions and events.
3. Some categories of stories are told more often than others.
4. The stories that are told more often are more likely to be used to construct people's self-narratives.
5. When people appropriate stories to construct self-narratives, desired goal states and ways of attaining them in terms of sequence of actions and events, which are contained in the stories, are also appropriated.

In short, the appropriation of culturally circulated stories results in the adoption of the stories' goals.

Thus, the central hypothesis of the narrative conception of human motivation is that narratives mediate the acquisition of certain states of the world and self as desired and desirable goals. This emphasis on goals is reminiscent of Lewin's (1938) theory of human motivation, though the present conception does not inherit Lewin's fascination with physical science. As suggested by D'Andrade (1992), once acquired, a loosely organized hierarchy of goals and subgoals may then become the proximal motivator of human action. To the extent that goals embedded in narratives are "genuinely" internalized and that such goals can realistically function as goals, they may provide a motivational basis of human action (D'Andrade, 1992). The well-established finding that the setting of a realistic goal acts as a strong motivator (Locke & Latham, 1990) attests to the psychological force of internalized goals.

Within the present conception, goals embedded in narratives become the central motivator. However, narrativized goals should be distinguished from the folk psychological notion of goals, which Brody (1983) criticized as inadequate for scientific psychology. According to Brody, laypeople explain human action by citing the actor's goal. The question "Why did you walk across the street?" may be answered, "In order to buy a pack of cigarettes." In the folk psychological explanation, the actor is supposed to know what his or her goal is, and a given action is taken to be an instrumental activity to attain it. Brody argued that the actor is not always aware of his or her own goal as clearly as folk psychology presumes.

In a similar vein, McClelland, Koestner, and Weinberger (1989) introduced the distinction between self-attributed and implicit motives. Roughly, self-attributed motives are goals that are clearly recognized by the actors as such; implicit motives are goals that are discernible from stories people tell but of which the actors are not necessarily aware as goals. According to McClelland and associates, self-attributed motives predict specific actions, whereas implicit motives predict spontaneous behavioral trends over time. The researchers likened their notion of implicit motives to unconscious motives of Freudian psychoanalysis (p. 700).

A narrative conception of motivation can accommodate both self-attributed and implicit motives. Narrativized goals may not always be recognized by the actor as his or her own goals. When certain narratives are adopted as self-narratives, the actor may simply act out those narratives without reflective appreciation of the main protagonist's motives. It is perhaps akin to children's play and acting out of some stories: the actor simply carries out the sequence of action described in the narratives. To the extent that self-narratives stay at this level, narrativized goals remain implicit. However, if self-narratives are reflected upon, and the main protagonist's goals are cognized as such, the narrativized goals may become self-attributed motives.

The narrative conception of human motivation has theoretical affinities with many past and present theoretical frameworks of human motivation. For instance, Freud's psychoanalysis can be understood as narratives. According to Schafer (1980–1981), Freud's theory is a kind of metapsychology, which consists of two major narratives: a narrative of the beast (the Id) beaten into submission by the civilization and a narrative of the Newtonian physics of a closed energy system. Schafer suggested that Freudian psychoanalysis provides a language to narrativize an analysand's story.

A narrative conception of human motivation may provide a way of expanding on Weiner's attributional theory of motivation (1986). The literature on attributional processes in the achievement context is mainly concerned with how cognitive processes may be prompted by success and failure experiences, and mediate subsequent achievement-related activities. One of the drawbacks of this approach is that it focuses too narrowly on a set of perceived causes of success and failure. No doubt causes such as ability, effort, task difficulty, and luck play a significant role in everyday explanations of success and failure. However, the attributional approach tended to look too closely at "causes" to the exclusion of any other types of explanations. By contrast, narratives, which are often used to explain everyday experiences, include a much broader range of explanations in addition to causes.

Implications and Concluding Remarks

A NARRATIVE conception has methodological, theoretical, and metatheoretical implications for examining the relationship between culture and motivation. Methodologically, a narrative conception suggests that psychologists should take people's stories seriously. This trend is already here: in 1994, *Personality and Social Psychology Bulletin* (vol. 20, no. 6) had a special section in which a number of researchers' efforts in using narratives were reported.

More to the point, motivation psychology has a long tradition of using narratives in measuring people's motives. The Thematic Apperception Test (TAT), developed by Murray (1938) and used extensively by McClelland, Atkinson, and colleagues (e.g., McClelland, Atkinson, Clark, & Lowell, 1953), uses stories told by people in assessing needs. As Sorrentino and Higgins (1986) noted, TAT may be reinterpreted within a contemporary cognitive-motivational framework. Stories people tell about ambiguous stimuli may reflect their goals that are accessible at the time. Such accessible goals may reflect or even determine human motivation. The coding scheme developed in certain cultures may have some cultural biases and may not be uncritically generalizable; however, a culturally more sensitive coding procedure may be developed (Kornadt, Eckensberger, & Emminghaus, 1980).

Theoretically, the link between culture and motivation may be fruitfully investigated by examining stories that are often told in a culture. McClelland (1961) used the imaginative method of measuring nAch (Need for Achievement) by coding children's stories in terms of achievement themes, and showed that the economic growth of a country from 1925 to 1950 (measured by a composite index of per capita national income and per capita electricity produced) was significantly predicted ($r = .46$ across twenty-one nations) by thus measured nAch for around 1925. This finding is especially intriguing because nAch measured in the same manner for 1950 did not predict the economic gain ($r = -.08$).

McClelland (1961) also reviewed studies that examined the connection between the rise of various Western nations and nAch measured by archival data including stories from those nations. He asserted that the rise of nations such as ancient Athens, Spain in the Middle Ages, Britain around the time of the Industrial Revolution, and the United States from 1800 to 1950 may be in part explained by need for achievement. Whether McClelland's theory of nAch and entrepreneurial behavior is tenable, the empirical relationships stand. Although a subsequent study yielded some negative results (Beit-Hallahmi, 1980), a reexamination of McClelland's research program may be due within the context of psychology's contribution to national development.

Metatheoretically, a narrative approach may be taken as a counterweight to the so-called logical positivist paradigm (Bruner, 1990; Sarbin, 1986), or a reconfiguration of the social sciences as a humanly relevant endeavor (Smith, 1991). Logical positivism stifled the development of human sciences by restricting the meaning of meaning to empirical verifiability (or its Popperian refiguration as empirical falsifiability), thereby narrowly focusing on the literalness of meaning.[3] The meaning of a narrative, however, is not exhausted by its literal meaning (i.e., reference) but is significantly shaped by its plot. At the same time, while acknowledging the importance of the imaginary, a narrative approach does not exclusively emphasize the lack of literalness. To this extent, a narrative approach *expands* on the current focus on literal meaning rather than *replaces* it.

Recently, a number of psychologists have examined how figurative meaning such as metaphors and metonymies influences human thought (e.g., Gibbs, 1994; Ortony, 1993), redressing the imbalance created by the exclusive emphasis on literal meaning. Narrative, as a genre, sits between figurative and literal meaning, and touches on both. Likewise, human motivation stems from both internal and external sources, and depends on the real and imaginary. Narrative perhaps plays an important role in the story about human motivation.

Notes

1. I take that both D'Andrade (1981) and Shweder (1992) expressed a similar discontent, though their criticism is directed to the analytical separation between ideational content and affective force, or cultural content and cultural force, respectively.

2. I wish to emphasize the point that narratives are *indifferent* to truths. Surely, narratives may be "true" or "false" in some sense.

3. Logical positivism (or logical empiricism) as a philosophy of science requires a complex discussion, which goes beyond the scope of this paper. I focus on the aspect of logical positivism as a theory of meaning here.

References

Auerbach, E. (1953). *Mimesis: The representation of reality in western literature* (R. Trask, Trans.). Princeton: Princeton University Press.

Bartlett, F. C. (1932). *Remembering.* Cambridge: Cambridge University Press.

Baumeister, R. F., & Newman, L. S. (1994). How stories make sense of personal experiences: Motives that shape autobiographical narratives. *Personality and Social Psychology Bulletin, 20,* 676–690.

Baumeister, R. F., Wotman, S. R., & Stillwell, A. M. (1993). Unrequited love: On heartbreak, anger, guilt, scriptlessness, and humiliation. *Journal of Personality and Social Psychology, 64,* 377–394.

Beit-Hallahmi, B. (1980). Achievement motivation and economic growth. *Personality and Social Psychology Bulletin, 6*, 210–215.

Bourdieu, P. (1977). *Outline of a theory of practice* (R. Nice, Trans.). Cambridge: Cambridge University Press.

Bower, G. H., Black, J. B., & Turner, T. J. (1979). Scripts in memory for text. *Cognitive Psychology, 11*, 177–220.

Brody, N. (1983). *Human motivation: Commentary on goal-directed action.* New York: Academic Press.

Bruner, J. (1986). *Actual minds, possible worlds.* Cambridge: Harvard University Press.

Bruner, J. (1990). *Acts of meaning.* Cambridge: Harvard University Press.

Burke, K. (1945/1969). *A grammar of motives.* Berkeley: University of California Press.

D'Andrade, R. G. (1981). The cultural part of cognition. *Cognitive Science, 5*, 179–195.

D'Andrade, R. G. (1992). Schemas and motivation. In R. G. D'Andrade & C. Strauss (Eds.), *Human motives and cultural models* (pp. 23–44). Cambridge: Cambridge University Press.

Ewick, P., & Silbey, S. S. (1995). Subversive stories and hegemonic tales: Toward a sociology of narrative. *Law and Society Review, 29*, 197–226.

Gergen, K. J., & Gergen, M. M. (1988). Narrative and the self as relationship. *Advances in Experimental Social Psychology, 21*, 17–56.

Gibbs, R. W., Jr. (1994). *The poetics of mind: Figurative thought, language, and understanding.* New York: Cambridge University Press.

Gick, M. L., & Holyoak, K. J. (1980). Analogical problem solving. *Cognitive Psychology, 12*, 306–355.

Gick, M. L., & Holyoak, K. J. (1983). Schema induction and analogical transfer. *Cognitive Psychology, 15*, 1–38.

Goodman, N. (1978). *Ways of worldmaking.* Indianapolis: Hackett.

Graesser, A. C., Woll, S. B., Kowalski, D. J., & Smith, D. A. (1980). Memory for typical and atypical actions in scripted activities. *Journal of Experimental Psychology: Human Learning and Memory, 6*, 503–515.

Greimas, A. J. (1966/1983). *Structural semantics: An attempt at a method* (D. McDowell, R. Schleifer, & A. Velie, Trans.). Lincoln: University of Nebraska Press.

Greimas, A. J. (1990). *The social sciences: A semiotic view.* (P. Perron & F. H. Collins, Trans.). Minneapolis: University of Minnesota Press.

Greimas, A. J., & Courtés, J. (1976). The cognitive dimension of narrative discourse. *New Literary History, 7*, 433–447.

Harvey, J. H., Weber, A. L., & Orbuch, T. L. (1990). *Interpersonal accounts: A social psychological perspective.* Cambridge, MA: Basil Blackwell.

Hastie, R., Park, B., & Weber, R. (1984). Social memory. In R. Wyer, Jr., & T. Srull (Eds.), *Handbook of social cognition,* Vol. 2 (pp. 151–212). Hillsdale, NJ: Erlbaum.

Holland, D. C. (1992). How cultural systems become desire: A case study of American romance. In R. G. D'Andrade & C. Strauss (Eds.), *Human motives and cultural models* (pp. 61–89). Cambridge: Cambridge University Press.

Holland, D. C., & Quinn, N. (1987). *Cultural models in language and thought.* New York: Cambridge University Press.

Kahler, E. (1973). *The inward turn of narrative* (R. Winston & C. Winston, Trans.). Princeton: Princeton University Press.

Kornadt, H.-J., Eckensberger, L. H., & Emminghaus, W. B. (1980). Cross-cultural research on motivation and its contribution to a general theory of motivation. In H. C. Triandis & W. Lonner (Eds.), *Handbook of cross-cultural psychology: Basic processes,* Vol. 3 (pp. 223–321). Boston: Allyn & Bacon.

Labov, W. (1972). *Language in the inner city.* Philadelphia: University of Pennsylvania Press.

Lewin, K. (1938). *The conceptual representation and the measurement of psychological forces.* Durham, NC: Duke University Press.

Locke, E. A., & Latham, G. P. (1990). *A theory of goal setting and task performance.* Englewood Cliffs, NJ: Prentice-Hall.

Lonner, W. J. (1980). The search for psychological universals. In H. C. Triandis & W. W. Lambert (Eds.), *Handbook of cross-cultural psychology: Perspectives,* Vol. 1 (pp. 143–204). Boston: Allyn & Bacon.

Lucariello, J. (1990). Canonicality and consciousness in child narrative. In B. K. Britton & A. D. Pellegrini (Eds.), *Narrative thought and narrative language* (pp. 131–149). Hillsdale, NJ: Erlbaum.

Lukes, S. (1973). *Individualism.* Oxford: Basil Blackwell.

McClelland, D. C. (1961). *The achieving society.* Princeton, NJ: D. Van Nostrand.

McClelland, D. C., Atkinson, J. W., Clark, R. A., & Lowell, E. (1953). *The achievement motive.* New York: Appleton-Century-Crofts.

McClelland, D. C., Koestner, R., & Weinberger, J. (1989). How do self-attributed and implicit motives differ? *Psychological Review, 96,* 690–702.

Michaels, S. (1991). The dismantling of narrative. In A. McCabe & C. Peterson (Eds.), *Developing narrative structure* (pp. 303–351). Hillsdale, NJ: Erlbaum.

Miller, P. J., Potts, R., Fung, H., & Hoogstra, L. (1990). Narrative practices and the social construction of self. *American Ethnologist, 17,* 292–311.

Murray, H. A. (1938). *Explorations in personality.* New York: Oxford University Press.

Murray, S. L., & Holmes, J. G. (1994). Storytelling in close relationships: The construction of confidence. *Personality and Social Psychology Bulletin, 20,* 650–663.

Nelson, K. (1993). The psychological and social origins of autobiographical memory. *Psychological Science, 4,* 7–14.

Ortony, A. (1993). *Metaphor and thought* (2nd ed.). New York: Cambridge University Press.

Pennington, N., & Hastie, R. (1986). Evidence evaluation in complex decision making. *Journal of Personality and Social Psychology, 51,* 242–258.

Pennington, N., & Hastie, R. (1988). Explanation-based decision making: Effects of memory structure on judgment. *Journal of Experimental Psychology: Learning, Memory and Cognition, 14,* 521–533.

Pennington, N., & Hastie, R. (1992). Explaining the evidence: Tests of the story model for juror decision making. *Journal of Personality and Social Psychology, 62,* 189–206.

Polkinghorne, D. E. (1988). *Narrative knowing and the human sciences.* Albany: State University of New York Press.

Propp, V. (1968). *Morphology of the folktale.* Austin: University of Texas Press.

Ricoeur, P. (1981). The narrative function. In J. B. Thompson (Ed. & Trans.), *Paul Ricoeur: Hermeneutics and the human sciences* (pp. 274–296). Cambridge: Cambridge University Press.

Ricoeur, P. (1984). *Time and narrative,* Vol. 1 (K. McLaughlin & D. Pellauer, Trans.). Chicago: University of Chicago Press.

Sarbin, T. R. (1986). The narrative as a root metaphor for psychology. In T. R. Sarbin (Ed.), *Narrative psychology: The storied nature of human conduct* (pp. 3–21). New York: Praeger.

Schafer, R. (1980–1981). Narration in the psychoanalytic dialogue. In W. J. T. Mitchell (Ed.), *On narrative* (pp. 25–49). Chicago: University of Chicago Press.

Schank, R. C., & Abelson, R. P. (1995). *Knowledge and memory: the real study.* In R. Wyer & T. Srull (Eds.), *Advances in social cognition,* Vol. 8 (pp. 1–85). Hillsdale, NJ: Erlbaum.

Shweder, R. A. (1992). Ghost busters in anthropology. In R. G. D'Andrade & C. Strauss (Eds.), *Human motives and cultural models* (pp. 45–57). Cambridge: Cambridge University Press.

Smith, B. H. (1980–1981). Narrative versions, narrative theories. In W. J. T. Mitchell (Ed.), *On narrative* (pp. 209–232). Chicago: University of Chicago Press.

Smith, M. B. (1991). *Values, self, and society: Toward a humanist social psychology.* New Brunswick, NJ: Transaction.

Sorrentino, R. M., & Higgins, E. T. (1986). Motivation and cognition: Warming up to synergism. In R. M. Sorrentino & E. T. Higgins (Eds.), *Handbook of motivation and cognition,* Vol. 1 (pp. 3–19). New York: Guilford Press.

Todorov, T. (1977). *The poetics of prose.* Ithaca, NY: Cornell University Press.

Valsiner, J. (1989). *Human development and culture: The social nature of personality and its study.* Toronto: Lexington Books.

Weiner, B. (1986). *An attributional theory of motivation and emotion.* New York: Springer-Verlag.

White, H. (1980–1981). The value of narrativity in the representation of reality. In W. J. T. Mitchell (Ed.), *On narrative* (pp. 1–23). Chicago: University of Chicago Press.

Wrong, D. H. (1961). The oversocialized conception of man in modern sociology. *American Sociological Review, 26,* 183–193.

Social and Interpersonal Processes

Chapter Three

Social Motivation and Culture

RUSSELL GEEN *and* JOHN D. C. SHEA

otivation refers, in a general sense, to processes involved in the initiation, direction, and energization of individual behavior. The term *social motivation* refers to the activation of these processes by situations in which other people are in close contact with the individual. It is usually assumed that the social situation does not provide specific cues for the behavior of the individual. Such topics as direct social influence, persuasion, conformity, and social reinforcement are not, therefore, considered to be part of social motivation (Geen & Gange, 1977).

The study of social motivation was begun by Triplett (1898), who observed that sport bicyclists pedaled with greater speed when they rode in the company of other cyclists than they did when riding alone. This study introduced to psychology the phenomenon of social facilitation of performance, in which the presence of others produces an increase in individual motivation. Triplett studied situations in which the other persons present performed a task in concert with the individual; these became known as coaction settings. In 1904, Meumann reported the first study in which social facilitation was achieved by a passive audience that merely observed the individual perform (Cottrell, 1972). Several years later, Ringelmann reported a series of studies (which had actually been conducted prior to Triplett's research) in which the presence of others appeared to lead to decreased individual productivity (Kravitz & Martin, 1986). Ringelmann showed that when people are added to a group engaged in a physical task like rope pulling, the amount of force exerted per person decreases as the size of the group increases. Although Ringelmann thought that this effect was due chiefly to loss of coordination as the group grew in size, he conceded that loss of motivation could also be involved. The earliest studies in social motivation, therefore, showed that under some conditions the presence of others leads to motivational gains, whereas under other conditions it produces motivational decrements. Interest in motivation losses in social settings—the so-called Ringelmann effect—declined sharply in the decades immediately following the original reports, but investigations of social facilitation, involving both the coaction and audience paradigms, were conducted sporadically during that period. The findings from these studies were mixed, however, and tended to show that the presence of audiences or coactors facilitated performance or had the opposite effect—what might be designated as social inhibition of performance—about equally often. This research was seriously hampered by a lack of theoretical formulations that could explain the contradictory effects with a single set of premises.

Social Facilitation

THE modern era of research on social facilitation began with a major theoretical paper by Zajonc (1965). Attempting to explain the mixed evidence from previous studies, Zajonc proposed that (1) the presence of others elicits a drive-like state of arousal, (2) drive multiplies with habit strength for all responses in a situation, increasing the probability of a dominant response relative to a subordinate one, and (3) the dominant response is more likely to be the correct one on easy tasks than on a difficult ones. From this, Zajonc concluded that the presence of others leads to social facilitation of performance on easy or overlearned tasks but to social inhibition of performance on difficult ones. The decade following the appearance of Zajonc's paper yielded numerous experimental investigations of social facilitation, most of them animated by Zajonc's arguments. Some sought to test his viewpoint and others to challenge it with alternative explanations. In 1977 Geen and Gange reviewed this literature and concluded that at that time the most parsimonious explanation for both social facilitation and social inhibition was the drive-theoretical viewpoint. In the years since that review the situation has changed, and today such a confident conclusion of the primacy of drive theory is no longer warranted.

Evaluation Apprehension

An early criticism of Zajonc's position concerned the nature of the social presence required for increased drive. Whereas Zajonc (1965) had concluded that the mere presence of others is sufficient to have this effect on the individual, certain investigators argued that the others must be regarded by the individual as potential judges and critics. The immediate precursor of increased drive was therefore thought to be anxiety or evaluation apprehension. (Cottrell et al., 1968; Henchy & Glass, 1968). For example, Seta and associates (1989) showed that the status of other persons present plays a role in generating arousal. Whereas the addition of high-status persons to an observing group leads to increased arousal in the observed individual, the addition of lower-status persons may actually reduce arousal by diminishing the overall level of anxiety over being evaluated.

Two other explanations of social facilitation/inhibition were built on the idea of increased arousal in social settings. Baron and his associates (Baron, 1986) showed that audiences may induce conflict in a performing subject by distracting him or her from the task at hand. Guerin (1986) concluded that arousal elicited by the presence of others is due mainly to feelings of uncertainty over what those others may do. Both of these theories are supported by considerable evidence, but, as Geen (1991) has argued, separating the effects of evaluation apprehension from those of conflict and uncertainty is often difficult on methodological grounds, and experimental studies designed to test one explanation often can be adduced as support for the others as well.

Cognitive Overload

More recent formulations of social facilitation have departed from the once-dominant view that drive constitutes the major intervening variable in the process (Geen, 1989). In an extension of his distraction/conflict model, Baron (1986) has argued that the distraction caused by being observed by others results in stimulus overload. This is a departure from the previously held idea that distraction engenders drive because the consequences of cognitive overload are different from those of increased drive. Whereas drive energizes all responses in a situation (manifesting the second of the two steps in the social facilitation process outlined above), cognitive overload produces selectivity and narrowing of attention.

This argument assumes that every person has a finite attentional capacity and that as demands arise, the spare capacity left over for such activities as problem solving decreases. One result of overload is increased effort to pay attention, which can produce a momentary increase in arousal. The significance of this arousal does not lie in its energizing task-related responses, however, as drive theory would hold. Instead, it is a concomitant of effortful attention. The main functional response to cognitive overload is a narrowing of attention to a relatively narrow range of central cues, thereby reducing the load on the attentional system. In a study supporting this proposition, Geen (1976) found that subjects who were observed during a task were less distracted by the addition of irrelevant information than were subjects working alone. On the other hand, when potentially helpful additional information was provided, observed subjects were helped less by it than were those who performed in isolation. These findings suggest that being observed led subjects to be less able to utilize additional information than they would have been if left alone. This is what would be expected if being observed produced a narrowing of attention to central task cues.

Self-Presentational Concerns

The presence of others has effects on the individual that go beyond both arousal and cognitive overload by engaging and activating a need to present a desired or idealized self-image to others. Self-presentation motives have been shown to play a role in several studies. The findings of these studies are sometimes cited as evidence against the drive-theory explanation of social facilitation, and it is true that they often report effects that cannot be accounted for by that approach. For example, Bond (1982) designed an experiment in which drive theory and self-presentation theory made directly opposite predictions and found that the latter accounted for the social facilitation effect. Other studies, while being less directly crucial in comparing the two theories, have adduced evidence that under some conditions the self-presentation theory can explain results that are inexplicable in terms of drive theory. Three approaches to social facilitation that employ the concepts of self-presentation have been proposed.

Self-awareness. Carver and Scheier (1981) have proposed that the effect of the presence of others increases the individual's sense of self-awareness, making him or her more cognizant of not only personal behavior but also an ideal standard of performance for the task at hand. In keeping with their general theory of behavior, in which action is generated to reduce or eliminate discrepancies between one's actual level of performance and a standard, Carver and Scheier proposed further that the decision to undertake such action depends on the perceived probability of successful matching-to-standard. When the task is easy and the probability of successfully matching the ideal is high, the person proceeds to complete the task; in this case, the presence of others, by bringing the real-ideal discrepancy into focus, facilitates performance. However, when the task is difficult, the person is more likely to think that the probability of success is too low and, hence, to give up. Under these conditions, the presence of others causes task performance either to be terminated or to become minimal.

Impression management. Another self-presentational approach to social facilitation is based on the premise that people strive to present the best possible appearance to others so that they may make a favorable impression. Observers or coactors may not only motivate individuals to work hard at tasks but also exacerbate the person's sense of embarrassment when performance leads to failure. Such failure is less likely when the task is easy than when it is hard, so that the increased motivation may be sufficient to produce performance of high quality. Difficult tasks often result in failure, however, at least at the outset. Embarrassment evoked by such failure may cause stress and cognitive interference that disrupts subsequent performance. The previously cited study by Bond (1982) was conducted in the context of this approach. Thus, evaluation apprehension, which was earlier shown to be an antecedent of arousal, also plays an important role in presentation of the self. Baumeister (1982) makes this point in asserting that the desire to make a good impression is a fundamental motive and that fear of negative evaluation arises whenever the person has some concern over being able to present the self adequately.

Consistent with this line of reasoning, several studies have shown that when the person is subjected to an experience of failure just before performing a task (which should increase feelings of evaluation anxiety), subsequent performance before observers is poorer than it is when no prior failure is experienced (e.g., Seta & Hassan, 1980). Geen (1979) obtained similar findings among observed subjects who had first been exposed to failure, and in addition found that when a success experience preceded the task, performance among observed subjects was superior to that of subjects who performed the task without preliminary treatment. Because the task used by Geen was a difficult one, this finding goes against what would have been predicted from drive theory, but it is consistent with the self-presentational approach.

Response withholding. Evaluation apprehension arising from the presence of others can also influence performance by motivating the individual to refrain from behaving in ways that may be socially undesirable. Response suppression has been demonstrated in a series of studies by Berger and his associates (1981), who found that the presence of an audience motivates subjects to suppress overt practice (e.g., moving one's lips while reading, counting out loud) while performing a task. Because these devices assist learning, their suppression should inhibit performance on difficult tasks.

Elimination of such overt practice on easy tasks may have the beneficial effect of compelling the person to use more symbolic processing, which should improve performance on such tasks. The upshot of all this is that if for any reason the person feels constrained to inhibit overt motoric practice, learning unfamiliar material will be hindered but learning familiar material will not. Berger further suggests that persons who are observed while learning will feel such constraints because of a cultural norm that discourages such overt activity. Thus, the presence of an audience should facilitate performance on familiar tasks but inhibit performance on unfamiliar ones. In several experiments, Berger and his associates have found support for this hypothesis.

Additional findings linking the presence of an audience to response inhibition are contained in several studies by Geen (1985, 1987) on the relationship of evaluation apprehension to passive avoidance. Briefly stated, the major hypothesis of this research is that when people are anxious in an evaluative situation and are also unable to leave the situation physically, they withhold or restrain responding in an effort to avoid making errors. If the presence of observers elicits evaluation apprehension, one reaction to audience settings may be cautiousness in responding, reflected in a low response rate. Furthermore, because complex and difficult tasks evoke more anxiety than simple ones, the greatest amount of response withholding should come on

difficult tasks. This would lead to relatively poor performance, whereas on simple tasks the relatively moderate response withholding would have no such effect. Instead, a slightly slower response rate could facilitate greater attention to simple tasks because the person is not distracted by his or her own action, and this could lead to a slight facilitation of performance.

Conclusion

From this brief and selective review of the literature on social facilitation, two conclusions may be drawn. The first is that audiences can evoke feelings of evaluation apprehension in observers and that these feelings mediate subsequent social facilitation or inhibition of performance. The second is that evaluation apprehension can produce direct effects on behavior by initiating efforts at impression management, including the withholding of behaviors likely to embarrass or otherwise discomfit the person. The significance of these conclusions for a cultural analysis of social motivation will be the subject of the final section of this chapter.

Social Loafing

THE phenomenon of apparent motivation loss in groups studied by Ringelmann (see above) was resurrected in the late 1970s by Latané and his associates, who gave the phenomenon the name of social loafing. Early tests of social loafing involved simple physical acts such as shouting and hand clapping individually or in groups, with the general result that the intensity of output per person declined as additional members were added (e.g., Latané et al., 1979). Later studies showed considerable generality in the effect, with loafing occurring in several nonphysical activities. The data on social loafing are consistent with one of the major premises of social impact theory (Latané & Nida, 1980): when a person is a member of a group subjected to social forces, the impact of those forces on each person in the group is diminished in inverse proportion to, among other things, the number of people in the group.

Geen (1991) has concluded that social loafing involves the same processes related to evaluation apprehension that explain the social facilitation/inhibition effect. The argument may be summarized briefly. Social loafing is a normal response to tasks that are tiring, uninteresting, and otherwise not likely to make a person feel involved. The tasks commonly used in experimental research on social loafing are boring and meaningless (cf. Brickner, Harkins, & Ostrom, 1986). People therefore try to avoid doing them, and will do so unless social constraints are implemented. Kerr and Bruun (1981) call this the "hide-in-the-crowd" explanation, indicating that group members provide a cover of anonymity for the unmotivated individual. This cover is usually facilitated in experiments on loafing by the usual practice of pooling the outputs of the group members. Making each person's output identifiable eliminates social loafing (Williams et al., 1981).

This finding introduces the possibility that subjects become apprehensive about being evaluated by the experimenter (as has already been demonstrated in research on social facilitation), and that this is why they do not loaf under nonanonymous conditions. Such is especially the case when subjects believe that their performance is being compared to that of their coactors, so that they are effectively in competition with the others. This will be more likely to occur, moreover, when all of the persons in the group are performing the same task than when they are working on different tasks. Harkins and Jackson (1985) found support for this hypothesis by showing that social loafing was least likely to occur in a group when the outputs of the individuals were identifiable and when all subjects worked at the same task. Thus, the condition in which the highest level of evaluation apprehension was created was also the one in which the least loafing occurred.

If experiments on group performance involve tasks that engage the interest or concern of the individual, a necessary condition for social loafing is absent and the effect is not obtained (Brickner et al., 1986). Social loafing is, therefore, attributable not so much to a loss of motivation in the group setting as to an absence of motivation due to the nature of the task that becomes manifest in behavior under group conditions. Evaluation apprehension in this setting causes the individual to suppress the preferred response—inactivity—in favor of more socially desirable behavior. Viewed in this way, absence of social loafing appears to represent a special case of response withholding under conditions of evaluation anxiety quite similar to that shown in studies reviewed above.

A related explanation of social loafing involves the concept of matching-to-standard. This explanation assumes that apprehension over the possibility of being evaluated by the experimenter causes the person to match a standard for performance set by the experimenter (and that this matching is avoided under conditions that allow social loafing). Several studies have shown in addition that even when cues signalling evaluation by the experimenter are not present, social loafing may be eliminated by the invocation of other salient standards to which the person's output can be compared. These standards need not be social. Harkins and Szymanski (1988), for example, found that merely reminding the persons in a group of a personal performance standard for the behavior in question was sufficient to eliminate social loafing, and Harkins and Szymanski (1989) obtained the same result by reminding individuals of a group standard.

Social loafing, once thought to be the product of a loss in motivation under group conditions, now appears to be a form of avoidance behavior prompted by uninteresting and noninvolving tasks. It is reduced or eliminated by establishing conditions that either remove the anonymity of the persons involved or remind the persons of certain standards of behavior pertinent to the activity. The idea that the introduction of social, personal, or group standards increases motivation is consistent with certain theoretical formulations pertaining to the self. For example, Breckler and Greenwald (1986) have proposed that individuals select their behaviors in order to secure a favorable self-image, to make a good impression on other people, and to live up to the standards of important reference groups. People avoid social loafing in spite of low motivation for the task because of salient personal, social, and collective standards for behavior. These three standards may, in turn, all be the products of a larger superordinate motive: the motive to be included in the social collective. To understand this, we must consider the motivational bases for evaluation apprehension, social anxiety, and self-presentation.

The Need for Social Inclusion
THEORY and research on both social facilitation and social loafing suggest that evaluation apprehension is an important motive for human behavior in

social settings. Each phenomenon may therefore be thought of as a manifestation of a more general influence of social anxiety, which has been defined as a state brought about by a person's being motivated to make a certain impression on others but doubting that this impression can be made (Schlenker & Leary, 1982). To avoid this state the person adopts various strategies of self-presentation and impression management in the hopes of creating a favorable impression and, as a consequence, of maintaining self-esteem. That is, the person adopts a course of action that enables him or her to overcome doubts about securing a desirable social outcome.

The impression-management strategy in social facilitation, seen in such behavior as trying harder to succeed in the presence of an audience following success than following failure, typifies such activity. The person appraises the social situation as one that threatens to be embarrassing should he or she fail and, as a consequence, increases effort to avoid failure. Inhibiting socially undesirable responses in social settings may also be seen as behavior calculated to avoid the possibility of making a bad impression and hence avoiding social anxiety. Suppressing a desire to loaf in a group during a boring task because of fear of exposure or of not meeting an internalized standard may also be interpreted as behavior aimed at avoiding anxiety.

Why should the fear of making a bad impression be such a powerful motive for individual behavior? One answer is that people may wish to make a good impression in order to avoid social rejection or exclusion. Humans have a strong need to be accepted by, and included within, society (Baumeister & Leary, 1995). Because of this need, social anxiety may be adaptive by supplying a warning signal that social disapproval will occur unless an ongoing course of action is modified (Baumeister & Tice, 1990). Any behavior that might make the person seem unattractive or useless to the group could invite social exclusion and thereby elicit the warning signal. Anxiety therefore interrupts behavior, focuses attention on what is being done wrong, and motivates the person to seek an alternative course of action. Among these alternatives, as already noted, are acts that help the person avoid failure or other negative outcomes by controlling behavior, becoming more motivated to do some things and to refrain from doing others. The phenomena of social facilitation and social loafing fall within this broad domain of behavior. However, it is also possible that the person will resort to other courses of action and sample from a wide range of cognitive strategies demonstrated in recent research on the maintenance of self-esteem, such as self-handicapping, a self-serving attributional bias, excuse making, or symbolic self-completion (Geen, 1991). Each strategy can be thought of as a process whereby the person attempts to escape blame or criticism from others for failure or other socially undesirable outcomes.

Why do people need to belong to social groups? One reason may be psychoevolutionary. Homo sapiens evolved as a member of small hunting or gathering groups, so that certain traits associated with sociability may have become dominant through natural selection (Hogan, 1983). Another reason may be cultural. According to an interesting thesis proposed by Solomon and his colleagues (1991), people need to be included within the collective because human culture, which society represents, provides a buffer against facing one's own vulnerability and mortality. Society provides a "cultural drama" that gives meaning to life and without which the person would experience existential dread. The person is therefore motivated to fulfill an approved role in that drama. Meeting cultural standards brings approval, social acceptance, and self-esteem; failing to meet those standards and social expectations invites rejection. Avoiding failure and suppressing socially undesirable action is only part of the motivational complex elicited by fear of death and nonbeing. The same motive also elicits positive prosocial behaviors aimed at enhancing and strengthening the authority of social customs and demands.

Social Motivation Across Cultures

FOLLOWING on from the notion that a need for inclusion in the social collective may be an important determinant of social anxiety in general and therefore of social motivation in particular, we might expect some differences in the way that social motivation appears in different cultures when the quality or intensity of social demands differs from Western countries. It has been argued that cultural norms shape the manner in which people from a given cultural group behave in order to win basic approval from their peers (Bond, 1991) and that these styles of embodying the cultural ideal often do not "translate" across cultural lines.

The effect of cultural constraints on limiting social facilitation in some contexts while amplifying it in others is suggested in the description by Savishinsky (1982) of the common participation in vicarious forms of affective experience by the Hare Indians of Coleville Lake, a sub-Arctic village of about seventy persons. People observed in this community were reluctant to express a range of positive and negative emotions such as anger, jealousy, affection, and resentment, in normal day-to-day matters. They maintained an ethic of nonintervention in the lives of others. However, social facilitation of emotional expressiveness was displayed through drinking, aggression, gossip, reactions to movies, and the narrative recitation of folklore and personal adventures. Savishinsky sees this contrast as largely determined by the isolation of the community, and high levels of daily intimacy. Social harmony is maintained by expressing and experiencing affective states only through indirect means in social situations that reduce inhibitions and lead to social facilitation.

Social Loafing/Social Facilitation

Although metanalysis of social loafing studies has demonstrated that it is a robust phenomenon that generalizes across tasks and subject populations, a large number of variables have been shown to moderate social loafing and among these culture is particularly important (Karau & Williams, 1993). It has been asserted that the impact of culture is so great that social loafing may be universally revealed only when examined through the most trivial types of experimental task (Smith & Bond, 1993). Where the task becomes more important and meaningful, different cultures may respond differently. This seems reasonable on the face of it, but if we return to the idea that social loafing tasks are by design tiring, uninteresting, and unlikely to make a person feel involved (Geen, 1991), we might conclude that studies in which importance and meaning are given to some tasks, for some cultures, are studies of some aspect of social motivation other than social loafing.

When the experimental procedures of Latané, Williams, and Harkins (1979) involving how loudly people shout or clap alone or in groups have been repeated using schoolchildren in India, Thailand, Taiwan, and Japan, university students in Malaysia and Japan, and junior managers in Japan, some evidence of social loafing has been found (Smith & Bond, 1993).

Exploring the issue of differences in social loafing between cultures, Gabrenya, Latané, and Wang (1983) examined the hypothesis that group-oriented cultures would show less social loafing because of a tendency to form more cohesive groups and a greater willingness to place group benefit over individual benefit compared to an individualistic culture like that of the United States. In a study of Chinese schoolchildren in Taiwan, using the original task demonstrated by Latané and associates (1979), the authors failed to obtain a cross-cultural difference. However, in a later study (Gabrenya, Wang, & Latané, 1985), using an auditory tracking task that the authors hoped would better meet the requirements of a social loafing task across different cultures, social loafing was found for American schoolchildren but not for Chinese children. The Chinese children actually performed better in pairs than alone, an effect that the authors called "social striving." This observation seems to place the influence of culture for the Chinese subjects within the field of social facilitation rather than that of social loafing.

Studies of social loafing in male Japanese undergraduates (Matsui et al., 1987; Shirakashi, 1985) have led to the conclusion that Japanese subjects do not engage in social loafing in the way that American subjects do. In a comparative study between Japanese and American subjects on a letter-matching task, Yamagishi (1988) reported that in a situation in which subjects could not monitor how much work others were putting in, Japanese subjects more frequently chose to be rewarded on the basis of their individual performance than did American subjects. He argued that they did this in order to avoid the situation wherein they had no information on how hard the others in the group were working. By selecting the individual reward, they could be certain that they would not be penalized by any social loafing that was occurring. Thus, though there is evidence that social loafing is less likely to occur in Japanese than in American subjects, there has been no report of the kind of social facilitation effect that Chinese subjects have revealed when working in groups.

Using a more real-life task than is typical of the classic social loafing studies, Earley (1989) examined the effect of individualism and collectivism on work completed in an organizational setting, comparing managerial trainees from the United States and the People's Republic of China. Subjects were given in-basket tasks such as prioritizing interviews, filling out requisition forms, and rating job applications. Earley reported reduced output for the American subjects but not for the Chinese. The Chinese managers actually worked harder in the group condition than when alone. Again, it appears that working in groups has a social facilitation effect for Chinese subjects.

If we consider the notion, expressed earlier, that the social loafing observed in Western samples in the classic studies of the phenomenon may be attributable to the boring and meaningless nature of the experimental tasks (Brickner et al., 1986), which in turn leads to an absence of motivation manifest in group conditions, we might speculate that when the task is more meaningful, in some collectivist cultures an increase in motivation may occur in a group context. Thus, we might see Earley's (1989) study, in which the experimental task seems more meaningful than the typical social loafing experiment, as demonstrating a difference in social facilitation across cultures rather than a difference in social loafing.

In a similar study comparing American, Israeli, and Chinese managers, Earley (1993) found no difference in work output in the group condition for the "collectivist" Israeli and Chinese managers when they believed they were working with an in-group of similar others, but some reduction in work if they believed they were working with an out-group of dissimilar others. The American managers showed an equal reduction in output whether they were working with an in-group or an out-group. Thus, the social context may determine whether or not social motivation effects occur for people from collectivist cultures, as is the case for people from individualist cultures.

Differences in cultural meaning and value in self-presentation may be reflected in different levels of self-monitoring and even in personality qualities in collectivist versus individualistic cultures. In a study of the characteristics of daily encounters in Chinese and "European" New Zealand college students as a function of self-monitoring and locus of control, Hamid (1994) observed that Chinese subjects showed higher self-monitoring, and higher locus-of-control scores. Their daily social contacts were less task-oriented and involved higher levels of self-disclosure. These observations are consistent with Yang's (1986) conclusion from a review of the research, that Chinese tend to be shyer and less extroverted than other cultural groups and more "socially oriented." A relationship between such social orientation and the extent of self-monitoring behavior may be part of the explanation for the differences observed in the social facilitation data from studies of Chinese groups (Bond, 1986).

Conclusion

Social motivation phenomena have been reported in Japanese, Chinese, Malaysian, Indian and Thai, and Israeli "collectivist" subject groups that are not unlike those reported with Western "individualistic" subject samples. Evidence of both social facilitation effects and of social loafing has been reported. However, experimental situations that purported to demonstrate social loafing in Western subjects often did not produce the same decrease in performance in subjects from collectivist societies and sometimes, specifically with Chinese subjects, produced a "social-striving" effect. Because group performance tasks that engage the interest or concern of the individual do not contain the necessary condition (of boredom) for the absence of motivation that characterizes social loafing, and at least some of the studies here involved such tasks, we might more properly describe such increases in output as social facilitation. Social facilitation effects from group involvement that occur in some collectivist groups may be related to increased self-monitoring that comes from the higher social orientation in such groups.

Summary

A COMMON thread that connects the problem of social facilitation with that of social loafing is the construct of evaluation apprehension. Situations that evoke this affective state can elicit a number of intervening processes that lead in turn to the improvement or inhibition of performance. Such situations can also eliminate tendencies toward social loafing that may be evoked in group settings by boring or uninvolving tasks. Evaluation apprehension, in turn, is a facet of social anxiety, a state called forth whenever the person wishes to make a good impression on others but fears that others' evaluations will be negative. Finally, social anxiety may be a product of a larger and more general motivational state based on a need for inclusion in the social collective and the corresponding fear of social exclusion. Social motivation may, therefore, be a manifestation of basic social processes that have adaptive and even existential consequences.

References

Baron, R. S. (1986). Distraction-conflict theory: Progress and problems. In L. Berkowitz (Ed.), *Advances in experimental social psychology,* Vol. 19 (pp. 1–40). New York: Academic Press.

Baumeister, R. F. (1982). A self-presentational view of social phenomena. *Psychological Bulletin, 91,* 3–26.

Baumeister, R. F., & Leary, M. R. (1995). The need to belong: Desire for interpersonal attraction as a fundamental human motivation. *Psychological Bulletin, 117,* 497–529.

Baumeister, R. F., & Tice, D. M. (1990). Anxiety and social exclusion. *Journal of Social and Clinical Psychology, 9,* 165–195.

Berger, S. M., Hampton, K. L., Carli, L. L., Grandmaison, P. S., Sadow, J. S., & Donath, C. (1981). Audience-induced inhibition of overt practice during learning. *Journal of Personality and Social Psychology, 40,* 479–491.

Bond, C. F. (1982). Social facilitation: A self-presentational view. *Journal of Personality and Social Psychology, 42,* 1042–1050.

Bond, M. H. (1986). The social psychology of the Chinese people. In M. H. Bond, *The psychology of the Chinese people* pp. 213–266. Hong Kong: Oxford University Press.

Bond, M. H. (1991). Cultural influences on modes of impression management: Implications for the culturally diverse organization. In R. A. Giacalone & P. Rosenfeld (Eds.), *Applied impression management: How image-making affects managerial decisions* (Sage Focus editions, 135, pp. 195–215). Newbury Park, CA: Sage.

Breckler, S. J., & Greenwald, A. G. (1986). Motivational facets of the self. In R. M. Sorrentino & E. T. Higgins (Eds.), *Handbook of motivation and cognition,* Vol. 1 (pp. 145–164). New York: Guilford Press.

Brickner, M. A., Harkins, S. G., & Ostrom, T. M. (1986). Effects of personal involvement: Thought-provoking implications for social loafing. *Journal of Personality and Social Psychology, 51,* 763–769.

Carver, C. S., & Scheier, M. F. (1981). The self-attention-induced feedback loop and social facilitation. *Journal of Experimental Social Psychology, 17,* 545–568.

Cottrell, N. B. (1972). Social facilitation. In C. G. McClintock (Ed.), *Experimental social psychology* (pp. 185–236). New York: Holt.

Cottrell, N. B., Wack, D. L., Sekerak, G. J., & Rittle, R. H. (1968). Social facilitation of dominant responses by the presence of an audience and the mere presence of others. *Journal of Personality and Social Psychology, 9,* 245–250.

Earley, P. C. (1989). Social loafing and collectivism: A comparison of the United States and the People's Republic of China. *Administrative Science Quarterly, 34,* 565–581.

Earley, P. C. (1993). East meets West meets Mideast: Further explorations of collectivistic and individualistic work groups. *Academy of Management Journal, 36,* 319–348.

Gabrenya, W. K., Latané, B., & Wang, Y. (1983). Social loafing in cross-cultural perspective: Chinese on Taiwan. *Journal of Cross-Cultural Psychology, 14,* 368–384.

Gabrenya, W. K., Wang, Y., & Latané, B. (1985). Social loafing on an optimizing task: Cross-cultural differences among Chinese and Americans. *Journal of Cross-Cultural Psychology, 16,* 223–242.

Geen, R. G. (1976). Test anxiety, observation, and the range of cue utilization. *British Journal of Social and Clinical Psychology, 15,* 253–259.

Geen, R. G. (1979). Effects of being observed on learning following success and failure experiences. *Motivation and Emotion, 3,* 355–371.

Geen, R. G. (1985). Evaluation apprehension and response withholding in solution of anagrams. *Personality and Individual Differences, 6,* 293–298.

Geen, R. G. (1987). Test anxiety and behavioral avoidance. *Journal of Research in Personality, 21,* 481–488.

Geen, R. G. (1989). Alternative conceptions of social facilitation. In P. Paulus (Ed.), *The psychology of group influence* (2nd ed., pp. 15–51). Hillsdale, NJ: Erlbaum.

Geen, R. G. (1991). Social motivation. *Annual Review of Psychology, 42,* 377–399.

Geen, R. G., & Gange, J. J. (1977). Drive theory of social facilitation: Twelve years of theory and research. *Psychological Bulletin, 84,* 1267–1288.

Guerin, B. (1986). Mere presence effects in humans: A review. *Journal of Experimental Social Psychology, 22,* 38–77.

Hamid, P. N. (1994). Self-monitoring, locus of control, and social encounters of Chinese and New Zealand students. *Journal of Cross-Cultural Psychology, 25,* 353–368.

Harkins, S. G., & Jackson, J. M. (1985). The role of evaluation in eliminating social loafing. *Personality and Social Psychology Bulletin, 11,* 456–465.

Harkins, S. G., & Szymanski, K. (1988). Social loafing and self-evaluation with an objective standard. *Journal of Experimental Social Psychology, 24,* 354–365.

Harkins, S. G., & Szymanski, K. (1989). Social loafing and group evaluation. *Journal of Personality and Social Psychology, 56,* 934–941.

Henchy, T., & Glass, D. C. (1968). Evaluation apprehension and the social facilitation of dominant and subordinate responses. *Journal of Personality and Social Psychology, 10,* 446–454.

Hogan, R. (1983). A socioanalytic theory of personality. In M. Page & R. Dienstbier (Eds.), *Nebraska Symposium on Motivation,* Vol. 31 (pp. 55–89). Lincoln: University of Nebraska Press.

Karau, S. J., & Williams, K. D.(1993). Social loafing: A meta-analytic review and theoretical integration. *Journal of Personality and Social Psychology, 65,* 681–706.

Kerr, N. L., & Bruun, S. E. (1981). Ringelmann revisited: Alternative explanations for the social loafing effect. *Personality and Social Psychology Bulletin, 7,* 224–231.

Kravitz, D. A., & Martin, B. (1986). Ringelmann rediscovered: The original article. *Journal of Personality and Social Psychology, 50,* 936–941.

Latané, B., & Nida, S. (1980). Social impact theory and group influence: A social engineering perspective. In P. Paulus (Ed.), *The psychology of group influence* (1st ed., pp. 3–34). Hillsdale, NJ: Erlbaum.

Latané, B., Williams, K., & Harkins, S. G. (1979). Many hands make light the work: The causes and consequences of social loafing. *Journal of Personality and Social Psychology, 37,* 822–832.

Matsui, T., Kakuyama, T., & Onglatco, M. L. (1987). Effects of goals and feedback on performance in groups. *Journal of Applied Psychology, 72,* 407–415.

Savishinsky, J. S. (1982). Vicarious emotions and cultural restraint. *Journal of Psychoanalytic Anthropology, 5,* 115–135.

Schlenker, B. R., & Leary, M. R. (1982). Social anxiety and self-presentations: A conceptualization and model. *Psychological Bulletin, 92,* 641–669.

Seta, J. J., Crisson, J. E., Seta, C. E., & Wang, M. A. (1989). Task performance and perceptions of anxiety: Averaging and summation in an evaluative setting. *Journal of Personality and Social Psychology, 56,* 387–396.

Seta, J. J., & Hassan, R. K. (1980). Awareness of prior success or failure: A critical factor in task performance. *Journal of Personality and Social Psychology, 39,* 70–76.

Shirakashi, S. (1985). Social loafing of Japanese students. *Hiroshima Forum for Psychology, 10,* 35–40.

Smith, P. B., & Bond, M. H. (1993). *Social psychology across cultures. Analysis and perspectives.* Hemel Hempstead, U.K.: Harvester Wheatsheaf.

Solomon, S., Greenberg, J., & Psyzczynski, T. (1991). A terror management theory of social behavior: The psychological functions of self-esteem and cultural worldviews. In M. P. Zanna (Ed.), *Advances in experimental social psychology,* Vol. 24, (pp. 93–159). San Diego: Academic Press.

Triplett, N. (1898). The dynamogenic factors in pacemaking and competition. *American Journal of Psychology, 9,* 507–533.

Williams, K., Harkins, S. G., & Latané, B. (1981). Identifiability as a deterrent to social loafing: Two cheering experiments. *Journal of Personality and Social Psychology, 40,* 303–311.

Yamagishi, T. (1988). Exit from the group as an individualistic solution to free rider problem in the United States and Japan. *Journal of Experimental and Social Psychology, 24,* 530–542.

Yang, K. S. (1986). Chinese personality and its changes. In M. H. Bond (Eds.), *The psychology of the Chinese people* (pp. 106–170). Hong Kong: Oxford University Press.

Zajonc, R. B. (1965). Social facilitation. *Science, 149,* 269–274.

Chapter Four

Cross-Cultural Personal Relationships

ROBIN GOODWIN

The theme of "crisis" in social psychology is not a new one but is one that has gained a renewed momentum in recent years following a shift in emphasis from methodological to theoretical concerns (Parker, 1989). One recurrent problem has been the inability of researchers to extend their models and findings beyond the confines of the Western experimental settings that have been the locations for most of the work in this field (Bond, 1988). This is despite the fact that the available cross-cultural work that does exist indicates that far from being general, many of the findings of previous researchers are in fact highly culture-specific (Rosenblatt & Anderson, 1981; Winkler & Doherty, 1983).

In few areas has this lack of cross-cultural research been more evident than in the area of personal relationships (Rosenblatt, 1974; Kagitçibasi, 1990). Such an omission is regrettable for a number of reasons. First, a cross-cultural examination of relationships can help answer important questions concerning the way in which the different conceptual "levels" of individual, dyadic, and societal interact (Gudykunst & Ting-Toomey, 1988; Huston & Levinger, 1978). Second, cross-cultural analysis allows us to test competing theories under particularly stringent conditions and, where negative aspects of relationships are under investigation, to learn from cultures where such behavior is absent (Levinson, 1989). Third, acculturation processes in new or changing societies have important implications for relationship behavior and subsequent mental health (e.g., Ghaffarian, 1987; Hanassab & Tidwell, 1989). Finally, it is widely recognized by those outside the traditional academic boundaries of personal-relationship investigation that personal relationships play a strategic role in the wider issues of cultural change and political transition. It is thus evident that cross-cultural investigations of personal relationships are invaluable not only to those working within traditional psychology/sociology frameworks but also to those aiming at wider interdisciplinary connections within the social science and humanity disciplines.

This chapter begins by looking at two theoretical approaches to the study of personal relationships across cultures. First, I consider sociobiological interpretations that stress the universality of relationship practices and beliefs, and some criticisms of this approach. I then outline work from a more social psychological tradition that emphasizes systematic differences in values across cultures and provide examples of the way in which studies of cultural variants can be used to understand some basic variations in personal relations across cultures. I also point to the way in which many of these values can be seen as transient and argue that relationship practices are in many ways at the forefront of cultural change and debate. For the sake of brevity, cross-cultural issues in polygamy and divorce are omitted; interested readers should consult the large anthropological data on this subject (e.g., Betzig, 1989; Goody, 1976).

Arguing for Universals: The Sociobiological Perspective

THE idea that there are fundamental psychological characteristics common to all humans is an old one; Jahoda (1990) traces it back at least as far as Condorcet (1743–94). In the past century, the work has been more empirically rigorous, with researchers having been intrigued by the prospect of finding cultural universals: worldwide patterns in language acquisition or facial expressions of emotion and so forth (Brown, 1991; Rohner, 1984). For sociobiologists, reproductive behavior has been argued to be "the first line of evolutionary pressure" (Kenrick & Keefe, 1992, p. 75), providing a valuable insight into the workings of sociobiological processes in what has previously been considered as a social psychological domain. These approaches assume that each species has a genetically organized set of strategies and tactics for survival, growth, and reproduction (Kenrick & Keefe, 1992, p. 77). Traits that maximize gene replication are considered fit and assumed to be targets of mate choice (Thiessen & Gregg, 1980); further, the sex investing the most in the offspring is generally assumed to be the more selective in choosing a mate (p. 78). Although males may invest more energy in trying to attract a mate, females invest more resources in parenting. In recent years, two studies conducted from this sociobiological perspective have stimulated a great deal of heated debate.

David Buss and his colleagues (1985; 1988; 1989; Buss & Barnes 1986; Buss and forty-nine others, 1990) have taken a sociobiological approach to understanding partner selection. They argue that a "selective advantage" is afforded those who prefer mates capable of reproductive investment (Buss & Barnes, 1986, p. 569), and, accordingly, potential partners with preferred attributes are those most frequently chosen for mating. Thus, across cultures men should value the features that correlate with female reproductive capability, in particular, female youth and beauty (Buss, 1988, 1989). Similarly, women should choose men who can "provide" the family with social and material resources, usually reflected through earning potential, ambition, and industriousness.

To test these hypotheses in a cross-cultural setting, Buss (1989; Buss et al., 1990) gathered data from more than ten thousand respondents in thirty-seven cultures and a vast diversity of samples in probably the largest-ever study of human relationships across cultures. The critical questions included the desired age of marriage, desired age difference between spouses, the rating of a set of eighteen characteristics, and the rank ordering of a further thirteen. In thirty-six of the cultures, females valued "good financial prospects" more highly than males did, and in twenty-nine valued ambition and industriousness significantly more. In all the cultures men rated physical attractiveness higher than women did, and in twenty-three chastity in potential mates more than did females. There were no significant differences in the other cultures. In each of the cultures, men preferred young females, and younger women preferred older men. Demographic data seemed to support these preferences, with females being younger than males at actual age of marriage.

In a second application of sociobiological theory, this time focusing on age differences in partner preferences, Kenrick and Keefe (1992) predicted that males' preferences for relatively young females would be minimal during early mating years but become more pronounced as the male ages. Young females were predicted to prefer older males both during early years and as they grew older. The researchers conducted six studies, using a variety of data sources (advertisements in newspapers, marriage statistics) and analyzing data from different generations and cultures (the United States, Germany, Holland, Philippines, India). Their interpretation is a relatively complex one that allows for individual factors (such as attractiveness) and environmental factors (such as the availability of opposite-sex partners and social norms) and for cognitive considerations, such as self-perceptions.

A number of questions can be raised about both Buss's and Kenrick and Keefe's conclusions. First, Buss's principal finding seems to be that both men and women have the same order of mate preference: for a kind and understanding and intelligent partner. This finding is also consistent with other explorations into mate selection using other samples (e.g., Goodwin, 1990a; Howard, Blumstein, & Schwartz, 1987) and is also consistent with Buss's finding that the tactics of mate selection are also very similar across the sexes (Buss, 1988). This (understandable) tendency to "overplay" the sex differences that most strongly support evolutionary theory is less present in the age-difference data, but here it is the considerable variability in the age of choice (with women preferring men who are "too old" to offer suitable parenting) that is the most challenging for these theorists. It is possibly in this variance that the most fascinating social psychological processes occur.

Second, Buss's own cross-cultural data show that far more variability in his responses was explained by cultural variability than by sex differences (Buss et al., 1990), a factor that may be linked to degree of modernity (as Buss and associates suggest) or the partly related concept of societal development (Glenn, 1989). Similar questions must be raised concerning the cross-cultural generalizability of the age data presented by Kenrick and Keefe (1992). Their sample was drawn predominantly from the United States and Europe, together with advertisers in a high-status Indian newspaper, with females over forty omitted. It is thus questionable whether their data fit societies such as hunter-gatherers, where older women are often preferred despite their reduced protective capabilities (Stephan, 1992).

Third, the speed at which partner preferences seems to have changed over the past fifty years, at least in Western cultures, also makes an evolutionary account more problematic. The extensive partner-preference literature shows a steady growth in similarity of preferences over the years (Goodwin, 1989). A similar change has been shown in age preferences over the past century; in the United States at least there has been a marked increase in the tendency for women to marry older men (Stevens, 1992). From this author's viewpoint (as well as that of many others; see, for example, Howard and associates' {1987} article using homosexual couples), the shift makes it easier to interpret these sex differences in terms of relatively short-term societal values and norms rather than in rather more ambitious sociobiological terms. The same normative argument may also be applied to the findings of Kenrick and Keefe (1992), although, if it is desirable for human beings to marry and have children, then they are likely to seek partners of child-producing and child-rearing ages, so biological imperatives produce a sex difference. However, this difference may be seen as part of the wider "exchange" process by which a woman's ability to have children is rated alongside other characteristics that are less directly biological (such as social standing with peers) in determining her "market" value. Other cultural imperatives still operate by providing acceptable minimal ages of marriage, the stigmas attached to "lechery," and so on.

Variations in Values Across Cultures

IN contrast, a set of studies of values over the past two decades have sought to examine the manner in which cultures differ in values, and the implications these value variations have for a variety of social behaviors. In one of the largest empirical studies ever undertaken in the social sciences, Geert Hofstede (Hofstede, 1980) collected data on employees' work experience from more than a hundred thousand employees of IBM across forty countries during 1967 and 1973. He discovered that approximately half the differences between countries could be explained by four dimensions, which he termed individualism-collectivism, power distance (large versus small), uncertainty avoidance, and masculinity versus femininity (Hofstede, 1994). Following the work of the Chinese Culture Connection (1987; Bond, 1988) on Chinese values, he added the fifth dimension: Confucian dynamism.

Hofstede's dimensions have been used differently in different disciplines (Hofstede, 1994). In cross-cultural psychology, the two most widely employed cultural variants have been those of individualism-collectivism and power distance (Smith & Bond, 1993), with the former attracting the most attention (for example, see Kim, Triandis, Kagitçibasi, Choi, & Yoon, 1994). Individualism-collectivism refers to societies "in which the ties between individuals are loose: everyone is expected to look after himself or herself and his or her immediate family" (Hofstede, 1991, p. 2). Collectivism is usually taken as referring to the opposite pattern: societies "in which people from birth onwards are integrated into strong, cohesive ingroups, which throughout people's lifetime continue to protect them in exchange for unquestioning loyalty."

Individualist societies emphasize the "I", "this interests me" (Yang, 1981). In these cultures, the stress is on an individual's goals, and preference is for only a loosely knit social framework. In collectivist societies, the group is all-important, and there is a need for group solidarity and shared activity (Hui & Triandis, 1986). It is thus the "we" that dominates. People in such societies are keen to protect and aid their in-group members and are less helpful to those outside the group. Western Europe, Australasia, and North America have traditionally been viewed as mainly "individualist" cultures, and East Asia as stereotypically "collectivist" (Hofstede, 1980). Power distance represents "the extent to which members of a society accept [as legitimate] that power in institutions and organisations is distributed unequally" (Hofstede, 1983, p. 336), and examines prevailing norms of inequality within a culture. People in high-distance cultures see power as a basic fact of society and stress coercive power. Those in low-power-distance societies believe power should be used only when it is legitimate, and they prefer legitimate power.

Several other studies have made large-scale comparisons of values across cultures, although these are yet to have the impact of Hofstede's work. The Chinese Culture Connection (1987; Bond, 1988) attempted to look at values from a specifically Chinese perspective, deriving a questionnaire using just Chinese concepts. A factor analysis of this questionnaire revealed four factors termed by the researchers integration, human-heartedness, moral discipline, and Confucian work dynamism. Three of these factors overlapped with Hofstede's previous dimensions, but instead of uncertainty avoidance, the new dimension of Confucian work dynamism was identified. Schwartz (e.g., 1990, 1994) collected data from some eighty-six samples taken from forty-one cultural groups and thirty-eight nations. He established two basic dimensions: openness to change versus conservation (security, conformity, tradition) and "self-enhancement" (hedonism, power, achievement) versus self-transcendence (universalism and benevolence). Schwartz (1994) found that although, as expected, individualism positively correlated with autonomy and negatively correlated with conservatism, individualism also positively correlated with egalitarian commitment, reflecting the importance of voluntary action in an autonomous society.

Finally, Douglas (1978, 1982) proposes four sets of worldviews and attendant social relations (egalitarian, fatalist, individualist, and hierarchical) that vary along two dimensions: grid (extent of regulation in a societal structure) and group (the extent to which an individual is incorporated and influenced by a group). A belief in egalitarianism (high on group, low on grid) indicates the rejection of role differentiations and a belief in shared and equal social relations. Such egalitarianism can be seen as the predominant approach to in-group personal relationships in Japan. At the other extreme, a fatalistic outlook (low group, high grid) is one of dependency, powerlessness, and isolation, reflecting a sense of social isolation. Individualists (the prototypical capitalist, low on both grid and group) seeks continuous alliances with others, but relationships with these others may be relatively narrow and shallow. Finally, the social relationships of the hierarchist (high on grid and group) are strongly demarcated and ordered by status. In Hofstede's terms, there is a strong overlap here with the concept of power distance. Douglas's theory is particularly valuable in that it offers distinct possibilities for the analysis of social change (Gross & Rayner, 1985) and has been used explicitly to map the relationship between broad cultural ideals, subcultural norms, and individual and dyadic values and behaviors (e.g., Dake, 1991; Grendstad, 1990; Mars, 1982). Thus, this model is an ambitious attempt to predict the consequences of multilevel cultural variation.

A Selective Review
of Relationship Formation and Maintenance

THE above works all provide means of categorizing societies. Related work has also provided means of categorizing individuals within those societies, using similar schemas: for example, Triandis, Leung, Villareal, and Clark (1985) on the "individual-level" measures of individualism-collectivism termed idiocentrism-allocentrism; Schwartz's (1992) individual-level analysis of his values data; and Dake's (1991) use of Douglas's cultural theory to provide individual-difference analyses. I now turn to consideration of some previous cross-cultural relationship research and try to use these theoretical schemas for interpreting the findings presented. Because of the overwhelming emphasis on individualism and collectivism in the existent cross-cultural literature, as well as the strong argument for the conceptual overlap of this divide with the other schemes for analyzing cultural variation, the emphasis here will be primarily on this dimension.

Western research on partner preferences has a long history of research (cf. Goodwin, 1990b), and has increasingly stressed the primacy of the "abstract" qualities of kindness and honesty as desired traits in a partner (Buss & Barnes, 1986; Goodwin, 1990b; Woll, 1987). Cross-cultural investigation has been scarce, with the most comprehensive study to date being Buss's study of 37 cultures (Buss, 1989; Buss et al., 1990) cited above. One way of interpreting Buss's findings is to focus on the divide between "romantic" (usually more abstract) preferences and more "pragmatic" (usually concrete) desires. Evidence from a variety of cultures suggests that economic development is associated with the more "romantic" approach to relationships (Glenn, 1989; see also Gupta, 1976; Stones & Philbrick, 1989). In rural China, pragmatic attributes (e.g., income and kinship obligations) are stressed above notions such as "romance" (Dion & Dion, 1988). "The ideal wife in Communist China is socialized for society ... romantic ties to the husband (are not) of any great importance; indeed, they can be a nuisance or threat" (Fried, 1976); and in a recent study of the romantic preferences of college students, Goodwin and Tang (1991) found that Chinese students stressed a more pragmatic money-mindedness than

British participants, who in turn emphasized a more abstract sensitivity and sense of humor. Similarly, in her study of Malay villagers, Strange (1976) found that an increase in a couple's economic power led to a greater freedom in mate selection, with a corresponding decrease in emphasis on more "pragmatic" priorities. Because individualistic values are usually associated with greater gross domestic product (Hofstede, 1980), it is probably reasonable to assume that those societies where psychological assets are desired are generally the more individualist societies, and those where economic factors are vital are the more collectivist societies. The limited evidence on this subject indeed supports this (Dion & Dion, 1988; Zebrowitz-McArthur, 1988).

Of course, the luxury of choice of partner is often unavailable. Historically, individualistic values have also been associated with freedom of marital choice, with little control from the wider kinship network (Buunk, 1986). Marriage throughout the world can be arranged along a continuum from societies where everything is totally arranged to those where individuals have a complete freedom of choice, often also known as "love marriages," but there are relatively few societies at either extreme (Rosenblatt & Anderson, 1981). In Iran, dating and free choice are largely nonexistent; parents dictate the opportunities for any partner choice (Hanassab & Tidwell, 1989). Many Asian couples are presented with a prospective partner deemed to be suitable by families and elders; although they may be able to reject a particular individual, the "pool" of available choices may be limited (Stopes-Roe & Cochrane, 1990).

Romantic Love

THE notion of "romantic love" is widely recognized as being culture-tied (e.g., Jahoda, 1988), and although love rules seem to apply in most cultures concerning partner suitability (Rosenblatt & Anderson, 1981), love, particularly romantic love, has tended to be viewed as a largely Western concept (e.g., K. K. Dion & K. L. Dion, 1993; K. L. Dion & K. K. Dion, 1988; K. L. Dion & K. K. Dion,, 1993). In Western individualistic societies love is "a passionate spiritual-emotional-sexual attachment between two people that reflects a high regard for the value of each other person" (Branden, 1988, p. 220). Intimacy is a major component (Sternberg, 1988), as is reciprocity (Levinger, 1988) and the freedom to choose your partner, ideally from a completely "open field" of candidates (Murstein, 1986). Yet, in many other cultures, love can be seen as a disrupting influence on kinship ties, and the very term can imply illicit, nonapproved liaisons (cf. Hsu, 1971, on China). Here, choosing a partner is far too important to be left to the individual alone, and a variety of kinship or tribal networks become significant in partner choice (Fried, 1976).

There is some debate as to whether or not "love marriages" are becoming more common across cultures. Some (e.g., Fox, 1975; Murstein, 1986) point to the way in which an increase in educational standards, especially among women, has led to the greater desirability of, and opportunity for, "affairs of the heart." However, the picture is rarely a simple one; many cultures recognized the importance of love even before the birth of the "romantic ideal" in the West (Oppong, 1980), with love-based selection often permitted within a framework of strategic religious and family alliances. Furthermore, freedom to "love match" does not necessarily preclude consideration of pragmatic factors; evidence from a number of societies suggests that passion and pragmatics frequently run in parallel, for example, in Egypt (Abu-Loghod & Amin, 1961).

An interesting example of the way in which centuries-old (Confucian) concepts of love complement more modern, Westernized notions of romance is in the case of the idea of *yuan-fen,* or "relational fatalism"—the Chinese belief that personal relationships are predestined to succeed or fail, and that the interactants themselves have only limited control over this (Yang & Ho, 1988). From this perspective, couples are together because of *yuan* and their coupling is inevitable, and even before individuals meet, telepathic *yuan* (*shenjiao*) may develop, with the partners sensing the extent to which they are (or are not) compatible. This notion of a mysterious predestined love is arguably also strongly present in Western conceptions of romantic love (Keller, 1992). Indeed, a study of Hong Kong Chinese and British respondents (Goodwin & Findlay, in submission) found that although the notion of *yuan* was more strongly endorsed by the Chinese respondents, the notion had clear resonance too with the Western (British) sample, reflecting a fatalistic resignation in the face of love across very different cultures.

Attitudes Toward the Family

SOCIOLOGICAL and anthropological writings have generated a vast literature concerned with attitudes toward the family, but the majority of writers identify a tension between cultures and subcultures in which family power and influence are dominant and others that stress individual autonomy (e.g., Kagitçibasi, 1990). Family honor is a fundamental hallmark of a collectivist culture (Bond & King, 1985), with the family retaining significant influence (Feldman & Rosenthal, 1990; Fried, 1976). In contrast, the rejection of the traditional advisory and statutory role of the family, and the greater right of the individual to privacy is a prevalent tendency in the individualist society (e.g., Georgas, 1989), although a synthesis of these values is evident in many societies.

Other work has shown how such family attitudes can represent a key ideological battleground. Georgas (1989) found in Greece that although all his respondents rejected traditional family authority to some extent, those most critical of this authority were, surprisingly, the rurally reared respondents— possibly because this authority was "at the top of the agenda" for these informants. In India, a twenty-year study of change among Havik Brahmins showed a similar rejection of the family as a vehicle for traditional values, again surprisingly, led as much by older females as by the young and educated (Ullrich, 1987). In yet other cultures, governments have attempted explicitly to promote or curtail "traditional" family values, which offers a fascinating insight into the malleability of such values. Tashakkori and Thompson (1988, 1991) collected three comparable data sets in Iran in 1982, 1984, and 1986, three, five, and seven years after the Islamic Revolution. Intentions and aspirations of high school seniors regarding education, marriage, and careers were examined through a range of indices. Although the results are complex, they provide evidence of some movement toward traditionalization following the revolution, contrary to that found elsewhere in transitional societies, and demonstrate the significance of ideological forces in promoting family ideals.

Finally, the author's own work on family values in the Russian Union shows how the complex interplay of gender, worldviews, and occupational status contributed toward overall attitudes toward the family in this transitional society (Goodwin & Emelyanova, 1995a, 1995b). Using Douglas's cultural theory, we found beliefs in individualism and hierarchy were negatively related to family commitment, and disclosure about family issues was best predicted by examining the interaction between gender and occupation. This gender x occupation interaction was also significant in the kind of child-rearing values expressed by the respondents: education and independence were important values for entrepreneurs and students, and the encouragement of communal values was more stressed by the manual workers. An analysis of the December 1995 election results across Russia suggest that such divergence in child-rearing values may reflect wider attitudinal divides.

Friendship

SOME of the most sophisticated work on the individualist-collectivist divide has addressed the issue of friendship. My review here will focus on patterns of self-disclosure and mutual activity, a major source for the comparative psychological research on friendship.

Western, individualist friendship is generally seen as a "noninstitutional-ized institution," in which there are relatively few ritualistic ties and rela-tionships are built on "voluntary interdependence." Although the relationships may vary in terms of intimacy and reciprocity, both are common in most friendships (Hays, 1988). Sex differences in disclosure have been widely reported, with men usually less willing to disclose than women (e.g., Williams, 1985).

In contrast, work in India, a collectivist society, has found that sex differ-ences in same-sex friendship disclosures are less evident; men and women share similarly "expressive" communications (Berman, Murphy-Berman, & Pachauri, 1988). Work in China and Hong Kong suggests that where strong family ties exist casual friends and acquaintances become less necessary and even less desirable, because they can be seen as interfering in family relations (Wheeler, 1988). Wheeler found that although Chinese students interacted in larger groups than Americans did, they interacted less frequently and often more by chance than design, with opposite-sex interactions being particularly problematic. Other evidence suggests that Chinese friends in general are less willing than British friends to disclose in "taboo" areas, despite the fact that there are few cross-national differences in identification of such areas (Goodwin & Lee, 1993).

However, to conclude simply that the Chinese disclose less is misleading. Members of Eastern, primarily individualist cultures also form very close friendships that are determined by relationships established at an earlier time (Gudykunst & Ting-Toomey, 1988; Triandis et al., 1986). These relationships may take some time to mature, but they are highly intimate (Hsu, 1953; Hui & Villareal, 1989). Thus, whereas people in Western cultures make friends easily, "close friend" means something rather less intimate than the term does in Eastern cultures, and the apparent sociability of Westerners is less "deep" than the friendship relationships of the Chinese.

Personal Relationships in a Changing World

ANY summary of differences in personal relationships across cultures must emphasize the very fluidity of such relationships across the world. For example, as I argued above, "family values" is a "hot" issue in many nations, and there is evidence too that dating and mating patterns are showing evidence of increasing individualism (Rosenblatt & Anderson, 1981; Murstein, 1986), with the "love match" (as opposed to the arranged marriage) becoming increasingly common.

Yet, however "Westernized," "modernized," or "industrialized" a nation becomes, unique and culturally adaptive configurations are likely to emerge that make simplistic cross-cultural assumptions problematic (cf. Kagitçibasi, 1990). An example of this is the "lonely hearts column," now evident in the most obscure corners of the world and frequently cited as evidence of increased individualization. More careful examination reveals that such columns are predominantly couched in materialistic and status-sensitive terms (Kenrick & Keefe, 1992), recalling rather more traditional matchmakings methods and priorities common to collectivist societies too. A second example is the way in which family life has adapted to deal with modern economic demands. Hildenbrand (1989) examined such issues in his analysis of the family farm in (Western) Germany. Here, the situation seemed ripe for conflict: traditional models of orientation toward the farm and its continuity were echoed in traditional patriarchal family lifestyles, and the modernization of labor seemed likely to induce new lifestyles and attitudes that would endanger the traditional family-run structure. However, individual parties concerned seemed able to maintain two apparently opposing orientations: on one hand, they embraced modernization, learning the new skills necessary to ensure the farm survived, and on the other hand, they maintained traditions such as the communal sharing of income from any work outside the farm. Thus, the older patriarchal and authoritarian family format disappeared but was replaced by a strong core family apparently well suited to modern agri-cultural demands.

Such a coexistence between the old and new relationship organization represents just one example of the complexity of relationship-pertinent values that are now evident in most societies. The only certainty seems to be that the future adoption of relationship values is likely to be uneven and that adaptation processes are also likely to be variable, with the frequently cited evils of modern society likely to be at least ameliorated by greater economic benefits and the possibility of new, nontraditional alliances (Inkeles, 1977).

Such complexities clearly challenge the simplistic "data fishing expeditions" that dominate the area at present (Fletcher & Ward, 1988; Wheeler et al., 1989). Future researchers should attempt to integrate broad theoretical frameworks into their research, frameworks that can provide both testable hypotheses and, it is hoped, further impetus for future research. Such a process will assure that cross-cultural research is seen less as an interesting sideline and more as a vital backdrop for both the development and testing of the field of personal relationships as a whole.

References

Abu-Loghod, J., & Amin, L. (1961). Egyptian marriage ads: Microcosm of a changing society *Marriage and Family Living, 23,* 127–136.

Berman, J., Murphy-Berman, V., & Pachauri, A. (1988). Sex differences in friendship patterns in India and in the US. *Basic and Applied Social Psychology, 9,* 61–71.

Betzig, L. (1989). Causes of conjugal dissolution: A cross-cultural study. *Current Anthropology, 30,* 654–676.

Bond, M. (1988). Finding universal dimensions of individual variation in multicultural studies of values: The Rokeach and Chinese Value Surveys. *Journal of Personality and Social Psychology, 55,* 1009–1015.

Bond, M., & King, A. (1985). Coping with the threat of westernization in Hong Kong. *International Journal of Intercultural Relations, 9,* 351–364.

Branden, N. (1988). A vision of romantic love. In R. Sternberg & M. Barnes (Eds.), *The Psychology of Love.* New Haven: Yale University Press.

Brown, D. E. (1991). *Human Universals.* Philadelphia: Temple University Press.

Buss, D. M. (1985). Human mate selection. *American Scientist, 73,* 47–51.

Buss, D. M. (1988). The evolution of human intrasexual competition: Tactics of mate attraction. *Journal of Personality and Social Psychology, 54,* 616–628.

Buss, D. M. (1989). Sex differences in human mate preferences: Evolutionary hypotheses tested in 37 cultures. *Behavioral and Brain Sciences, 12,* 1–49.

Buss, D. M., Abbott, A., Angleitner, A., Biaggio, A., Blanco-Villasenor, A., Bruchon-Schweitzer, M., et al. (1990). International preferences in selecting mates: A study of 37 cultures. *Journal of Cross-Cultural psychology, 21,* 5–47.

Buss, D. M., & Barnes, M. (1986). Preferences in human mate selection. *Journal of Personality and Social Psychology, 50,* 559–570.

Buunk, B. (1986). Autonomy in close relationships: A cross-cultural study. *Family Perspective, 20,* 209–221.

Chinese Culture Connection. (1987). Chinese values and the search for culture-free dimensions of culture. *Journal of Cross-Cultural Psychology, 18,* 143–164

Dake, K. (1991). Orienting dispositions in the perception of risk: An analysis of contemporary worldviews and cultural biases. *Journal of Cross-Cultural Psychology, 22,* 61–82.

Dion, K. L., & Dion, K. K. (1988). Romantic love: Individual and cultural perspectives. In R. Sternberg & M. Barnes (Eds.), *The psychology of love.* New Haven: Yale University Press.

Dion, K. K., & Dion, K. L. (1993). Individualistic and collectivistic perspectives on gender and the cultural context of love and intimacy. *Journal of Social Issues, 49,* 53–69.

Dion, K. L., & Dion, K. K. (1993). Gender and ethnocultural comparisons in styles of love. *Psychology of Women Quarterly, 17,* 463–473.

Douglas, M. (1978). *Cultural bias.* Occasional Paper, no. 35. London: Royal Anthropological Institute.

Douglas, M. (1982). Introduction to grid/group analysis. In M. Douglas (Ed.), *Essays in the sociology of perception.* London: Routledge & Kegan Paul.

Feldman, S., & Rosenthal, D. (1990). The acculturation of autonomy expectations in Chinese high schoolers residing in two Western nations. *International Journal of Psychology, 25,* 259–281.

Fletcher, G., & Ward, C. (1988). Attribution theory and processes: A cross-cultural perspective. In M. Bond (Ed.), *The cross-cultural challenge to social psychology.* Newbury Park, CA: Sage.

Fox, G. (1975). Love match and arranged marriage in a modernizing nation: Mate selection in Ankara, Turkey. *Journal of Marriage and the Family, 37,* 180–193.

Fried, M. (1976). Chinese culture, society and personality in transition. In G. De Vos (Ed.), *Responses to change: Society, culture and personality.* New York: Van Nostrand.

Georgas, J. (1989). Changing family values in Greece: From collectivist to individualist. *Journal of Cross-Cultural Psychology, 20,* 80–91.

Ghaffarian, S. (1987). The acculturation of Iranians in the US. *Journal of Social Psychology, 127,* 565–571.

Glenn, N. (1989). Intersocietal variation in the mate preference of males and females (Commentary on D. Buss (1989), Sex differences in human mate preferences: Evolutionary hypotheses tested in 37 cultures). *Behavioral and Brain Sciences, 12,* 21–23.

Goodwin, R. (1989). *Striking the perfect match: Preferences for a partner as predictors of relationship initiation and quality.* Unpublished doctoral thesis, University of Kent.

Goodwin, R. (1990a). Taboo topics amongst close friends: A factor-analytic investigation of two samples. *Journal of Social Psychology, 130,* 691–692.

Goodwin, R. (1990b). Sex differences amongst partner preferences: Are the sexes really very similar? *Sex Roles, 23,* 501–513.

Goodwin, R., & Emelyanova, T. (1995a). The perestroika of the family? Gender and occupational differences in family values in modern day Russia. *Sex Roles, 32,* 337–351.

Goodwin, R., & Emelyanova, T. (1995b). The privatisation of the personal? II: Attitudes to the family and child-rearing values in modern-day Russia. *Journal of Social and Personal Relationships, 12,* 132–140.

Goodwin, R., & Findlay, C. (in submission). We were just fated together ... Chinese love and the concept of yuan in two cultures.

Goodwin, R., & Lee, I. (1993). Taboo topics amongst Chinese and British Friends: A cross-cultural comparison. *Journal of Cross-Cultural Psychology, 25,* 325–328.

Goodwin, R., & Tang, D. (1991). Preferences for friends and close relationship partners: A cross-cultural comparison. *Journal of Social Psychology, 131,* 579–581.

Goody, J. (1976). *Production and reproduction.* Cambridge: Cambridge University Press.

Grendstad, G (1990). *Europe by culture: An exploration of grid/group analysis.* Unpublished graduate thesis, Department of Comparative Politics, University of Bergen.

Gross, J., & Rayner, S. (1985). *Measuring Culture: A paradigm for the analysis of social organisations.* New York: Columbia University Press.

Gudykunst, W., & Ting-Toomey, S. (1988). *Culture and interpersonal communication.* Newbury Park, CA: Sage.

Gupta, G. (1976). Love, arranged marriage and the Indian Social Structure. *Journal of Comparative Family Studies, 7,* 75–85.

Hanassab, S., & Tidwell, R. (1989). Cross-cultural perspective on dating relationships of young Iranian women: A pilot study. *Counseling Psychology Quarterly, 2,* 113–121.

Hays, R. (1988). Friendship. In S. Duck (Ed.), *Handbook of personal relationships.* Chichester, U.K.: Wiley.

Hildenbrand, B. (1989). Tradition and modernity in the family farm: A case study. In K. Boh, G. Sgritta, & M. B. Sussman (Eds.), *Cross-cultural perspectives on families, work, and change.* New York: Haworth Press.

Hofstede, G. (1980). *Culture's consequences: International differences in work-related values.* Beverly Hills, CA: Sage.

Hofstede, G. (1983). Dimensions of national cultures in fifty cultures and three regions. In J. B. Deregowski, S. Dziurawiec, & R. C. Annis (Eds.), *Expiscations in cross-cultural psychology* (pp. 335–355). Lisse, The Netherlands: Swets & Zweitlinger.

Hofstede, G. (1991). *Cultures and organizations.* London: McGraw-Hill.

Hofstede, G. (1994). Foreword. In U. Kim, H. C. Triandis, C. Kagitçibasi, S-C. Choi, & G. Yoon, *Individualism and collectivism: Theory, method and applications.* Thousand Oaks, CA: Sage.

Howard, J., Blumstein, P., & Schwartz, P. (1987). Social or evolutionary theories? Some observations on preferences in human mate selection. *Journal of Personality and Social Psychology, 53,* 194–200.

Hsu, F. (1953). *American and Chinese.* New York: Schuman.

Hsu, F. (1971). Psychosocial homeostasis and jen: Conceptual tools for advancing psychological inquiry. *American Anthropologist, 73,* 23–44.

Hui, C., & Triandis, H. (1986). Individualism-collectivism: A study of cross-cultural researchers. *Journal of Cross-Cultural Psychology, 17,* 225–248.

Hui, C., & Villareal, M. (1989). Individualism-collectivism and psychological needs: Their relationships in two cultures. *Journal of Cross-Cultural Psychology, 20,* 310–323.

Huston, T., & Levinger, G. (1978). Interpersonal attraction and relationships. *Annual Review of Psychology, 29,* 115–156.

Inkeles, A. (1977). Understanding and misunderstanding individual modernity. *Journal of Cross-Cultural Psychology, 8,* 135–176.

Jahoda, G. (1988). J'accuse. In M. Bond (Ed.), *The cross-cultural challenge to social psychology.* Newbury Park, CA: Sage.

Jahoda, G. (1990). Our forgotten ancestors. In J. Berman (Ed.), *Cross-cultural perspectives: The Nebraska Symposium on Motivation, 1989.* Lincoln: University of Nebraska Press.

Kagitçibasi, C. (1990). Family and socialization in cross-cultural perspective: A model of change. In J. Berman (Ed.), *Cross-cultural perspectives: The Nebraska Symposium on Motivation, 1989.* Lincoln: University of Nebraska Press.

Keller, J. D. (1992). Schemes for schemata. In T. Schwartz, G. White, & C. Lutz (Eds), *New directions in psychological anthropology*. Cambridge: Cambridge University Press.

Kenrick, D. T., & Keefe, R. C. (1992). Age preferences in mates reflect sex differences in human reproductive strategies. *Behavioral and Brain Sciences, 15,* 75–133.

Kim, U., Triandis, H. C., Kagitçibasi, C., Choi, S-C., & Yoon, G. (1994). *Individualism and collectivism: Theory, method and applications*. Thousand Oaks, CA: Sage.

Levinger. G. (1988). Can we picture "love"? In R. Sternberg & M. Barnes (Eds.), *The psychology of love*. New Haven: Yale University Press.

Levinson, D. (1989). *Family values in cross-cultural perspective*. Newbury Park, CA: Sage.

Mars, G. (1982). *Cheats at work: An anthology of the workplace*. London: Allen & Unwin.

Murstein, B. (1986). *Paths to marriage*. Beverly Hills, CA: Sage.

Oppong, C. (1980). From love to institution: Indications of change in Akan marriage. *Journal of Family History, 5,* 197–209.

Parker, I. (1989). *The crisis in social psychology—and how to end it*. London: Routledge.

Rohner, R. (1984). Toward a conception of culture for cross-cultural psychology. *Journal of Cross-Cultural Psychology, 15,* 11–38.

Rosenblatt, P. (1974). Cross-cultural perspective on attraction. In T. Huston (Ed.), *Foundations of interpersonal attraction*. New York: Academic Press.

Rosenblatt, P., & Anderson, R. (1981). Human sexuality in cross-cultural perspective. In M. Cook (Ed.), *The bases of human sexual attraction*. London. Academic Press.

Schwartz, S. (1990). Individualism-collectivism: Critique and proposed refinements. *Journal of Cross-Cultural Psychology, 21,* 139–157.

Schwartz, S. (1994). The universal content and structure of values: Towards an understanding of national differences. In U. Kim, H. Triandis, & G. Yoon (Eds.), *Individualism and collectivism: Theoretical and methodological issues*. Newbury Park, CA: Sage.

Smith, P., & Bond, M. (1993). *Social psychology across cultures: Analysis and perspectives*. New York: Harvester Wheatsheaf.

Stephan, W. G. (1992). Sexual motivation, patriarchy and compatibility. *Behavioral and Brain Sciences, 15,* 111–112.

Sternberg, R. (1988). Triangulating love. In R. Sternberg & M. Barnes (Eds.), *The psychology of love*. New Haven: Yale University Press.

Stevens, G. (1992). Mortality and age-specific patterns of marriage. *Behavioral and Brain Sciences, 15,* 112–113.

Stones, C., & Philbrick, J. (1989). Attitudes towards love among Xhosa university students in South Africa. *Journal of Social Psychology, 129,* 573–575.

Stopes-Roe, M., & Cochrane, R. (1990). *Citizens of this country: The Asian-British*. Clevedon, U.K.: Multilingual Matters.

Strange, H. (1976) Continuity and change: Patterns of mate selection and marriage ritual in a Malay village. *Journal of Marriage and the Family, 38,* 561–571

Tashakkori, A., & Thompson, V. (1988). Cultural change and attitude change: An assessment of postrevolutionary marriage and family attitudes in Iran. *Population Research and Policy Review, 7,* 3–27.

Tashakkori, A., & Thompson, V. (1991). Social change and change in intentions of Iranian youth regarding education, marriage and careers. *International Journal of Psychology, 26,* 203–217.

Thiessen, D., & Gregg, B. (1980). Human assortative mating and genetic equilibrium: An evolutionary perspective. *Ethology and Sociobiology, 1,* 111–140.

Triandis, H., Bontempo, R., Betancourt, H., Bond, M., Leung, K., Brenes, A., Georgas, J., Hui, C., Marin, G., Setiadi, B., Sinha, J., Verma, J., Spangenberg, J., Touzard, H., & de Montmollin, G. (1986). The measurement of the etic aspects of individualism and collectivism across cultures. *Australian Journal of Psychology, 38,* 257–267.

Triandis, H. C., Leung, K., Villareal, M. V., & Clark, F. L. (1985). Allocentric versus idiocentric tendencies: Convergent and discriminant validation. *Journal of Research in Personality, 19,* 395–415.

Ullrich, H. (1987). Marriage patterns among Havik Brahmins: A twenty-year study of change. *Sex Roles, 16,* 615–635.

Wheeler, L. (1988). My year in Hong Kong: Some observations about social behavior. *Personality and Social Psychology Bulletin, 14,* 410–420.

Wheeler, L., Reis, H., & Bond, M. (1989). Collectivism-individualism in everyday social life: The Middle Kingdom and the melting pot. *Journal of Personality and Social Psychology, 57,* 79–86.

Williams, D. (1985). Gender, masculinity-femininity and emotional intimacy in same-sex friendships. *Sex Roles, 12,* 587–600.

Winkler, I., & Doherty, W. (1983). Communication styles and marital satisfaction in Israeli and American couples. *Family Process, 22,* 221–228.

Woll, S. (1987). *Improper linear models of matchmaking.* Paper presented at the Iowa Conference of Personal Relationships, Des Moines, 1987.

Yang, K. (1981). Social orientation and individual modernity among Chinese students in Taiwan. *Journal of Social Psychology, 113,* 159–170.

Yang, K. S., & Ho, D. (1988). The role of yuan in Chinese social life: A conceptual and empirical analysis. In A. C. Paranjpe, D. Ho, & R. C. Reiber (Eds.), *Asian contributions to psychology.* New York: Praeger.

Zebrowitz-McArthur, L. (1988). Person perception in cross-cultural perspective. In M. Bond (Ed.) *The cross-cultural challenge to social psychology.* Newbury Park, CA: Sage.

Personal Values and Motives

Chapter Five

Values and Culture

SHALOM H. SCHWARTZ

Why do some people try to change the world but others seek to fit in? Why do some pursue wealth and power but others prefer sharing and equality? Why do some follow traditions but others strive for novelty and excitement? These are all questions about individual differences in motivation, but their answers depend only in part upon the unique personalities of individual persons. Groups of people also differ systematically in these ways of thinking, feeling, and acting. Findings we cite below suggest that in the current historical period, Americans are more likely to try to change the world than are people from most other nations, Chinese are more likely to pursue power and not equality, and Ghanaians are especially likely to follow tradition.

The Nature of Culture

WE all carry within us patterns of thinking, feeling, and acting that we acquire and modify throughout our lifetimes. Hofstede (1991) calls these our *mental programs*. Of course, this mental programming only partly determines our behavior; individuals are able to react in new and unexpected ways, especially under situational pressure. But knowing people's mental programs makes their behavior much more predictable and understandable.

Our mental programming begins with experiences in the family, continues in contacts in the neighborhood, school, workplace, recreational settings, and the wider community. In each situation, we learn what is possible, what is expected, and what are the consequences of expressing different thoughts and feelings in various actions. Each of us has unique sets of experiences and inherited traits that influence what we learn. As a result, we each have elements in our mental programming that we do not share with others. These unique elements constitute our individual personality.

Nonetheless, much of our mental programming is shared with other people in our society who have been exposed to similar situations, experienced similar opportunities, and been disciplined and rewarded for similar actions. This shared programming is what most social anthropologists and cross-cultural psychologists refer to as *culture*. Culture includes all the patterns of thinking, feeling, and acting that are shared by the members of a society or other bounded social group (ethnic, religious, national, and so on).

This concept of culture is broader than the common use of the word to describe such refined aspects of civilization as science, art, and literature. The broad concept of culture refers to the many everyday practices shared by the members of a society (ways of dressing, eating, conversing, expressing anger or joy), to the commonly understood symbols (words, gestures, pictures, objects), to the shared rituals (ways of showing respect, religious and civil ceremonies), and to the figures who are widely viewed as heroes or as villains (the founding fathers, the guru, the axe murderer).

The Nature of Values

ALL these aspects of culture can be seen by an outside observer, but their meaning remains unclear until the observer comes to understand how the members of a group evaluate particular practices, symbols, rituals, and figures. That is, the heart of culture is formed by *values*—what people believe is good or bad, what they think should and should not be done, what they hold to be desirable or undesirable. When we wish to characterize a culture in terms of values, we describe the ideas about what is good, right, and desirable that the members of a society or other cultural group share (Williams, 1970). These cultural values (e.g., freedom, prosperity, security) are the bases for the specific norms that tell people what behavior is appropriate in various situations.

A summary of the many definitions of values (Schwartz & Bilsky, 1987) suggests their main features:

- *Values are beliefs.* But they are not objective, cold ideas. Rather, when values are activated, they become infused with feeling. People for whom independence is an important value discuss it passionately, become aroused if their independence is threatened, despair when they are helpless to protect it, and are happy when they can express it.
- *Values refer to desirable goals and to the modes of conduct that promote these goals.* Social equality, for example, is a desirable goal for some people, one that can be promoted by such modes of conduct as acting fairly and helpfully. Thus, equality, fairness, and helpfulness are all values.
- *Values transcend specific actions and situations.* Obedience and honesty, for example, are values that may be relevant at work or in school, in sports or in business, with family, friends, or strangers. This feature of values distinguishes them from narrower concepts like norms and attitudes, which usually refer to specific actions, objects, or situations.
- *Values guide the selection or evaluation of behavior, people, and events.* That is, values serve as standards or criteria. We decide whether actions, people, or events are good or bad, justified or illegitimate, worth approaching or avoiding, by considering whether they facilitate or undermine the attainment of our cherished values.
- *Values are ordered by importance relative to one another.* The ordered set of values forms a system of value priorities. Cultures and individuals can be characterized by their systems of value priorities. Do people attribute more importance to achievement or to justice, to novelty or to tradition, to wealth or to spirituality? What is the relative importance of all the significant values that serve as guiding principles in life?

The various features in our conception of values suggest that they are important sources of motivation. Motivation refers to the determinants of goal-directed behavior, its initiation, direction, intensity, and duration (Heckhausen, 1990). Values, as broad goals of varying importance, render available action alternatives more or less attractive according to the likelihood that these alternatives will promote goal attainment. Hence, they can account for both the initiation and direction of action. The importance of the values pursued through an action influences the intensity with which it is carried out and the persistence of action in the face of obstacles. Expectancy-value theories explicate these connections between values and motivation as applied to individual decision making (e.g., Feather, 1992) and can be used to explain the relations of individuals' values to their behavior (Schwartz, 1996). In this chapter, we focus on the prevailing value priorities in society, that is, on cultural values. As elaborated next, cultural values can be seen as determinants and legitimizers of the actions taken in the name of social institutions.

How Do Value Priorities Function in Societies?

THE building blocks of society are its institutions—the family, the education system, religion, the economic and political systems, the armed forces, and so on. The ways these societal institutions function, their goals and modes of operation, express cultural value priorities. For example, in societies where complex knowledge and intellectual skills are important cultural values, provision is made for extensive formal education. Where traditional wisdom is valued more highly, education is less formal and is placed in the hands of the elders. If equality is also highly valued, education is open to almost everyone; if equality is unimportant, the educational system is likely to be elitist. Where individual ambition and success are highly valued, the organization of the economic and legal systems is likely to be competitive (e.g., capitalist markets and adversarial legal proceedings). In contrast, a cultural emphasis on group well-being is likely to be expressed in more cooperative economic and legal systems (e.g., socialism and mediation).

Cultural value priorities affect the way social resources are invested. The relative importance attributed to such values as wealth, justice, and beauty in a society partly determines how money, land, and human capital are spent. Are they invested more in industrialization, social welfare, or preserving the environment? As goals or criteria, cultural value priorities also determine how organizational performance is evaluated. The performances of industrial corporations, television stations, high schools, and museums, for example, might be evaluated according to how productive they are, how innovative, how socially responsible, or how supportive of existing authority structures. Which criteria are preferred depends on the values that are dominant in the culture. An emphasis on innovation versus maintaining authority or on productivity versus social responsibility would lead to radically different, even contradictory, evaluations of the same performance.

When people carry out their roles in social institutions, they draw upon cultural values to decide what behavior is appropriate and to justify their choices to others. Government leaders base decisions about whether to conduct nuclear tests, for example, on the cultural importance of values like national security, power, and world peace. Moreover, leaders invoke such values to justify their actions. When parents, teachers, bosses, and commanding officers punish or reward those for whom they are responsible, they guide and justify their behavior by calling upon the values that define the goals of families, schools, workplaces, and armies.

The explicit and implicit value emphases that characterize a culture are imparted to societal members through everyday exposure to customs, laws, norms, scripts, and practices that are shaped by the cultural values (Bourdieu, 1972; Markus & Kitayama, 1994). Cultural values are built into people's mental programming, often without their conscious awareness, as they adapt to life in the societal institutions. But societies are not homogeneous. They consist of numerous groups or categories that may have somewhat different sets of value priorities and ways of seeing the world—different subcultures. There are ethnic, religious, and occupational groups, for example, and generational, class, and gender categories. People are usually members of a number of these groups and categories at the same time. So they are likely to carry with them multiple and possibly contradictory mental programs that can complicate their decision making.

Measuring Cultural Values

IDEALLY, the subcultures of ethnic, regional, and other groups within nations should be studied. Practically, however, the vast majority of cross-cultural work on values has examined national differences. National boundaries do not necessarily correspond to the boundaries of organically developed, relatively homogeneous societies with a shared culture, but there are strong forces toward integration in nations that have existed for some time (Hofstede, 1991, p. 12). There is usually a single dominant language, educational system, army, and political system, and shared mass media, markets, services, and national symbols (e.g., flag, sports teams). These can produce substantial, shared mental programming among those with a common passport. This is less the case, of course, in nations with sharp cleavages among ethnic groups.

The values that characterize a society cannot be observed directly; rather, they must be inferred from various cultural products. For example, researchers have inferred the value emphases of societies by studying folktales, children's textbooks, typical methods of formal and informal learning, legal systems, games, and many other behavior patterns. The most common approach infers the prevailing value emphases in societies by averaging the value priorities of individuals (e.g., Hofstede, 1980; Morris, 1956). This approach views individual value priorities as a product both of shared culture and of unique individual experience.

As noted above, shared cultural value emphases help to shape the contingencies to which people must adapt in everyday life in social institutions. As a result, the members of each cultural group share many value-relevant social experiences and they come to accept similar values. Within cultural groups, of course, there are individual differences in value priorities due to unique experiences and temperaments. However, the average of the value priorities of the members of a cultural group is determined by their shared enculturation. Hence, the average priorities point to the underlying, common cultural values.

Cultural Dimensions of Values

THERE are hundreds, perhaps thousands, of values on which societies could be compared. Some values are relevant in all societies, others are known only in particular societies. Hence, a way must be found to organize the profusion of cultural values into a limited number of dimensions on which to compare societies effectively. The value dimensions on which cultures vary may well differ from the value dimensions on which individual persons can be compared (Hofstede, 1980; Schwartz, 1994a). For identifying critical cultural value dimensions, an approach that starts with societies is needed.

Theorists have made the following assumption in their search for cultural value dimensions: cultural dimensions of values reflect the basic issues or problems that societies must confront in order to regulate human activity (Hofstede, 1980; Kluckhohn & Strodtbeck, 1961; Schwartz 1994a). Societal members, especially decision makers, recognize and communicate about these problems, plan responses to them, and motivate one another to cope with them. Values (e.g., success, justice, freedom, social order) are the vocabulary of socially approved goals they use to motivate action and to express and justify the solutions they choose.

We present two major lines of current research on cultural value dimensions. Both derived cultural dimensions from theorizing at the level of societies rather than of individuals; both verified the cultural dimensions they derived through empirical research on data from many nations around the world; both have examined some of the possible sources of these cultural differences in values; and both have considered implications of cultural differences for nations and for individuals.

Hofstede

Hofstede (1980, 1991) suggested that four basic problems that all societies face, identified by Inkeles and Levinson (1954), underlie cultural value dimensions. He defined four cultural dimensions that reflect the way members of a society typically cope with each of these problems.

- *Power Distance:* accepting an unequal distribution of power in institutions as legitimate versus illegitimate (from the viewpoint of less-powerful persons).
- *Individualism/Collectivism:* valuing loosely knit social relations in which

individuals are expected to care only for themselves and their immediate families versus tightly knit relations in which they can expect their wider in-group (e.g., extended family, clan) to look after them in exchange for unquestioning loyalty.

- *Masculinity/Femininity:* valuing achievement, heroism, assertiveness, and material success versus relationships, modesty, caring for the weak, and interpersonal harmony.
- *Uncertainty Avoidance:* feeling uncomfortable or comfortable with uncertainty and ambiguity and therefore valuing or devaluing beliefs and institutions that provide certainty and conformity.

Hofstede examined responses of about 117,000 IBM employees from fifty nations and three regions, obtained during 1967–1973, to questions that he interpreted as reflecting each of these value dimensions. For each question, he computed an average score for each nation. Factor analyses of these average national scores supported the view that nations differ on these four cultural dimensions. He then computed nation scores for each dimension by combining the questions that represented it. Of course, the scores of IBM employees do not reveal the actual averages for their nations. Hofstede assumed, however, that the *order* of nations on the four dimensions, based on the IBM samples, is close to the "true" *order* traceable to cultural differences. He reasoned that because the samples were well matched on a large variety of variables other than nationality, nationality itself is the most likely explanation for consistent differences between the national groups.

Table 1 provides the ranking of exemplary nations from highest to lowest on Hofstede's four cultural value dimensions. In general, nations high in Power Distance are low in Individualism/Collectivism and vice versa; these may constitute a single dimension.

Hofstede suggests how these cultural differences are expressed in the workplace, schools, families, and in politics and ideas. For example, in the workplace, tasks are presumably more important than relationships in more Individualist cultures (I), but relationships are more important than tasks in more Collectivist cultures (C). In schooling, the main objective is to learn how to *learn* (I) versus to learn how to *do* (C). In families, children come to think in terms of "I" (I) versus "we" (C). In politics, power is exercised by voters (I) versus interest groups (C). The ultimate goal is self-actualization in (I) versus social harmony and consensus in (C). Individuals' own goals are expected to take precedence over group goals in (I), but the reverse is expected in (C). People discriminate less sharply between their own in-group and out-groups in (I) than in (C).

Individualism/Collectivism is the dimension that has most strongly caught the imagination of researchers. Many view East Asian cultures as prototypical of Collectivism, and Western cultures, especially American, as prototypical of Individualism (e.g., Kim et al., 1994; Markus & Kitayama, 1994; Triandis, 1990). Ideas about the effects of living in Individualist versus Collectivist cultures have been used to predict and/or explain many differences between people from nations that score high or low on this cultural dimension, differences in, for example, judgments, emotions, communication and choice behaviors, conformity, and stereotyping (summaries in Gudykunst & Bond, in press; Kagitcibasi & Berry, 1989). Most of these studies compare only a few nations, however. It is therefore easy to find other variables on which the nations differ that could also explain the findings.

Hofstede offers numerous speculations about possible origins of national differences on his cultural dimensions. For example, he traces high Power Distance to a heritage shaped by life in centralized empires such as the Roman and Chinese empires. He connects Individualism to the effects of urbanization, industrialization, and national wealth. He conjectures that moderate and cold climates promote cultural Individualism and low Power Distance because survival in such climates requires greater personal initiative.

Hofstede's causal reasoning about the origins of national differences on the

Table 1. National Ranks on the Hofstede Cultural Value Dimensions, Selected Countries

Rank	Power Distance	Individualism/ Collectivism	Masculinity/ Femininity	Uncertainty Avoidance
1	Malaysia	U.S.	Japan	Greece
2	Guatemala	Australia	Austria	Portugal
3	Panama	Great Britain	Venezuela	Guatemala
12	Yugoslavia	Ireland	Colombia (15–U.S.; 16–Australia)	Spain
20	Belgium	Spain	India	Colombia
30	Taiwan (38–U.S.)	Greece	Indonesia	Thailand (37–Australia)
40	Netherlands (41–Australia)	Singapore	Salvador	New Zealand (43–U.S.)
51	Denmark	Panama	Netherlands	Denmark
52	Israel	Ecuador	Norway	Jamaica
53	Austria	Guatemala	Sweden	Singapore

SOURCE: Adapted from G. Hofstede, *Cultures and Organizations: Software of the Mind* (New York: McGraw-Hill, 1991).

cultural value dimensions is supported by correlational evidence, though correlations cannot demonstrate causality. However, the work has been the subject of many critiques (e.g., Kagitcibasi, 1994, in press; Schwartz, 1994a). This is only natural for a research tradition that has been the central focus of attention for fifteen years. Critics argue that (1) the items used to measure the cultural dimensions do not fit the conceptual definitions of the dimensions very well; (2) Individualism/Collectivism is a catch-all that includes so many elements that it can be used to explain everything and, therefore, nothing; (3) IBM employees may not provide well-matched samples for comparing nations because they do not have the same relative status in more and in less affluent societies; (4) the nations sampled do not represent the world's nations well (e.g., no East European), which may bias the dimensions found; (5) the items used to measure the dimensions may have different rather than equivalent meanings in the different cultures; and (6) the dimensions have been widely misused to characterize individuals, whereas Hofstede applied them only to cultures. Despite these problems, Hofstede's work has stimulated an astonishing number and variety of cross-cultural studies. It has helped to move the field from treating culture merely as a way to describe group differences to treating culture as an explanatory variable.

Schwartz

The initial objective of this line of research was to identify the potentially universal types of individual human values and the relations of compatibility and conflict among values (Schwartz & Bilsky, 1987, 1990). Ten types of individual values were derived by reasoning that values express, in the form of words, the different goals inherent in human existence about which people have to communicate. These goals arise from the needs of individuals as biological organisms, as participants in coordinated social interaction, and as members of ongoing groups. Research in a wide variety of cultures supported the near-universality of the ten types of individual values and of the structure of relations among them (Schwartz, 1992).

When moving to the level of cultural values, Schwartz assumed that nations might well be differentiated on dimensions that differ from those on which individual persons vary. He therefore sought issues that all societies confront that are likely to underlie cultural value dimensions (Schwartz, 1994a; Schwartz & Ros, 1995). He identified three basic issues:

1. The relationship between individual and group: to what extent are persons autonomous versus embedded in groups?
2. Assuring responsible social behavior: how to motivate people to consider

others' welfare and coordinate with them to manage their unavoidable interdependencies?

3. The role of humankind in the natural and social world: is it more to submit, to fit in, or to exploit?

The different cultural adaptations that evolve to resolve each of the basic issues are arrayed along bipolar cultural dimensions. These adaptations are each expressed, maintained, and justified by a particular set of value priorities called value types.

Conservatism versus Autonomy. In cultures at the Conservatism pole of this dimension, the person is viewed as embedded in a collectivity, finding meaning in life largely through social relationships, through identifying with the group and participating in its shared way of life. This value type emphasizes maintenance of the status quo, propriety, and restraint of actions or inclinations that might disrupt the solidary group or the traditional order. Exemplary specific values are social order, respect for tradition, family security, and self-discipline.

In cultures at the Autonomy pole of this dimension, the person is viewed as an autonomous, bounded entity who finds meaning in his or her own uniqueness, who seeks to express his or her own internal attributes (preferences, traits, feelings, motives) and is encouraged to do so. Schwartz distinguishes two related types of Autonomy. *Intellectual Autonomy* emphasizes the independent ideas and rights of the individual to pursue his or her own intellectual directions (exemplary values: curiosity, broadmindedness, creativity). *Affective Autonomy* emphasizes the individual's independent pursuit of affectively positive experience (pleasure, exciting life, varied life).

Hierarchy versus Egalitarianism. In high Hierarchy cultures, a hierarchical system of ascribed roles assures socially responsible behavior. People are socialized and sanctioned to comply with the obligations and rules attached to their roles. The Hierarchy value type emphasizes the legitimacy of an unequal distribution of power, roles, and resources (social power, authority, humility, and wealth). High Egalitarianism cultures portray individuals as moral equals who share basic interests as human beings. People are socialized to internalize a commitment to voluntary cooperation with others and to feel concern for everyone's welfare. The Egalitarian value type emphasizes transcendence of selfish interests (equality, social justice, freedom, responsibility, honesty). Egalitarianism values are a focus of socialization in cultures where the person is viewed as autonomous rather than interdependent because autonomous persons have no natural commitment to others.

Mastery versus Harmony. In high Mastery cultures, people actively seek to master and change the natural and social world, to assert control, bend the world to their will, and exploit it in order to further personal or group interests. The Mastery value type emphasizes getting ahead through active self-assertion (ambition, success, daring, competence). High Harmony cultures accept the world as it is, trying to preserve rather than to change or exploit it. The Harmony value type emphasizes fitting harmoniously with the environment (unity with nature, protecting the environment, a world of beauty). In contemporary national cultures, the potential adaptation of submitting to the environment is uncommon.

Schwartz obtained ratings of the importance of fifty-six values, intended to measure the full range of human values across cultures, from about 44,000 respondents, during 1988–1995. These included two sets of matched samples—urban schoolteachers from forty-seven nations and college students from forty-eight, largely from the dominant cultural group in each nation. Teachers were the focal occupational group because they play a key role in value socialization. By replicating all analyses with two sets of samples, Schwartz and Ros (1995) supported the assumption that different kinds of samples from the same nations yield a similar *order* of nations on the three cultural value dimensions. Analyses used only the forty-five values demonstrated to have relatively stable cross-cultural meanings in studies within each nation (Schwartz, 1992, 1994b). Multidimensional scaling analyses of the average national scores on these values supported the theoretical specification of seven value types, organized into three bipolar dimensions. Nation scores for each value type and dimension were computed by combining the values that represented it.

Table 2 provides the ranking of exemplary nations from highest to lowest on Schwartz's three cultural value dimensions for the teacher samples. On these dimensions, the set of the world's nations studied here form five distinctive cultural groups: Western Europe, Eastern Europe, East Asia, English-speaking nations, and Islamic nations (Schwartz, 1994a, in press; Schwartz & Ros, 1995). For example, West European nations are especially high on Autonomy and Egalitarianism and low on Hierarchy and Conservatism, whereas East Asian nations show the opposite pattern of priorities. The value patterns of East Asia and West Europe suggest a simple East-West cultural dichotomy resembling Collectivism versus Individualism. However, the patterns for the English-speaking nations indicate that this would be a misreading of world culture. These nations differ substantially from West Europe in the higher importance they attribute to Mastery and Hierarchy values at the expense of Harmony, Conservatism, Egalitarianism, and Intellectual Autonomy values.

Schwartz and his associates offer explanations for these cultural patterns. For example, Schwartz and Bardi (1997) attribute a distinctive East European pattern to adaptation to the life circumstances imposed by communist regimes—pervasive demands for conformity, close surveillance, unpredictable application of rules, suppression of initiative, and rewards not contingent on effort and performance. They suggest that Conservatism and Hierarchy became more important in Eastern Europe because these values were compatible with life circumstances, while Intellectual and Affective Autonomy, Mastery, and Egalitarianism values became less important because pursuit of these values was largely self-defeating. The resulting value priorities were adaptive under the communist social system even though some were clearly contrary to communist ideology (e.g., high Hierarchy, low Egalitarianism). Comparisons of value priorities in Eastern Europe with those in other countries with different social systems support this reasoning.

Sociohistorical developments that can account for the patterns of cultural values prevalent in West Europe and in the United States are also discussed (Schwartz & Ros, 1995). For example, the Protestant Reformation and secularization, as well as the impact of the philosophies of Hobbes, Locke, and Kant, are seen as playing a role in the rise of Autonomy and Egalitarianism

Table 2. National Ranks on the Schwartz Cultural Value Dimensions, Selected Countries

Rank	Conservatism/ Autonomy	Egalitarianism/ Hierarchy	Mastery/ Harmony
1	Ghana	Italy	Ghana
2	Cyprus (Greek)	Norway	Canada (England)
3	Bolivia	Denmark	Zimbabwe
			(8–U.S.)
12	Poland	Cyprus (Greek)	Nepal
20	Thailand	Venezuela	East Germany
	(23–Australia; 25–U.S.)	(22–Australia; 24–U.S.)	(24–Australia)
30	Italy	Malaysia/Brazil	Taiwan/Turkey
40	New Zealand	Japan/Turkey	Spain
45	Spain	China	Finland
46	France	Israel-Arabs	Estonia
47	Switzerland (France)	Nepal	Slovenia

SOURCE: Adapted from S. H. Schwartz, "Beyond Individualism-Collectivism: New Cultural Dimensions of Values," in U. Kim, C. Kagitcibasi, H. C. Triandis, and G. Yoon (Eds.), *Individualism and Collectivism* (Newbury Park, CA: Sage, 1994); pp. 85–119, and subsequent data.

values and the decline of Conservatism and Hierarchy values. Social and demographic correlates of national value priorities have also been examined. Cultural emphases on Conservatism, Hierarchy, and Mastery are associated with large families and multiple religious groups in a nation, and cultural emphases on Autonomy and Egalitarianism are associated with greater socioeconomic development and more democratic political systems. Reciprocal causal influences that may explain these and other associations are discussed in Schwartz (1993) and Schwartz & Ros (1995).

Schwartz's theory of cultural values has yet to be applied widely. A few generalizations that have some empirical support point to its potential. Individual differences in values have more influence on attitudes and behavior in cultures high on Autonomy, as one would expect because of the greater encouragement for individual expression of internal attributes (Barnea & Schwartz, 1994, July). On the other hand, conformity is greater in cultures high on Conservatism (Bond & Smith, 1996). Work and religion are both more central to people's lives in cultures high on Hierarchy and Mastery (Schwartz, in press). People tend to view work as an obligation they owe to society in cultures high on Conservatism and Hierarchy but as an individual right in cultures high on Autonomy and Egalitarianism.

Because of its recency, this approach has also received little systematic criticism. How does it fare on the critical points raised above with regard to the Hofstede approach? (1) Items were selected a priori to represent the conceptual definitions of the dimensions. (2) Only items earlier shown to have reasonably similar meanings across cultures were used. (3) Elements often included in the catch-all Individualism/Collectivism concept were distinguished into five distinct value types that form two different dimensions. (4) Sample type did not seriously affect the order of nations on the dimensions. The orders replicated using two different sets of matched target samples. Moreover, for the eight nations in which roughly representative samples were available, similar orders were found (Schwartz & Ros, 1995). (5) Recent analyses of fifty-four nations that support the cultural dimensions represent the world's nations quite well, though Arab nations are substantially underrepresented. And (6) researchers may misuse the seven cultural value types to characterize individuals, as has been done with the Hofstede dimensions. Schwartz (1992) provides a separate theory and set of measures to characterize individual differences.

Integration and Conclusion

THE two main theories of cultural values differ in many ways (Schwartz, 1994a; Schwartz & Ros, 1995), but they have sufficient conceptual and empirical convergence to suggest that a valid understanding of cultural dimensions is emerging (Smith & Schwartz, in press). In particular, Individualism/Collectivism and Conservatism/Autonomy describe related resolutions of the issue of the relation of individual to group. Empirically, this similarity is reflected in a correlation of -0.62 between nation scores on these two dimensions for thirty-three overlapping nations. This is striking, given the gap of twenty years between studies and the different samples and instruments. Note, however, that the maximum shared variance among dimensions is only 38 percent, signifying that it makes a real difference which approach is used to order nations and to account for national differences in thoughts, feelings, and actions.

There is also empirical support for the conceptual relation of Power Distance with the broader dimensions of Egalitarianism/Hierarchy ($r = -0.48$). Conceptual relations of the other Hofstede dimensions with the Schwartz dimensions are less clear, and no empirical associations are found.

This chapter has described dimensions of mental programming that individuals are likely to share if they grow up in a particular society. Values—broad conceptions of the desirable—are a central feature of this programming. Values are an important linking concept between individual and cross-cultural psychology. Individual differences in value priorities underlie individual differences in attitudes and behavior (Feather, 1995; Schwartz, 1996), but cultural value priorities, expressed in the everyday functioning of social institutions, shape individual priorities. They contribute to the substantial commonalities within and differences across nations in thought, feeling, and action. They also serve as the common target against which members of a society construct unique selves (though less in conservative than in autonomous cultures), and prevailing cultural value priorities appear to change only gradually in response to historical and social structural changes (Hofstede, 1980; Inglehart, 1991; Schwartz & Bardi, 1997).

Note

Preparation of this chapter was supported by grant No. 94–00063 from the United States-Israel Binational Science Foundation (BSF), Jerusalem, Israel, and facilitated by the Leon and Clara Sznajderman Chair in Psychology.

References

Barnea, M., & Schwartz, S. H. (1994, July). *Value dimensions of political conflict: A cross-national perspective.* Paper presented at the XII Congress of the International Association of Cross-Cultural Psychology, Pamplona, Spain.

Bond, R. A., & Smith, P. B. (1996). Culture and conformity: A meta-analysis of studies using the Asch line judgement task. *Psychological Bulletin, 119,* 111–137.

Bourdieu, P. (1972). *Outline of a theory of practice.* Cambridge: Cambridge University Press.

Feather, N. (1992). Values, valences, expectations and actions. *Journal of Social Issues, 48,* 109–124.

Feather, N. (1995). Values, valences and choice: The influence of values on the perceived attractiveness and choice of alternatives. *Journal of Personality and Social Psychology, 68,* 1135–1151.

Gudykunst, W. B., & Bond, M. H. (in press). Intergroup relations across cultures. In C. Kagitcibasi & M. H. Segall (Eds.), *Handbook of cross-cultural psychology* (2nd ed.), Vol. 3. Boston: Allyn & Bacon.

Heckhausen, H. (1990). *Motivation and action.* Berlin: Springer-Verlag.

Hofstede, G. (1980). *Culture's consequences: International differences in work-related values.* Beverly Hills, CA: Sage.

Hofstede, G. (1991). *Cultures and organizations: Software of the mind.* New York: McGraw-Hill.

Inglehart, R. (1991). *Culture change in advanced industrial societies.* Princeton, NJ: Princeton University Press.

Inkeles, A., & Levinson, D. J. (1954). National character: The study of modal personality and socio-cultural systems. In G. Lindsey & E. Aronson (Eds.), *Handbook of social psychology* (2nd ed.), Vol 4 (pp. 418–506). Reading, MA: Addison-Wesley.

Kagitcibasi, C. (1994). A critical appraisal of individualism and collectivism: Toward a new formulation. In U. Kim, C. Kagitcibasi, H. C. Triandis, & G. Yoon (Eds.), *Individualism and collectivism* (pp. 52–65). Newbury Park, CA: Sage.

Kagitcibasi, C. (in press). Individualism and collectivism. In C. Kagitcibasi & M. H. Segall (Eds.), *Handbook of cross-cultural psychology* (2nd ed.), Vol. 3. Boston: Allyn & Bacon.

Kagitcibasi, C., & Berry, J. (1989). Cross-cultural psychology: Current research and trends. *Annual Review of Psychology, 40,* 493–531.

Kim, U., Triandis, H. C., Kagitcibasi, C., Choi, S-C., & Yoon, G. (Eds.). (1994). *Individualism and collectivism: Theory, method, and applications.* London: Sage.

Kluckhohn, F., & Strodtbeck, F. (1961). *Variations in value orientations.* Evanston, IL: Row, Peterson.

Markus, H. R., & Kitayama, S. (1994). A collective fear of the collective: Implications for selves and theories of selves. *Personality and Social Psychology Bulletin, 20,* 568–579.

Morris, C. W. (1956). *Varieties of human value.* Chicago: University of Chicago Press.

Schwartz, S. H. (1992). Universals in the content and structure of values: Theoretical advances and empirical tests in 20 countries. In M. Zanna (Ed .), *Advances in experimental social psychology,* Vol. 25 (pp. 1–69). San Diego: Academic Press.

Schwartz, S. H. (1993). Explaining national differences in values. Address at the XXIV Congress of the Interamerican Society of Psychology, Santiago, Chile.

Schwartz, S. H. (1994a). Beyond individualism-collectivism: New cultural dimensions of values. In U. Kim, C. Kagitcibasi, H. C. Triandis, & G. Yoon (Eds.), *Individualism and collectivism* (pp. 85–119). Newbury Park, CA: Sage.

Schwartz, S. H. (1994b). Are there universals in the content and structure of values? *Journal of Social Issues, 50,* 19–45.

Schwartz, S. H. (1996). Value priorities and behavior: Applying a theory of integrated value systems. In C. Seligman, J. M. Olson, & M. P. Zanna (Eds.), *Values: The Ontario Symposium,* Vol. 8 (pp. 1–24). Hillsdale, NJ: Erlbaum.

Schwartz, S. H. (in press). Cultural value differences: Some implications for work. *Applied Psychology: An International Journal,*

Schwartz, S. H., & Bardi, A. (1997). Influences of adaptation to communist rule on value priorities in Eastern Europe. *Political Psychology,* Vol. 18.2.

Schwartz, S. H., & Bilsky, W. (1987). Toward a universal psychological structure of human values. *Journal of Personality and Social Psychology, 53,* 550–562.

Schwartz, S. H., & Bilsky, W. (1990). Toward a theory of the universal content and structure of values: Extensions and cross-cultural replications. *Journal of Personality and Social Psychology, 58,* 878–891.

Schwartz, S. H., & Ros, M. (1995). Values in the West: A theoretical and empirical challenge to the individualism–collectivism cultural dimension. *World Psychology, 1,* 91–122.

Smith, P. B., & Schwartz, S. H. (in press). Values. In C. Kagitcibasi & M. H. Segall (Eds.), *Handbook of cross-cultural psychology* (2nd ed.), Vol. 3. Boston: Allyn & Bacon.

Triandis, H. C. (1990) Cross-cultural studies of individualism and collectivism. In J. Berman (Ed.), *Nebraska Symposium on Motivation, 1989* (pp. 41–133). Lincoln: University of Nebraska Press.

Williams, R. M., Jr. (1970). *American society: A sociological interpretation* (3rd ed.). New York: Knopf.

Chapter Six

Self-Actualization and Culture

STEPHEN R. WILSON

Over the past thirty years, millions of people worldwide have adopted lifestyles that revolve around attaining what Abraham Maslow (1968) called self-actualization. Although Maslow was aware of this phenomenon and later in his career commented on the cultural conditions that might account for it, his view that self-actualization is motivated by instinct prevented him from developing a sociocultural theory of self-actualization (Marks, 1979; Whitson & Olczak, 1991). Although critics of Maslow's biological bias have called for a more sociological approach to self-actualization, there have been very few responses to this challenge. Thus, there is still no answer to the question of what sociocultural changes could explain why, at this point in time, so many people have begun a quest for self-actualization.

In this paper I will suggest that most sociologists have ignored this phenomenon because they hold two assumptions that are central to the sociological tradition. I will go on to review the work of four social scientists— John Hewitt (1989), Anthony Giddens (1991), Kenneth Gergen (1991), and Stephen Marks (1979)—who have freed themselves of these assumptions. Although none of these scholars intended to develop a fully developed sociocultural theory of self-actualization, I suggest they offer the building blocks for such a theory, one that would both account for the emerging interest in self-actualization and complement Maslow's theory.

In formulating his famous hierarchy of needs, Maslow saw self-actualization as one of several biological needs influencing human behavior. However, the need for self-actualization was characterized by Maslow as weaker than the needs further down on the hierarchy and thus the organismic signals of this need were easily drowned out by the more basic needs. Maslow's theory suggests that the higher needs, like self-actualization, are sensitive to environmental influence, but he never clearly spells out the conditions that facilitate or hinder the drive toward self-actualization or, for that matter, what the process of self-actualization involves (Marks, 1979; Wilson, 1988).

The topic of self-actualization, and more specifically why so many people are interested in it today, has been overlooked by most sociologists because they subscribe to two assumptions that are central to the sociological perspective. The first is that humans are primarily motivated by their quest for status, power, and financial gain, which could all be regarded as "lower needs" in terms of Maslow's hierarchy. Research by Inglehart (1990) could conceivably convince sociologists that this assumption is no longer tenable. Through the analysis of cross-cultural surveys on values, Inglehart has documented the waning of what he calls "materialistic" cultural values and the waxing of "postmaterialistic" values. According to Inglehart, the materialistic values resemble Maslow's "lower needs" and the postmaterialistic values reflect an interest in Maslow's "higher needs," such as self-esteem and self-actualization. Although his research does not support Maslow's hierarchy theory, it does suggest that when cultures can provide for the lower physiological needs, members are free to develop an interest in higher-level pursuits, including self-actualization. However, his data show that not everybody in such cultures adopts postmaterialist values and even those who do are not necessarily drawn to self-actualization. Inglehart's work suggests that sociologists should consider the importance of self-actualization in contemporary societies, but it does not really identify the mechanisms by which culture contributes to the growing interest in self-actualization (Tamney, 1992).

The second assumption that has hindered the development of a sociological theory of self-actualization has been what Hewitt (1989) calls the "pessimistic" view of self and culture found in sociology. This perspective involves the belief that the evolution from traditional to modern societies has led to unbridled individualism and self-absorption. This assumption, shared by authors such as Schur (1976), Lasch (1978, 1984), and Yankelovich (1981), has led to the view that quests for self-actualization are nothing more than narcissistic attempts to withdraw from a sick culture. Although these authors explore the ways in which modern culture influences the self, their pessimistic bias stands in the way of acknowledging that it could motivate healthy, life-affirming responses.

Since Maslow's death a number of alternative theories dealing with self-transformation have emerged and have been received by the wider public with some success (see Miller, 1991). Of these newer theories, Ken Wilber's (1984) is the most sociological in that it is not based on the assumptions mentioned above and acknowledges that the evolution of consciousness is linked to sociocultural evolution. Wilber suggests that for individuals to be transformed to the level of consciousness representing self-actualization, they must "accept the *death* of the present level of adaptation" (p. 53), which in today's culture is characterized by rationality and self-reflexivity. Wilber's scheme seems to suggest that the symbolic death of an identity grounded in rationality and self-awareness can be initiated by cultural changes, but he does not specify how or why this occurs.

In the remainder of the paper I will review the work of four social scientists whose work on self and culture is not restricted by the assumptions mentioned above. Although all of these authors are interested in the connection between self and culture, they vary in the extent to which they are explicitly interested in developing a sociocultural theory of self-actualization. All, however, point to ways in which features of modern culture could facilitate the quest for self-actualization and so provide building blocks for the development of such a theory in the future.

Hewitt's Dilemmas of the American Self

JOHN HEWITT'S (1989) approach to culture and the self consciously avoids viewing culture as a homogeneous monolith that leaves its stamp on the individual members of society and provides a view of motivation that acknowledges their active choice and reflection. According to Hewitt, "Although particular cultures may appear as uniform worlds of objects and thus motivationally consistent, there are always opposing objects and hidden streams of conduct" (p. 235). In Hewitt's view, identity becomes problematic whenever we are faced with situations or life circumstances in which there "is no self-evidently legitimate flow of life into which individuals can allow themselves to be swept" (p. 169). Such events force choices upon the individual, and these choices always have implications for how individuals conceive of themselves. When identity becomes problematic for individuals, they engage in verbalized reminders to themselves about who they are or who they want to be.

Hewitt does not directly deal with the topic of self-actualization but uses self-actualization theory as one of many texts about the self that can be used as a window into American culture. He treats self-actualization theory as an example of "optimistic" discourse wherein the individual is viewed as having the capacity to overcome repressive social constraints that hinder personal fulfillment. In this view, the modernization of society, which weakens ties to stable institutions and organic communities, is viewed as opening potential opportunities for self-development. In contrast to this are the social scientists and social critics assuming the "pessimistic" view mentioned above. They tend to be approving of the past stable social order and argue that current changes in society are leading to identity crises and other forms of pathology. Rather than take sides in this ongoing debate, Hewitt argues that both positions reflect the existence of an underlying dilemma posed by American culture: "whether to seek and accept dependence upon others or to go it alone as an independent being who has no need of others" (p. 105).

For Hewitt, culture influences the motives of individuals by constituting "an external and constraining world that attracts attention and effort at the same time as it both facilitates and interferes with humans acts" (p. 235). However, he argues that the way to understanding the connection between modern culture and the self is to understand that culture both facilitates and interferes with often opposite courses of action, the most important being the move toward independence and individuality and the move toward dependency and community. Such contradictions make identity problematic, and it is through making choices while facing such dilemmas that the individual constructs a self. Thus, we are constantly faced with momentary as well as lifelong decisions. On the one hand, how much time and energy should we devote to family, work, associations, and community? On the other hand, how much to the projects that we view as enhancing the self, such as pursuing a better career, better health, or a more healthy body? Hewitt suggests that although some people attempt to fashion their identity exclusively around one pole or the other (strategies of "exclusivity" and "autonomy"), most adopt a "pragmatic strategy," trying to balance both paths simultaneously.

Within this cultural context, says Hewitt, texts such as Maslow's theories of self-actualization, which promote themes of autonomy and individuality, are appealing to pragmatic identifiers who are searching for a way of balancing the conflicting demands that are inherent in contemporary culture. Those who are interested in the messages of Maslow and the hundreds of other authors who have elaborated upon his ideas are not interested because they are assuming a strategy of autonomy, opposing any commitment to community or group ties. Rather, argues Hewitt, they are simply looking for guidelines and skills that will help them in the daily struggle to balance the conflicting demands. Recognizing that the popularity of books, courses, lectures, and the like on issues of assertiveness and individuality could easily be dismissed as examples of narcissism and selfishness, Hewitt (1989, pp. 220-221) states:

> Such a dismissal is a poor analysis, for a concern with assertiveness—worries about whether one is too easily swayed by others and about how one can possibly learn to assert oneself more effectively—is inherent in the pragmatic mode of identification. To the extent that the individual is open to a variety of communities and their purposes, he or she is subject to cross-pressures and so more or less constantly has to deal with them and to find some solid ground from which to do so.

Thus, Hewitt suggests that the interest in self-actualization is motivated by those who are looking for guidelines and skills that will help them strike a balance between the cultural demands for constructing an identity based upon exclusivity and one based upon autonomy.

Giddens's *Modernity and Self-Identity*

IN *Modernity and Self-Identity,* Anthony Giddens (1991) continues his earlier efforts to characterize the nature of modern society and to outline the consequences of current institutional forms for the self (see Giddens, 1990). Giddens explicitly attempts to account for the current widespread interest in self-actualization by looking at the features of what he calls "late modern" culture. His comments on the process of self-actualization can be seen, following Hewitt (1989), as a discourse with Christopher Lasch (1978, 1984) and other "pessimistic" theorists of the self. The pessimists, he suggests, "mistake the new ethos of self-discovery for the 'old-modern' aggrandizing individual; they fail to distinguish between new impulses toward personal growth, on the one hand, and capitalistic pressures toward personal advantage and material accumulation on the other" (p. 209).

Like others who have commented on today's society, Giddens emphasizes the overwhelming number of choices available to individuals and the fact that there no longer exists an overarching authority to guide individual choice. Thus, "We are, not what we are but what we make of ourselves" (Giddens, 1991, p. 75), and each of us is responsible for creating and sustaining a personal biography that allows us to avoid shame and feel pride. Although Giddens sees the conditions of modernity as making this ongoing reflexive project challenging, he does not believe that the despair of Lasch and the other "pessimists" is warranted.

In what Lasch initially called the "culture of narcissism" and later called the "culture of survivalism," individuals are forced to deal with large bureaucracies with arbitrary powers and the influence of commodity production that fosters a "minimal self," defensively separated from the outer world. Individuals who feel they have no control over their lives become apathetic about the past and the future and become immersed in living one day at a time. Giddens (1991) feels this view fails to recognize that individuals never passively accept external conditions but rather "reflect upon them and reconstitute them in the light of their particular circumstances" (p. 175), and that this often is done collectively. According to Giddens (pp. 175-176):

> Modern social life impoverishes individual action, yet furthers the appropriation of new possibilities; it is alienating, yet at the same time, characteristically, human beings react against social circumstances which they find oppressive. Late modern institutions create a world of mixed opportunity and high-consequence risk. But this world does not form an impermeable environment which resists intervention.

Giddens (1991) admits that the pessimistic theorists' view of self-actualizing therapies and other modalities are partially true because they *can* involve self-indulgence and narcissistic withdrawal. However, for Giddens, such pursuits are better understood as part of the reflexive project of the self that is a natural and a healthy response to "modernity's reflexivity." He acknowledges that most forms of therapy developed as a means of helping individuals adjust to flawed social environments but believes that therapies in late modernity have taken a new direction: providing individuals with guidelines for life planning and encouraging "engagement and reappropriation" (p. 180). In a setting where the institutional frameworks for identity construction are weakening and conflicting, systems of self-actualization provide answers to the nagging questions of "who should I be?" and "how should I live my life?" (p. 180).

Giddens agrees with the pessimistic theorists' contention that modern life poses a constant threat of personal meaninglessness, but he views self-actualizing lifestyles as constructive means by which individuals counter that threat. In a time when morality is unavailable for identity-constructing, Giddens believes that individuals must develop new skills that enable them to exert control over those circumstances that potentially threaten identity.

Rather than withdrawing into a "minimal self," Giddens sees self-actualizers as engaging in "life politics," which he defines as a politics of choice and thus a politics of lifestyle. According to Giddens (1991, p. 214): "life politics concerns political issues which flow from processes of self-actualisation in post-traditional contexts, where globalising influences intrude deeply into the reflexive project of the self, and conversely where processes of self-realization influence global strategies." Some manifestations of life politics, according to Giddens, are the women's movement and the ecology movement, as well as the ongoing debates about abortion, sexuality, economic sustainability, and world peace. These movements and debates, he argues, raises into prominence the moral and existential questions that were repressed by the institutions of modernity. Because these issues are being discussed and acted upon by self-actualizing individuals as they seek a meaningful life and are not handed over to faceless institutional authorities, Giddens concludes that the self-actualizing process is one of individual and collective reappropriation and empowerment.

Gergen's *The Saturated Self*

FOR Gergen (1991), the emerging postmodern culture includes a blurring of traditional cultural boundaries, an increasing awareness of the social construction process, and a weakening of traditional sources of authority and "rational coherence," as well as the emergence of self-reflexive doubt. He suggests that the *modernist* view of the self, in which the essence of a person lies in his or her ability to reason, and be predictable, honest, and sincere, is being replaced with a new way of thinking about the self. According to Gergen, the emerging technologies that immerse us in information and relationships from around the world, as well as endless choices and conflicting opportunities discussed by Hewitt and Giddens, lead to *social saturation* and a new psychic state that he calls "multiphrenia." Under these conditions, says Gergen, "for everything we 'know to be true' about ourselves, other voices within respond with doubt and even derision" (pp. 6–7). Because the individual is pulled simultaneously in various directions—playing multiple roles, many of which seem contradictory, and engaging in shallow, disconnected relationships—the sense of being an "authentic self" becomes increasingly difficult to achieve. Indeed, says Gergen, "the fully saturated self becomes no self at all" (p. 7).

On the surface, Gergen's analysis sounds a great deal like that of Lasch and the other pessimistic theorists. Although he acknowledges his own ambivalence about the emerging postmodern culture, Gergen consciously makes an effort to consider the positive possibilities that this new way of life will offer the individual self. For example, he argues that to meet the challenges of postmodernity, individuals may begin to resemble the "strategic manipulator" described by Goffman (1959) or Riesman's (1950) *other-directed* personality: someone presenting a different self in every new situation or relationship. However, Gergen goes on to argue that the negative reactions we have to such people, (including ourselves)—as manifested in our tendency to label them as "insincere," "wishy-washy," "superficial," "chameleon-like," and so on—is based upon a leftover modernist worldview in which rational consistency, authenticity, and sincerity are valued. According to Gergen, the postmodern self is capable of being involved in various relationships in diverse settings, each of which calls forth distinct roles, and is capable of being involved in the "presentation" of vastly different selves without being concerned about these negative implications:

> Such relationships don't require full expression of self; one is free to express a delimited aspect without responsibility to the remainder, to coherence or consistency. One needn't worry that "this is only a misleading token of who I am," for in the context only a partial provisional self counts. (p. 179)

Following the lead of other postmodern theorists, Gergen suggests that postmodern culture is an invitation to play; that the self does not have to be defined by the usual markers of identity such as profession, gender, ethnicity, and so on; that consistency or integrity, so valued by romanticists and modernists, need not limit one's thoughts, feelings, and actions. The implication is that the "death of the self," as traditionally constituted, can be a liberating experience full of opportunities for self-development.

Stephen Marks's "Culture, Human Energy and Self-Actualization"

MARKS'S 1979 journal article was the first to address the possibility of a sociocultural theory of self-actualization, and is the one that does so most directly. It is useful to know that the article reviewed here followed an earlier one (1977) wherein Marks challenged the assumption that individuals playing multiple roles are the victims of "strain" or "overload." In the initial article, Marks observed that a minority of people facing multiple and conflicting role expectations do not run out of time and energy but are, in fact, "energized" by the situation and are able to rise to meet the occasion. In the second article, Marks further argues that humans are energized by carrying out the activities to which they are committed and "drained" by carrying out the activities to which they are not highly committed. In other words, if someone finds pleasure and joy from the demands of playing multiple roles, he or she becomes energized; if not, he or she loses energy. Marks then examines different cultures in terms of the systems of commitment that they engender. For our purposes here, it is important to know only that he views the culture of modern societies as possessing an "invidious system of commitments."

> This is a system of over- and undercommitments in which some of one's typical activities and role partners are supposed to be better, more important, more worthy of

oneself than others. Invidious cultures will therefore tend to energize their members in some activities and with some partners but enervate or drain them for others.... Overcommitments are the cultural analogue of obsessions, and they are not unlike addictions. Identity strength and self-esteem will rest disproportionately on "successful" performances in the overcommitted areas, and the culture will mobilize its arsenal of punishments and rewards (especially wealth, power, and prestige) on behalf of these performances, withholding support from those who "underachieve." (p. 33)

These overcommitted activities are inevitably accompanied by undercommitted activities, which because of their relatively low appeal, elicit effort, strain, and fatigue.

Marks points out that Maslow and others have characterized self-actualized individuals as having a sense of "aliveness" and a "zest for living." He goes on to suggest that such individuals are capable of responding to the demands of our "invidious system of commitments by finding pleasure and joy in all activities whether or not they are culturally rewarded." They do this, says Marks, because they possess what Carl Rogers (1961) called "openness to experience." Marks explicitly rejects both Maslow's notion that self-actualization is prompted by instinctual urges and Durkheim's (1965) belief that humans are energized by the "moral energy" of society:

> If human energy is a person/environment *relationship* and not an inherent property of anyone or anything, then we can produce it *whenever* we bridge the gap between the inside world and the outside world, that is, by opening, or, put differently, by communing (literally, "to make common"), or by being inspired (literally, "to be breathed in by"). (p. 37)

The challenge then, for persons living in a complex culture, is to find ways of remaining open to all experiences, no matter how routine or mundane, and therefore to be constantly reenergizing themselves. Marks suggests that one way of doing this is to discover ways of experiencing altered states of consciousness, which is consistent with Maslow's (1972) observations that self-actualizing individuals are especially prone to having and benefiting from "peak experiences."

Conclusions

DESPITE the very different agendas of the four theorists reviewed above, some common themes run through their work. Perhaps most striking is the suggestion that modern culture can induce or facilitate self-actualization by offering challenges to individual members. As Tamney (1992) points out, the self-actualization process involves deprivation, frustration, and pain. Although the four theorists acknowledge that modern culture may elicit pathological responses, all emphasize that this is not inevitable. Further, they all seem to suggest that those who do not retreat or withdraw in the face of the dilemmas and ambiguities presented by modern culture actually develop in ways that would fit Maslow's description of self-actualization.

Both Hewitt and Giddens, who see persons as actively constructing meaningful selves in a complex cultural field, view the philosophies and skills that constitute the self-actualization process as providing the individual with guidelines that enable him or her to maintain a sense of self-worth in the face of cultural forces that make this extremely difficult. Many of the programs, books, and therapies providing the knowledge and skills that Hewitt and Giddens see as promoting self-actualization include techniques, emphasized by Marks, for inducing altered states of consciousness and for "reenergizing" oneself while engaged in everyday routines.

Gergen's book does not deal with self-actualization per se, but his analysis strongly suggests that the conditions of postmodernity are creating an environment that facilitates changes in identity construction that are consistent with the self-actualization process. In discussing the possible stages a person passes through in transforming from a modern self to a postmodern self (or *relational self*), Gergen talks about the "nausea of dissimulation" (p. 150) giving rise to "exhilaration and potential in multiplicity" (p. 154). His language here resembles very closely the highs and lows of self-actualization as described by Westerners, like Maslow, as well as those writing within the context of the Eastern meditative disciplines. Most of these writers suggest that self-transformation usually occurs when individuals voluntarily enter a supportive environment such as therapy, a teacher-student relationship, or a spiritual community that also challenges and undermines the basis of a person's identity (see Wilson, 1990).

Gergen's work suggests that the larger postmodern culture itself may provide similar types of challenges to the self and thus have the potential to facilitate the social-psychological process promoting self-actualization. This view is consistent with Wilber's (1984) observation that self-transformation occurs when individuals accept the "death" of one's present mode of adapting to culture and progress to a higher level of adaptation.

Although he attempted to ground his theory upon positivism, Maslow's (1968) ideas about self-actualization were clearly influenced by Buddhism and Hinduism. His notion that the self-actualized state was one of selflessness or egolessness was central to the development of transpersonal movement in psychology. Wilson (1991) has argued that the state of selflessness, as attained through various self-actualizing modalities, is not so much a distinct or altered state of consciousness as an absence of the concern and anxiety that is a normal part of being a self, but this is heightened by the reflexivity of modern culture. Similarly, Epstein (1988) argues that the meditative practices do not lead to loss of either self-control or the ability to know oneself symbolically but to a loss of "ego feeling of an independent I" (p. 65), which results in "a more fluid ego able to constantly integrate potentially destabilizing experiences of insubstantiality and impermanence" (p. 68). In other words, the self-actualized person is open to change and ambiguity. The theorists reviewed here all point to the possibility that the conditions of modern culture actually provide the social conditions that encourage the development of the flexibility and fluidity of identity that is the essence of self-actualization.

It is doubtful that persons unwilling or unable to undergo this process will be "pushed" into self-actualization merely because they are living in a postmodern culture. For example, Gergen (1991) suggests that most people attempt to hold onto what they believe to be their "true" or "authentic" selves. Likewise, Hewitt (1989) argues that many people in today's society choose strategies of complete exclusivity or autonomy in fashioning their selves rather than becoming a pragmatic strategizer. Similarly, Giddens (1991) observes that many if not most people avoid the choices, the challenges, and the opportunity for self-actualization and empowerment that are offered by late modernity. According to Gergen, those who choose to hold onto a modernist worldview are destined to be "continuously ripped from the security of an essential or unified self" (p. 148). It is such individuals who are understandably thrown off balance by the emerging postmodern culture and it is they who are captured accurately by Lasch and the pessimistic theorists.

Toward the end of his life Maslow (1968) seemed puzzled by the fact that in societies where most people's lower needs were satisfied, so many people not only were not becoming self-actualized but were manifesting what he called "metapathologies." It seems clear that any theory of self-actualization must acknowledge that the cultural conditions that facilitate self-actualization for a small minority also contribute to unhealthy identities among the majority.

References

Durkheim, E. (1965). *Elementary forms of the religious life.* New York: Free Press.

Epstein, M. (1988). The deconstruction of the self: Ego and "egolessness" in Buddhist insight meditation. *Journal of Transpersonal Psychology, 20,* 61–69.

Gergen, K. J. (1991). *The saturated self.* New York: Basic Books.

Giddens, A. (1990). *The consequences of modernity.* Stanford, CA: Stanford University Press.

Giddens, A. (1991). *Modernity and self-identity.* Stanford, CA: Stanford University Press.

Goffman, E. (1959). *The presentation of self in everyday life.* Garden City, NY: Doubleday.

Hewitt, J. (1989). *Dilemmas of the American self.* Philadelphia: Temple University Press.

Inglehart, R. (1990). *Culture shift in advanced industrial society.* Princeton: Princeton University Press.

Lasch, C. (1978). *The culture of narcissism.* New York: Basic Books.

Lasch, C. (1984). *The minimal self: Psychic survival in troubled times.* New York: Norton.

Marks, S. (1977). Multiple roles and role strain: Some notes on human energy, time and commitment. *American Sociological Review, 42,* 921–936.

Marks, S. (1979). Culture, human energy, and self-actualization: A sociological offering to humanistic psychology. *Journal of Humanistic Psychology, 19,* 27–43.

Maslow, A. (1968). *Toward a psychology of being.* New York: Van Nostrand Reinhold.

Maslow, B. G. (Ed.) (1972). *Abraham H. Maslow: A Memorial Volume.* Monterey, CA: Brooks/Cole.

Miller, C. (1991). Self-actualization and the consciousness revolution. In A. Jones and R. Crandall (Eds.), Handbook of self-actualization [special issue]. *Journal of Social Behavior and Personality, 6,* 109–126.

Riesman, D. (1950). *The lonely crowd.* New Haven: Yale University Press.

Rogers, C. (1961). *On becoming a person.* Boston: Houghton Mifflin.

Schur, E. (1976). *The awareness trap.* New York: McGraw-Hill.

Tamney, J. B. (1992). Religion and self-actualization. In J. F. Schumaker (Ed.), *Religion and Mental Health* (pp. 132–137). New York: Oxford University Press.

Whitson, E. R., and Olczak, P. V. (1991). Criticism and polemics surrounding the self-actualization construct: An evaluation. In A. Jones and R. Crandall (Eds.), Handbook of self-actualization [special issue]. *Journal of Social Behavior and Personality, 6,* 75–95.

Wilber, K. (1984). *A sociable god.* Boulder, CO: Shambala Press.

Wilson, S. R. (1988). The "real self" controversy: Towards an integration of humanistic and interactionistic theory. *Journal of Humanistic Psychology, 28,* 39–65.

Wilson, S. R. (1990). Personal growth in a yoga ashram; A symbolic interactionist interpretation. *Research in the Social Scientific Study of Religion, 2,* 137–166.

Wilson, S. R. (1991). Self-actualization and selflessness: A social-psychological analysis. In A. Jones and R. Crandall (Eds.), Handbook of self-actualization [special issue]. *Journal of Social Behavior and Personality, 6,* 97–108.

Yankelovich, D. (1981). *New rules: Searching for self-fulfillment in a world upside down.* New York: Random House.

Chapter Seven

Conformity, Calculation, and Culture

JAMES VALENTINE

Conformity of Them Uersus Us

Conformity is thought to be a characteristic of certain cultures and subcultures, usually those that are considered different from "us." Although our own way of life is conceived as coming naturally, or from free choice, there is a tendency to explain away other ways of life as mere conformity. Those who act solely from conformity are seen as ridiculous and pitiable, and alternative ways of life are thus set apart and put down through humor and condescension. The characterization of "their" difference as conformity is part of a process of stereotypification. Breger (1992), in reviewing stereotyping processes in the German press, notes that stereotyping involves drawing a boundary between the in-group and out-group. A dichotomy is constructed between us and them, a collective Self and Other. A culture is thereby homogenized, "depicting it as undifferentiated" (p. 174).

The process of homogenization may lump together certain visible outsiders, while ignoring discrimination against less visible minorities. Rattansi (1992) finds this process in the homogenization of "blacks" in Britain, which further marginalizes the racialization of other British minorities, such as Irish and Jewish people. Outsiders who do not conform to the common identification may find themselves and their exclusion rendered insignificant. Stereotypification thus ordains conformity and significance.

Dyer (1984) sees stereotyping as especially confining for those whose difference puts them beyond the pale of normalcy. Stereotypes of excluded subcultures are markedly rigid, whereas typification of those within the boundaries of normalcy is "open-ended, more provisional, more flexible, to create the sense of freedom, choice, self-definition" (p. 29). Furthermore, this view of us in the mainstream as having a degree of choice in self-definition (unlike those condemned to stereotypical conformity) is compounded, as Dyer notes elsewhere (1993), by the notion that we have reached our consensus on others "independently and in isolation" (p. 14). The irony here lies in the conformity of thought about the conformity of others, and in the conformity of denial that our thinking is conformist.

The view of conformity as a characteristic of others means, moreover, that those who are seen as conforming too closely, even to traditional cultural ideals, are set apart. McKechnie (1993) noticed this in her study of Corsican ethnic identification. She found that demonstration of Corsican identity required dedication, but that the efforts of the more dedicated to conform to an ethnic norm merely distinguished them as out of place in the community, "their espousal of an ideal of Corsicanness excluded them from Corsican life" (p. 131).

In similar vein, to be a "dedicated follower of fashion" (as effectively mocked in the popular song by the Kinks) is derided as odd. Clearly overconformity is itself a deviation. Raz (1992) finds that an exaggerated conformity characterizes the epitome of deviant Japanese groups: the *yakuza*. The more intently they express their participation in Japanese culture, through closely observing traditional values and forms of speech, appearance, and organization, the more exclusive and excluded they become: "Eager expressions of inclusiveness ... often denote the opposite: that the actor is a marginal element or an outsider" (p. 213). The view of ardent conformists as deviant in Japan carries further irony, in that Japanese society is often characterized as differing from others through an exaggerated conformism.

Conformist Views of a Different Society: Japan

JAPAN is commonly viewed as a different society (Collick, 1981), yet difference can have meaning only in the context of a contrastive relationship. Here the difference that is established depends on a conventional contrast, in which Japan is set up as the "other" of Western societies, exotically far away from France (Barthes, 1982), holding mysterious secrets of success for Germany (Breger, 1992), a fresh opposition to place against the post–cold war American self (Robertson, 1990). There is considerable consensus on the characteristics that make Japan "different." The key quality is detected in a homogeneous society of eager conformists.

Theories of Japanese self and society are thus a prime example of the way in which conformity is considered to characterize a people viewed as other than a Western norm. From a Western point of view, Japanese people are routinely stereotyped as homogeneous, all alike in being different from a differentiated view of ourselves as distinct individuals. Yet, the traffic in stereotypes is not all one-way: images of Japan are not just passively imported into Japan but are produced for both home consumption and export. The most common Japanese self-image is in remarkable accord with Western views. Contributors to *Nihonjinron* (a theory of the Japanese people that emphasizes uniqueness) support the conception of Japanese selves as uniquely group oriented and homogeneous, thereby reinforcing the construction of a conformist Japanese society that contrasts with an individuated calculating Western self.

There is a double concordance here. The most common Western and Japanese images of Japan present the Japanese self (sometimes even the Japanese mind) as unique and conformist. A common Japanese view is that foreigners cannot understand the unique culture (Breger, 1992) that is characterized by the homogeneous group. Yoshino (1992) notes that this cultural nationalism sees Japan as unique among modern industrialized societies in preserving the supposedly preindustrial forms of solidarity of the *conscience collective* (Durkheim, 1964) and *Gemeinschaft* (Tönnies, 1963). The very spirit (*seishin*) of what it is to be Japanese is revealed in endurance and the willingness to regulate oneself for the sake of the group, thus contrasting with a Western individualism that is deemed selfish (Moeran, 1984; Hendry, 1992).

The ideal of active conformity cannot, however, be taken as an accurate description of everyday practice. Conformity may be a passive compliance for the sake of belonging. Unambiguous belonging is considered essential for successful interaction, and one is obliged to act according to where one belongs, to establish status propriety (Lebra, 1976). Lebra sees this as acquiescence, a passive conformism that does not necessarily entail active agreement. Moreover, such conformism is context-specific rather than located in a decontextualized self or mind. In an appropriate context, criticism, contention, and complaint may be freely exhibited.

Where a context demands conformity, the sanction that sustains this lies in the value of belonging, or remaining inside (*uchi*), and the threat of exclusion. Hendry (1984) observes how, from an early age, punishment comes to be seen as having its source outside (*soto*), and may take the form of being placed outside the group of insiders. The fear of exclusion is enough to encourage conformity, which is thereby secured by informal group sanctions rather than explicit regulation and law.

Nonconformity carries the risk not only of losing one's belonging inside (*uchi*) but also of losing reputation or face (*omote*), and these two controls are linked. Reputation depends largely on where one belongs, and belonging to a valuable group depends on maintaining a proper reputation. This leads groups to exert strong pressure on members to conform and to conceal any serious nonconformity from outsiders. Haley (1991) argues that "what emerges is a pattern of pervasive nonconformity, masked by outward conformity" (p. 182).

How can nonconformity be explained where a society is considered so homogeneous and conformist? Four regular explanations are consistent with the view of a conformist society. First, nonconformity is seen as resulting from odd individuals who have become disengaged from normal social integration and controls. The informal sanctions of the group cannot apply. Second, the very strength of conformity is assumed to account for its obverse in a nonconformist reaction: outbreaks of nonconformity are regarded as a reactive protest against insistent demands to conform. Third, attention is paid to the requirement of conformity in detail, which means that slight transgressions count as nonconformity. Exact regulation makes it easy to deviate. Fourth, nonconformity to mainstream culture is understood in terms of alternative allegiance. There is still conformity, but to a deviant group or subculture.

It is in these terms that juvenile delinquency is normally construed. The deviant style of Japanese youth gangs is explained as a conformist reaction against conformity, as where Kersten (1993) views such style both as "a statement against the ingrained and taken-for-granted rule of conformity during adolescence" and, nevertheless, as an alternative conformity, "another kind of uniformity," rule-governed rather than individualistic (p. 282). Studies of Japanese gangs indeed give evidence of their conformity to the predominant values and principles of Japanese social organization (Haley, 1991; Kersten, 1993; Raz, 1992). One of these principles is the emphasis on visual presentation (Valentine, 1986), which makes visible nonconformity a ready opportunity. Concern for the detailed regulation of appearance means that minor infringements are taken seriously (Kersten, 1993). White (1994) illustrates this with a Tokyo Metropolitan Police guide for parents and teachers, showing the "visual indicators" that a child might be on the road to juvenile delinquency (pp. 164–165).

A society with such a pronounced belief in conformity and homogeneity thus generates the very outsiders that belie the belief, and may in turn promote the insistency with which the conformist claims are made. Thus, what is special about Japanese culture is less the fact of conformity than its belief and the significance placed on belonging that accord peculiar distinction to those conceived as not clearly fitting, as marginal (Valentine, 1990).

Yet, an emphasis on belonging is not unique to Japanese society. For example, Day and Murdoch (1993) found that established locals in a Welsh rural valley were keen that incomers should fit in and be accepted as part of the community. "However, acceptance is conditional upon the 'correct' attitude being taken; there are certain implied 'terms of engagement' to which incomers must conform" (pp. 102–103). The value of belonging and the associated requirement of conformity cannot be seen as peculiar to Japan. Japanese society hence cannot be regarded as uniquely different through conformity, and indeed is far from unique in being considered different. A self-conception of uniqueness is not a uniquely Japanese trait.

Criticism and Calculation of Conformity

THE view of Japan as a uniquely conformist society has recently been subject to extensive criticism, and there now tends to be an emphasis on conflict and calculation. Rather than highlighting cultural specificity, supposedly universal models and theories are applied to the explanation of Japanese behavior, and these models are critical of notions of consensual motivation. Where conformity is acknowledged, it is accounted for in terms of masking and manipulation.

Far from the portrayal of a conformist society, Kamishima (1990) argues that divergence is so great in Japan that an official view or professed principle (*tatemae*) of convergence becomes essential. Social alignments are fragile, and heterogeneity is rife but hidden beneath a surface of conformity strategically adopted. Conformity is thus often seen as masking disagreement. Outright demonstrations of nonconformity are avoided. Surface compliance may be achieved through ambiguous expressions or through silence (Midooka, 1990), though Lebra (1987) notes the many meanings of silence in communication, including not only its use in maintaining propriety and social acceptance but also its potential for expressing "estrangement, hostility, or defiance" (p. 350).

The group model that sees Japanese society in terms of harmony, consensus, and conformity to group norms (Befu, 1990) can accordingly be attacked for considering only public statements and superficial views. In contrast, critiques of the group model have emphasized competition, conflict, and calculation. Yet, few of those who have been admonished as exponents of the group model ever ignored competition. Indeed, factional rivalry is seen as a corollary of group affiliation. For example, Roland (1988) adopts the group model but stresses the factionalism among groups of psychoanalytic therapists in Japan. Moreover, factional allegiance is recognized as involving strategic calculation.

Calculation is central to a model that Befu (1990) proposes as an alternative to the group model: the Social Exchange model in which actors "develop a strategy of action to maximize the benefit accruing to the action" (p. 226). Although Befu argues for a catholic attitude toward models, rather than the exclusive use of one, the currently predominant mode of interpretation of Japanese behavior is in terms of strategic calculation, even where conformity is apparent.

A calculating conformity means that the rewards of conformity and the penalties of nonconformity are carefully weighed. Conformity is here interpreted as a rational strategy pursued for personal gain or the avoidance of loss, and is thereby removed from the realm of collective consciousness and psychological disposition. It is no longer considered a trait of culture and personality but a rational choice given particular social conditions.

In this view, although choice is involved, the alternatives to conformity and continued acceptance may seem so limited and insufferable that choice appears as necessity, a compulsion that operates through awareness of fearful consequences. This is a "compulsion of perceived dependency or personal gain" (Haley, 1991, p. 180), whereby "there is really no alternative but to belong" (Hendry, 1984, p. 220).

The circumstances that make conformity appear essential may themselves be manipulated, so that conformity becomes a rational response to controls calculatedly exercised by the powerful. Alternatively, the conformist response to the technology of social control may become internalized as a "routinized psychic structure for compliance" (Sugimoto, 1986, p. 68), seen in Marxist terms as false consciousness. Allison (1991), following Althusser, sees this as the means by which the ideological state apparatus reaches into the realm of personal volition. Allison notes how her son learned that not adhering to nursery school routines leads to the penalty of rejection from the group: "Seeking the acceptance of his peers, the student develops the aptitude, willingness and ... even the desire to conform to the highly ordered and structured practices of nursery school life" (p. 201).

If Marxist accounts of conformity emphasize calculation on behalf of the controllers and manipulation by the powerful, who load the dice for any calculation of the gamble of nonconformity, interactionists focus on masking, the controlled manipulation of appearance with calculated effect on one's audience. Calculation is central to both accounts, as is manipulation and deception. Conformity emerges as a surface phenomenon whose explanation lies deeper. Conformity is appearance that masks calculation.

In Japanese culture there are common terms that express this perception.

These contrast surface, appearance, face, or front *(omote)* with what lies beneath or behind *(ura)*; they set professed views or officially correct tenets *(tatemae)* against actual feelings, real intentions, or underlying motives *(honne)*. Here, there is recognition of the importance of controlling emotions in order to foster and maintain rewarding social relationships (Lebra, 1976). Real feelings must be wrapped for propriety in public (Hendry, 1993).

Hendry (1993) also notes that Abu-Lughod's study *Veiled Sentiments* of the Awlad Ali Bedouin people, shows a similar concern with "individual sentiments and the need to mask or 'veil' these in everyday life" (p. 164). Hendry thus observes that, although wrapping constitutes a pervasive principle of Japanese life, in all societies "we use various forms of wrapping to express our opinions" (p. 172). This does not mean that form (and conformity thereto) takes precedence over content and intent. The wrapping itself may be what is significant. Thus, the use of highly polite language may indicate formality or deference but may equally be used among members of a high-status group to manifest belonging and to protect the group from outside intrusion (Hendry, 1990). More generally, as Weber (1968) would recognize, conformity to a style of life is a way for status groups to maintain prestige and exclusivity.

A calculated conformity of manner and expression that fosters belonging and attains status or other rewards may also be used to avoid detection of an unsuitable self. The nonconformist may feel compelled to take on the trappings of conformity. Conventional relationships may be used as a cover, as in a predicament cited by McKechnie (1993): a gay man, feeling obliged to conform to a traditional vision of Corsican masculinity, "went to bars with friends and picked up girls" (p. 130).

Such conformity may be seen as an "attempt to manipulate the gaze of others by acting out surface aspects of our selves" (Mita, 1992, p. 444), whether for self-defense or of self-advancement. Calculated conformity may not simply be a matter of appropriate self-presentation for the sake of belonging to a preexistent group; it may be the means of fostering useful connections. Such networks of obligatory relationships *(tsukiai)* in Japanese society are seen as deliberately cultivated as means to attain certain goals. An example is given by Atsumi (1980, p. 75): "Mr Sato must 'follow the rules' if he wants to be a successful company employee. This forces him to associate with his *tsukiai* associates even when he is tired or has something else to do. This is the social obligation of a good company employee."

Conformity may not just be the means of maintaining belonging and building alliances. It may be used as a strategy against others, whether in competition or conflict. This can occur in such an apparently insignificant obligation as the preparation of a child's lunchbox. This creation is the focus of considerable attention in Japanese preschools, and a mother who does not prepare a proper lunchbox feels publicly exposed. Social pressure here leads to a kind of competitive conformity. Maternal compliance in the painstaking preparation of articles for preschool is encouraged by "numerous subtle opportunities for mothers to compare each others' work" (Peak, 1991, p. 62). If such detailed conformity is demanded, a slight breach can signify great rebellion and indeed may be deliberately used in that way. Allison (1991) argues that a lunchbox that does not conform to prevailing conventions can subvert the ideological manipulation of motherhood by the state. Here, nonconformity is seen as the calculated means of political disorder.

The interpretation of conformity (along with nonconformity) in calculative terms, as means that are weighed for utility in achieving certain ends, itself conforms to predominant social scientific discourse, where rationalistic accounts explain social action with reference to motives that are clear, calculating, and self-centered. Conformity is thus regarded as form, outward appearance, masking an inner process of calculation. Rather than conformity constituting a motive in itself, it is considered as the means to other ends, and motives are assumed to be universally "selfish."

Selfish Rationalizations

THE explication of conformity as the calculated means to the achievement of selfish ends relies on the twin assumptions of rationality and egocentricity. The self is taken for granted as presocially constituted and (ironically) conforming to a universalized myth of what used to be termed rational man. Commonsense interpretations of motive may thus be part of a conformity of thought that passes unrecognized in Western self-images of independent individualism.

Such assumptions underlie even some sociological representations of the self. One of the most impressive accounts of the self in social action is given by Goffman (1971), who focuses on the presentation of self to others. Goffman treats conformity as manipulated appearance, in a way that recalls the common Japanese opposition of front and back, though his own fieldwork was in Shetland. For Goffman, the social self is a front, a dramatic performance that involves the elaboration of attributes "by means of a distinctive complex cultural configuration of proper ways of conducting oneself. To *be* a given kind of person, then, is not merely to possess the required attributes but also to sustain the standards of conduct and appearance that one's social grouping attaches thereto" (p. 81). Although Goffman is careful not to assume rationality, duplicity, and self-interest, these are evoked by his theme of impression management. The calculated management of appearance is given further significance where Goffman (1970) goes beyond dramaturgical models to draw on game theory. Here, he combines the dramatic presentation of self with the calculation of impression for the sake of winning against others. Interaction is treated as strategic where expression games entail the manipulation of what is manifested and concealed. Examples include the spy and the confidence trickster as extreme cases of calculated duplicity.

The strategic manipulation of appearance for personal gain has become the predominant mode of interpretation of conformity. Where this perspective is applied to Japan, it carries a double stereotype. Japanese people are portrayed as calculating conformists. This image supplements the fabrication of "them" as all alike with the equally pernicious myth of a universal human nature comprising calculated selfishness, which accords with an alternative stereotype of Japanese scheming inscrutability.

The assumption of scheming selfishness would be less dangerous if it were recognized as a model or metaphor (as in Goffman), but it tends to be put forward as a reality that is obvious to all. Its appeal lies in debunking a consensual myth, in order to reveal what we all "know" we do (an assumption that is further rationalized in the ideology of the new right). It thereby constructs another myth, a taken-for-granted common sense of Western societies that is supposed to be universally applicable but is as distortive in its application (whether to Japan or other societies) as the naïvely conformist models of Japanese society. The scheming construction implies an overrational, overcalculating attitude that is right for designing rational models but only if recognized *as* models from which actual human behavior diverges. Furthermore, a narrow individualism is presupposed in which advantage is calculated for self, individually conceived.

Weber, the key classical theorist of rationalization, would not have made this mistake. Indeed, his rational models are developed from a conception of types of action that include various possibilities for interpreting conformity, not only conformist action as means to an end but also conformity as the expression of a value, as an emotive response, and as following tradition. Although end-rationality may provide the clearest formulation for sociological understanding through ideal types, this is not to be seen "as involving a rationalistic bias of sociology, but only as a methodological device" (Weber, 1968, pp. 6–7). In these terms, calculative conformity may be a useful feature of models and types for the scientific interpretation of social action but must always be set against other possible sources of conformity, in values, emotions, or tradition. Through tradition or habit, conformist behavior may become taken for granted, and conformist thought can appear as common sense, even the common sense that conventionally attributes motives of selfish rationality.

Such unthinking conformity contrasts with the view of conformity (and indeed nonconformity) as a calculated achievement. It is important to remember that some conformity and nonconformity are ascribed rather than achieved. Some forms of disability can be seen as ascribed nonconformity to dominant conceptions of "proper" bodies (though labels must not be presumed to be passively accepted through ascription). In contrast, and as a challenge to naturalistic (rather than rationalistic) common sense, gender, even where conforming, may be seen as a performance (Butler, 1990), an accomplishment. The point is not to disparage models of ascribed or achieved conformity but to recognize them as models and question their assumptions.

Just as conformity may be only relatively unthinking tradition or habit (in Weberian terms, behavior rather than action), so may the motivation for conformity be more a matter of emotion than clear calculation. To complicate matters, emotional expression may be seen as rationally calculated, as in impression management. This does not necessarily imply a directly instrumental attitude to relationships. Befu (1990) points to the "building up of expressive debts and credits in relation to others" (p. 228), even where there may be no immediate payoff.

Whether rational or emotional, conformist action is still predominantly interpreted as self-interested, without specification of what "self" comprehends. A commonsense Western notion of individualism is assumed, which is not to be confused with Weber's methodological individualism, whose purpose is to avoid spurious notions of a group mind or a collective personality that acts. Weber's individualism, like his rationalism, is methodological rather than ideological:

> It is a tremendous misunderstanding to think that an "individualistic" *method* should involve what is in any conceivable sense an individualistic system of *values*. It is as important to avoid this error as the related one which confuses the unavoidable tendency of sociological concepts to assume a rationalistic character with a belief in the predominance of rational motives, or even a positive valuation of rationalism. (1968, p. 18)

Individualistically motivated rationalism is but one ideal type of action, as Tönnies (1963) also recognized when he contrasted the individualistic rational-calculative frame of mind (in *Gesellschaft*), with his vision of a supposedly traditional community (*Gemeinschaft*), where one is concerned with people, things, and activities for their own sake. Tönnies's simple opposition associates rationality with narrow selfishness. Yet, selfish motives can induce emotional action, and rational-calculative action may be conceived in terms of wider benefit or a broader conception of who we are. Goffman (1971) gives the example of the cynical individual, who deludes others for what is considered to be their own good rather than "for purposes of what is called 'self-interest' or private gain" (p. 29). Assumptions of self-interest are doubly flawed. They postulate a calculative rationality in conjunction with a self that is unexplicated but implicitly individualistic. To challenge interpretations of conformity with others as self-interested, a less narrowly delimited conception of self is required.

Wider Conceptions of Self and Other

CONFORMITY is not only a question of appearance, of front or outer form, that is manipulated for self-interest. If the self is conceived more widely, conformity can become an aspect of identification, assimilating self and other, sharing a sense of self. This dimension of identification with others is overlooked in narrowly selfish conceptions of conformity. Conformity that involves mutual identification promotes the sense of belonging that allows one to speak of "we," and expresses shared selves through participation in common symbols of who we are. Conformity motivated through such solidarity may still, of course, be calculated for benefits to an individual self, as where belonging provides one's material security, but it cannot automatically be reduced to this. Acting for "us" is no more illusory than acting for "myself," if recognition is accorded to the social construction of self, individual and collective. "Selfishness" has a different significance where the self is identified with others.

In Japanese culture there is a greater recognition of the social dimensions of self, the sharing of one's identity with others, than in Western individualistic ideology. Kondo (1990) suggests that relationally defined selves in Japan "mount a challenge to our own assumptions about fixed, essentialist identities" (p. 33). The study of Japanese culture can thus contribute to the realization of a broadly applicable concept of self that informs the process of conformity.

Similarly, conformity to social etiquette and ritual, which might be regarded from a Western point of view as irrational and uneconomical, may be recognized from a Japanese perspective as at least value-rational (in Weber's terms) if not end-rational. LaFleur (1992) observes how even inanimate objects, such as needles, chopsticks, and tea whisks, are humanized and personalized in proper compliance with memorial rituals "to express the intimacy of our relationship to them" (p. 146). Personhood is extended beyond the bounds of self and even of humanity, to encompass a wide circle of identification.

Acknowledgment of shared selves does not mean that there is no tension between narrower and wider identifications, or that conformity is any easier for Japanese people, which would be to resort again to a notion of conformist mentality. Conformity, even where apparently passive, may still require active, spirited control of expression to fit in rather than stick out; hence, the cultural recognition and evaluation of the spirit to endure. Kondo (1987) observes that ethical movements in Japan rely and play on notions of the connectedness of self and other. Through acts of endurance at an ethics retreat, the heart is strengthened to fit in with others. Promoting recognition of one's connection and indebtedness to others, and of the importance of conforming to expectations is also a notable feature of Japanese psychotherapy (Lebra, 1976, 1986). Such efforts suggest that conformity is not simple, automatic, or guaranteed.

Furthermore, a shared sense of self does not mean that individuality is lacking. Lebra (1992) argues that it is precisely because of the preoccupation with the interactional self that paradoxically a high evaluation is placed on a more private self. Hendry (1992) contrasts the Japanese recognition of individuality with the notion of individualism as a Western ideology, which features a self-assertion disparaged as selfish and regarded as a sign of immaturity, a failure to grow up and into one's social relationships. Similarly Plath (1980) observes that in Japan there is an emphasis on the growth of humans as social beings. Individuation (not to be confused with individualism) evolves through the unique set of social relationships cultivated through life.

Thus, Japanese culture acknowledges the social and fluid constitution of self. Identification of "us" on the "inside" (*uchi*) is constantly shifting. Although *uchi* locates the self in terms of group membership (Bachnik, 1990), its boundary is flexible (Hamabata, 1990). It is a variable frame that is drawn in opposition to those defined, in this context, as outside (*soto*). Thus, selves are defined (as everywhere, but significantly recognized in Japanese culture) both with and against others, "in the Japanese conception, the self, individual or collective, is defined always in relation to the other" (Ohnuki-Tierney, 1990, p. 198).

Just as self is defined flexibly, contextually, and in opposition, so is conformity. As Bachnik (1994) notes, the mutual constitution of "the contextually defined self and the contextually defined social order" (p. 5) has major relevance also beyond Japan. A contextual interpretation of conformity that comprehends flexibly framed social selves and contrastive definitions fits the experience (even if not the ideology) of Western identifications. Selves and conformities are relative.

Relative Conformities

CONFORMITY and nonconformity have to be seen as relative and pertaining to social context. Both will align you with some and distinguish you from others. The culturally available choices may be stark. A simple opposition is in some cases all that is presented. For example, in Britain in the 1950s, lesbian sexuality was interpreted in gender terms, for which the only role models were conventional masculinity and femininity, "The butch/femme divide was rigidly adhered to in the Fifties. You had to be one or the other" (McGregor, 1993, p. 41). Although those who do not conform can attempt to generate their own identities, these are constructed from material that is already socially constituted. They draw on available models. This is especially apparent in the realm of subculture, style, and fashion. Fashion is about the construction of our public selves from ready-mades (Chambers, 1986). The significance depends on how it is put together. A nonconformist construction may be made of conventionalized parts. It is the context that counts.

Fashion can simultaneously reveal both ostensible nonconformity and stylized conformity. The breaking of conventions requires knowledge of the codes, and is supported by participation with others in common styles and subcultures. As Wilson (1985) notes, dress can be "used as an indicator of social conformity" (p. 35) and as a vehicle for self expression, "to establish your membership of a group within the peer group" (p. 185). This again points to self and conformity as mutually constituted.

Conformity to subcultural conventions, making use of popular culture communicated through the media, can provide a valuable source of identity through solidarity, thereby giving rise to what Willis (1990) calls "proto-communities": "new, emergent or potential communication communities" (p. 141). These may involve both a challenge to convention, and conformity in a common pursuit, generated from the stock of consumer culture. Alternatively, models may be taken from others who do not conform to the dominant culture, as where Hebdige (1979) sees white youth subcultures adopting stylistic conventions of black youth for their symbolic value of oppositional solidarity. In subcultural revolt a self-conscious nonconformity is enacted in a conformist style. As with Japanese gangs, belonging does not have to be interpreted in terms of some individualistically conceived personal gain but may be valued for the shared identification, the sense of solidarity itself.

Just as deliberate nonconformity may rely and play on conformity, a self-conscious conformism may be regarded as nonconformist, because, according to common sense, conformity comes naturally and can be taken for granted, and its cultivation would indicate an unconventional desire to subordinate the individualism so highly valued in the West. Here, Japanese culture may give greater support to careful attempts at learning to conform. Ironically, given stereotypes of conformist selves, conformity appears to be "studied" in Japan and to come naturally in Western culture. This Western perspective is reflected in the fashionable affectation of indifference that is seen as "cool" (Wilson, 1985).

The converse of the appreciation of natural conformity is seen in the disdain for those who try too hard. This is especially noticeable in high-status groups, who look down on those whose overanxiety about fitting in with proper behavior shows that they are not included naturally within the charmed circle. Bourdieu (1984) sees the "concern for conformity which induces an anxious quest for authorities and models of conduct" as constituting the overconformism that he judges "petit bourgeois" (p. 331). Similarly, paying too much attention to style has been thought "unnatural" in men, signifying a narcissism that borders on effeminacy, disqualifying them from proper belonging.

The natural look, however contrived, contrasts with the exaggerated conformism of those disparaged as "obvious": prostitutes and gays. The overdressed and underdressed, the vulgar and the blatant, can stretch conformity into defiance. Superconformity is a common feature of subcultural resistance, as where overneatness is assumed to be a threat. The superconformist may be imposing. Superconformity to the measures of bodybuilding is regarded with ambivalence, as conventional yet outstanding, unnatural but potentially heroic. This again recalls the superconformity of Japanese gangs, exaggerating key characteristics of Japanese tradition (Raz, 1992). They are likewise treated with ambivalence and made the subject of heroic media representations.

Conformity is clearly a delicate construction that can fall over the edge into nonconformity, which is similarly constituted out of conformity. Like self and other, conformity and nonconformity are defined in relation to each other and in social context. Yet, discriminations are sustained with differential power and unequal resources, so that nonconformity with respect to mainstream social structures can be effectively marginalized. The conformity of shared mainstream selves is constructed in opposition to excluded others.

Conformity of Us versus Them

COMMON identification presupposes contrasting others. Our conformity implies their difference from us, even if their nonconformity is constructed as conforming to type. Conformity and nonconformity are constructed in terms of each other. Conformity already contains the possibility of transgression, and it is through conformity and transgression that we define ourselves with and against others. Transgression may be allowed in conformist terms, as an admissible infringement within a compartmentalized frame. Transgression defines the boundaries of the acceptable. Yet, crossing critical boundaries bears the mark of the nonconformist, who is seen as forming a group with others of that ilk.

Nonconforming others are thus already included in the identification of conforming selves. Fuss (1989, 1991) argues that identity always contains nonidentity within itself, as an interior exclusion. The excluded make clear the boundaries of belonging. Identity in community is formed through delimiting the bounds of similarity (Cohen, 1985). The demands for conformity may be especially rigorous in threatened or subordinated groups, where solidarity is of paramount importance. Here, failure to conform, whether to taste, manners, or morals, may be interpreted as illegitimate distinction, pretension, or betrayal. "That's not for the likes of us" is seen by Bourdieu (1984) to "reaffirm the principle of conformity" (p. 380). The excluded may thus themselves exclude ambiguity, deny choice and possibility in identity, and adopt a "political identity based on difference" (Lucas, 1994, p. 191).

Such exclusions must again be seen in the larger context of differential power that allows some to decide who "does or does not belong to a given society as a whole ... to define themselves as central and the rest as 'other,' peripheral or outcast" (Dyer, 1993, p. 14). All societies exclude, and some are particularly excluding. Samuel (1989) argues that "British society remains peculiarly excluding to those who, for whatever reason, fail to fit in" (p. xiv), among whom he includes lesbians and gays, disabled people, and Gypsies. A society that sees itself in conformist terms may portray outsiders as lacking the requisite constraint and control. In sport, for example, British conformity is represented through "our" white players, who, in contrast with others, are characterized as controlled, disciplined, and stoical (Westwood, 1990).

Control of ourselves is inherent in the process that sees nonconformity as forming an alien identity, delineating a life that is unavailable to those who properly belong. Boundary markers, which contain the other, thereby imprison the self in its own fortifications (Valentine, in press). Thus, in a traditional male view, woman is constructed as other, and femininity is seen as strange or abnormal (Allen, 1992), and denied for the masculine self that is "reinforced by others like him" (Messer-Davidow, 1989, p. 81). This otherness may then be used to put down further others, as where colonized peoples are constructed as feminine or effeminate (Cobham, 1992). Likewise, homosexuality can be passed off as endemic to foreigners (Ratti, 1993). The conviction "we cannot be like that" is further reinforced through ritual attacks that, though strictly beyond the bounds of conformity, may be tacitly or explicitly accepted in the wider community, as Lafont (1985) notes in his study of Paris gangs.

Such vehement rejection implies a prior familiarity with the other, who is central to our own identification but projected outside (Rutherford, 1990).

Marginality is (ironically) centrally significant, integral to the culture that denounces it (Dollimore, 1991). Nonconformity is inherent in conformity; those who do not conform are employed to establish the criteria of conformity, in a collective definitional process characterized by Miles (1989) as "a dialectic of representational inclusion and exclusion" (p. 38).

Collective representations of nonconformity are crucial in establishing conceptions of those who do not belong, in contrast to the shared identification of "us" within the boundaries. It is here that media portrayals of nonconformity are crucial, acting as ways of framing mainstream and marginalized identities (Valentine, in press). Framing those who step over the mark of conformity, in representations that judge them as heroic, threatening, or pathetic, operates to contain nonconformity so that it conforms to prevailing expectations. Those who do not fit are made to conform to stereotypes, in order to be recognizable (Dyer, 1993), which may allow nonconformity that does not match stereotypes to pass unnoticed (Valentine, in press).

The framing of nonconformity may act as warning or consolation. Rejection as a threat may be less effective than reincorporation into conformity, where "the difference is simply denied" (Hebdige, 1979, p. 97). Hebdige notes the transformation of challenging styles into conventional commodities. Jeans, for example, became "increasingly uncoupled from their former significance as a signal of revolt" (Scheuring, 1989, p. 231). Framed nonconformity can be safely sold. Nonconformity may be licensed within strictly confined limits, as in shows and spectacles (Fiske, 1989), where conspicuous nonconformists may be treated as freaks who are meant to evoke a conformist response in the audience.

The framing process may lump together several categories of the unfitting, as where the British film *Mona Lisa* assembles "pathologised Blacks, working classes, lesbians and prostitutes" (Young, 1990), or may homogenize all those within one category. Russo (1987) analyzes the differential credit given to actors playing homosexuals: "When a homosexual actor plays a homosexual, then, it is not acting because all homosexuals are alike and can be played only as stereotypes; when a heterosexual actor plays a heterosexual character, it is acting because heterosexuals are different individuals and can be played as people" (p. 213). As seen in representations of "the Japanese," others are conventionally constructed as all alike in contrast to ourselves.

Recognition of the collective process of identification of self, in conformity with and distinction from others, would preclude the one-sided representation of others in conformist terms, and would equally avoid the uniform application of a rationalistic individualism to the interpretation of conformity. The debunking of myths about Japan has been accompanied by a diminished understanding of identification that ranges beyond the individual, a sharing of self *and* other, that is recognized more fully in Japanese culture. Indeed, an exploration of Japanese conceptions of self, along with contrasts of inside and outside, back and front, can aid the interpretation of other societies. Japanese representations have wider relevance for the understanding of conformity, not necessarily because Japanese society "is" more conformist but because the motivation to conform is more readily acknowledged in Japanese culture, just as the social dimension of selves is more widely appreciated. "The difference may be less one of psychology than of ethnopsychology, less a difference between Japanese and Western psyches than in the way the dimensions of the self are portrayed and evaluated in Japan and the West" (Tobin, 1992, p. 24). Instead of assuming Western notions of rationality and individuality and applying them universally, they can be recognized as models that have limited applicability even in Western contexts.

References

Allen, R. (1992). Analysing representations. In F. Bonner, L. Goodman, R. Allen, L. Janes, & C. King (Eds.), *Imagining women: Cultural representations and gender* (pp. 21–42). Cambridge, U.K.: Polity Press and Open University.

Allison, A. (1991). Japanese mothers and *obentōs*: The lunch-box as ideological state apparatus. *Anthropological Quarterly, 64,* 195–207.

Atsumi, R. (1980). Patterns of personal relationships: A key to understanding Japanese thought and behaviour. *Social Analysis, 5/6,* 63–78.

Bachnik, J. M. (1990). Being in the group: Spatio-temporal "place" in Japanese social organization. In A. Boscaro, F. Gatti, & M. Raveri (Eds.), *Rethinking Japan,* Vol. 2 (pp. 192–197). Folkestone, U.K.: Japan Library.

Bachnik, J. M. (1994). Introduction: *Uchi/Soto,* Challenging our conceptualizations of self, social order, and language. In J. M. Bachnik & C. J. Quinn (Eds.), *Situated meaning: Inside and outside in Japanese self, society, and language* (pp. 3–37). Princeton: Princeton University Press.

Barthes, R. (1982). *Empire of signs.* London: Cape.

Befu, H. (1990). Four models of Japanese society and their relevance to conflict. In S. N. Eisenstadt & E. Ben-Ari (Eds.), *Japanese models of conflict resolution* (pp. 213–238). New York: Kegan Paul International.

Bourdieu, P. (1984). *Distinction.* New York: Routledge & Kegan Paul.

Breger, R. (1992). The discourse on Japan in the German press: Images of economic competition. In R. Goodman and K. Refsing (Eds.), *Ideology and practice in modern Japan* (pp. 171–195). London: Routledge.

Butler, J. (1990). *Gender trouble.* New York: Routledge.

Chambers, I. (1986). *Popular culture: The metropolitan experience.* London: Methuen.

Cobham, R. (1992). Misgendering the nation: African nationalist fictions and Nuruddin Farah's

113

maps. In A. Parker, M. Russo, D. Sommer, & P. Yaeger (Eds.), *Nationalisms and sexualities* (pp. 42–59). New York: Routledge.

Cohen, A. P. (1985). *The symbolic construction of community.* Chichester, U.K.: Ellis Horwood & Tavistock.

Collick, M. (1981). A different society. In H. Smith (Ed.), *Inside Japan* (pp. 9–58). London: British Broadcasting Corporation.

Day, G., & Murdock, J. (1993). Locality and community: Coming to terms with place. *Sociological Review, 41,* 82–111.

Dollimore, J. (1991). *Sexual dissidence: Augustine to Wilde, Freud to Foucault.* Oxford, U.K.: Clarendon Press.

Durkheim, E. (1964). *The division of labor in society.* New York: Free Press.

Dyer, R. (1984). Stereotyping. In R. Dyer (Ed.), *Gays and film,* (rev. ed., pp. 27–39). New York: New York Zoetrope.

Dyer, R. (1993). *The matter of images: Essays on representations.* London: Routledge.

Fiske, J. (1989). *Understanding popular culture.* Boston: Unwin Hyman.

Fuss, D. (1989). *Essentially speaking.* New York: Routledge.

Fuss, D. (1991). Inside/Out. In D. Fuss (Ed.), *Inside/Out* (pp.1–10). New York: Routledge.

Goffman, E. (1970). *Strategic interaction.* Oxford, U.K.: Basil Blackwell.

Goffman, E. (1971). *The presentation of self in everyday life.* Harmondsworth, U.K.: Penguin.

Haley, J. O. (1991). *Authority without power: Law and the Japanese paradox.* Oxford: Oxford University Press.

Hamabata, M. M. (1990). *Crested kimono: Power and love in the Japanese business family.* Ithaca: Cornell University Press.

Hebdige, D. (1979). *Subculture: The meaning of style.* London: Methuen.

Hendry, J. (1984). Shoes: The early learning of an important distinction in Japanese society. In G. Daniels (Ed.), *Europe interprets Japan* (pp. 215–222). Tenterden, U.K.: Paul Norbury.

Hendry, J. (1990). Humidity, hygiene, or ritual care: Some thoughts on wrapping as a social phenomenon. In E. Ben-Ari, B. Moeran, & J. Valentine (Eds.), *Unwrapping Japan: Society and culture in anthropological perspective* (pp. 18–35). Manchester, U.K.: Manchester University Press.

Hendry, J. (1992). Individualism and individuality: Entry into a social world. In R. Goodman & K. Refsing (Eds.), *Ideology and practice in modern Japan* (pp. 55–71). London: Routledge.

Hendry, J. (1993). *Wrapping culture.* Oxford: Oxford University Press.

Kamishima, J. (1990). Society for convergence: An alternative for the homogeneity theory. *Japan Foundation Newsletter, 17,* 1–6.

Kersten, J. (1993). Street youth, *bosozoku,* and *yakuza:* Subculture formation and societal reactions in Japan. *Crime and Delinquency, 39,* 277–293.

Kondo, D. (1987). Creating an ideal self: Theories of selfhood and pedagogy at a Japanese ethics retreat. *Ethos, 15,* 241–269.

Kondo, D. (1990). *Crafting selves: Power, gender and discourses of identity in a Japanese workplace.* Chicago: University of Chicago Press.

LaFleur, W. R. (1992). *Liquid life: Abortion and Buddhism in Japan.* Princeton: Princeton University Press.

Lafont, H. (1985). Changing sexual behaviour in French youth gangs. In P. Ariès & A. Béjin (Eds.), *Western sexuality* (pp. 168–80). Oxford, U.K.: Basil Blackwell.

Lebra, T. S. (1976). *Japanese patterns of behavior.* Honolulu: University of Hawaii Press.

Lebra, T. S. (1986). Self-reconstruction in Japanese religious psychotherapy. In T. S. Lebra & W. P. Lebra (Eds.), *Japanese culture and behavior* (pp. 354–368). Honolulu: University of Hawaii Press.

Lebra, T. S. (1987). The cultural significance of silence in Japanese communication. *Multilingua, 6,* 343–357.

Lebra, T. S. (1992). Self in Japanese culture. In N. R. Rosenberger (Ed.), *Japanese sense of self* (pp. 105–120). Cambridge: Cambridge University Press.

Lucas, I. (1994). *Impertinent decorum.* London: Cassell.

McGregor, I. (1993). Iona McGregor. In B. Cant (Ed.), *Footsteps and witnesses: Lesbian and gay lifestories from Scotland* (pp. 38–45). Edinburgh: Polygon.

McKechnie, R. (1993). Becoming Celtic in Corsica. In S. Macdonald (Ed.), *Inside European identities* (pp. 118–145). Oxford, U.K.: Providence & Berg.

Messer-Davidow, E. (1989). The philosophical bases of feminist literary criticisms. In L. Kauffman (Ed.), *Gender and theory* (pp. 63–106). Oxford, U.K.: Basil Blackwell.

Midooka, K. (1990). Characteristics of Japanese-style communication. *Media, Culture and Society, 12,* 477-489.

Miles, R. (1989). *Racism.* London: Routledge.

Mita, M. (1992). *Social psychology of modern Japan.* New York: Kegan Paul International.

Moeran, B. (1984). Individual, group and *seishin:* Japan's internal cultural debate. *Man, 19,* 252–266.

Ohnuki-Tierney, E. (1990). The ambivalent self of the contemporary Japanese. *Cultural Anthropology, 5,* 197–216.

Peak, L. (1991). *Learning to go to school in Japan: The transition from home to preschool life.* Berkeley: University of California Press.

Plath, D. W. (1980). *Long engagements: Maturity in modern Japan.* Stanford: Stanford University Press.

Rattansi, A. (1992). Changing the subject? Racism, culture and education. In J. Donald & A. Rattansi (Eds.), *"Race," culture and difference* (pp. 11–48). London: Sage.

Ratti, R. (1993). Introduction. In R. Ratti (Ed.), *A lotus of another color: An unfolding of the South Asian gay and lesbian experience* (pp. 11–17). Boston: Alyson.

Raz, J. (1992). Self–presentation and performance in the *yakuza* way of life. In R. Goodman & K. Refsing (Eds.), *Ideology and practice in modern Japan* (pp. 210–234). London: Routledge.

Robertson, R. (1990). Japan and the USA: The interpenetration of national identities and the debate about orientalism. In N. Abercrombie, S. Hill, & B. S. Turner (Eds.), *Dominant ideologies* (pp. 182–198). London: Unwin Hyman.

Roland, A. (1988). *In search of self in India and Japan*. Princeton: Princeton University Press.

Russo, V. (1987). *The celluloid closet*. New York: Harper & Row.

Rutherford, J. (1990). A place called home: Identity and the cultural politics of difference. In J. Rutherford (Ed.), *Identity: Community, culture, difference* (pp. 9–27). London: Lawrence & Wishart.

Samuel, R. (1989). Introduction: The "little platoons." In R. Samuel (Ed.), *Patriotism: The making and unmaking of British national identity* (pp. ix–xxxix). New York: Routledge.

Scheuring, D. (1989). Heavy duty denim: "Quality never dates." In A. McRobbie (Ed.), *Zoot suits and second-hand dresses* (pp. 225–236). Basingstoke, U.K.: Macmillan.

Sugimoto, Y. (1986). The manipulative bases for "consensus" in Japan. In G. McCormack & Y. Sugimoto (Eds.), *Democracy in contemporary Japan* (pp. 65–75). New York: M. E. Sharpe.

Tobin, J. (1992). Japanese preschools and the pedagogy of selfhood. In N. R. Rosenberger (Ed.), *Japanese sense of self* (pp. 21–39). Cambridge: Cambridge University Press.

Tönnies, F. (1963). *Community and society (Gemeinschaft and Gesellschaft)*. New York: Harper & Row.

Valentine, J. (1986). Dance space, time, and organization: Aspects of Japanese cultural performance. In J. Hendry & J. Webber (Eds.), *Interpreting Japanese society* (pp. 111–128). Oxford, U.K.: JASO.

Valentine, J. (1990). On the borderlines: The significance of marginality in Japanese society. In E. Ben-Ari, B. Moeran, & J. Valentine (Eds.), *Unwrapping Japan* (pp. 36–57). Manchester, U.K.: Manchester University Press.

Valentine, J. (in press). Skirting and suiting stereotypes: Representations of marginalized sexualities in Japan. In *Theory, culture and society*.

Weber, M. (1968). *Economy and society*. New York: Bedminster Press.

Westwood, S. (1990). Racism, black masculinity and the politics of space. In J. Hearn & F. Morgan (Eds.), *Men, masculinities and social theory* (pp. 55–71). London: Unwin Hyman.

White, M. I. (1994). *The material child*. Berkeley: University of California Press.

Willis, P. (1990). *Common culture: Symbolic work at play in the everyday cultures of the young*. Milton Keynes, U.K.: Open University Press.

Wilson, E. (1985). *Adorned in dreams: Fashion and modernity*. London: Virago.

Yoshino, K. (1992). *Cultural nationalism in contemporary Japan*. London: Routledge.

Young, L. (1990). A nasty piece of work: A psychoanalytic study of sexual and racial difference in "Mona Lisa." In J. Rutherford (Ed.), *Identity: Community, culture, difference* (pp. 188–206). London: Lawrence & Wishart.

Intercultural Exchange in the Workplace

Chapter Eight

Work Motivation and Culture

HENRY S. R. KAO *and* NG SEK-HONG

I n the West, the term *motivation* normally refers to a behavioral process in which "an individual expends effort or energy in order to satisfy some need or attain some goal" (Herbert, 1976, p. 239). There is sometimes a social influence aspect to this process. In the workplace, motivation is often seen as a key managerial function whereby employees are induced to perform to achieve the results expected in their jobs and thereby to serve organizational goals. Managers are expected to acquire a working understanding of the inner forces that energize subordinates into a sequence of behaviors directed toward organizational goals, namely, by using individual satisfiers of one kind or another (Scott & Mitchell, 1976; Thurley & Wirdenius, 1989). The notion of satisfiers is a linchpin of classic need theories (Alderfer, 1972; Herzberg, Mausner, Peterson, & Capwell, 1957; Maslow, 1943; McClelland, 1961), balance theories (Adams, 1965), and expectancy theory (Vroom, 1964). Even the so-called human relations view (Mayo, 1949) embodies the assumption that the most "satisfying" work arrangement for the individual is also the most efficient for the organization (Filey, House, & Kerr, 1976; Likert, 1961). Overall, the prevailing ethos of work motivation is both self-serving and manipulative by managers and organizations (Boas, 1991).

This chapter describes an alternative and possibly complementary conceptualization of motivation, one that is rooted in Eastern rather than Western traditions. Motivation to act in the Chinese tradition, for instance, involves an imperative that is moralistic; that is, action is not necessarily driven by self-interest but is directed instead at fulfilling one's moral duty (Munro, 1977). This tradition contrasts sharply with the Western focus on improving workers' personal satisfaction. Even in the West, however, the empirical evidence has from the start been equivocal about a link between satisfaction and performance (e.g., Brayfield & Crockett, 1955; Herzberg et al., 1957; for a recent example, see Kelly, 1992). Thus, alternative views of motivation, such as those emanating from Eastern traditions, may potentially inform motivational theory in the so-called mainstream.

The Need for a New Departure

THE immediate postwar years brought the decasualization of employment and a greater sense of worker choice. Subtly motivational notions such as "corporate culture" and "psychological contract" emerged in the West in the 1960s and 1970s, reinforced by inspiration drawn from Japanese-style "welfare corporatism." This was the business environment in which mainstream work motivation theories developed, theories that are conspicuous for their optimism in assuming that opportunities are abundant and anyone interested and personally motivated can make it. Prescriptions seldom preach for austerity.

During the 1980s, however, this business optimism and industrial affluence steadily gave way to the agony of economic stagnation and subsequent high unemployment. During the 1990s, this has been compounded by the globalization of business and the subsequent need to continually restructure and change. Western managers of human resources are now seldom equipped, theoretically or practically, to manage the resulting potent sense of insecurity among workers. This feeling often curtails and impairs the latter's commitment to work, incentive to perform, and loyalty to the firm. In effect, the psychological contract has been broken.

Furthermore, the anchorage of motivational theories in Western culture, predominantly its orientation toward self-satisfaction and instrumentalism, has focused exclusively on rewarding persons who succeed. Those who are highly motivated but unable to achieve (due to overcompetition and limited opportunity) are neglected. By virtue of their "personal-success" bias, current motivational theories are incapable of instructing managers in how to deal with today's inevitable human failings. The result is widespread demotivation in the form of protests, resignations, and the like.

The advanced economies of North America and Western Europe are now confronted with a compelling agenda of self-reflection and revitalization, including a need to overhaul their approach to motivation in the workplace. In this context of Western economic stagnation and, by contrast, of rapid industrial growth experienced in Asia (especially in the newly industrialized economies along the Pacific Rim), attention increasingly shifted to the East, in search of inspiration from the spectrum of Oriental cultures and traditions there. Of all these, the cornerstone seems to be provided by the Chinese and Japanese cultures, which in turn share a common Confucian heritage. What are the discriminating motivational features of the Confucian cultural heritage that may account for the "high-froth" syndrome of some Asian economies?

The crux of motivating people to work in Eastern cultures is anchored in such nonmaterialistic properties as trust, altruistic sentiments, norms of reciprocity, and a moral duty obliging them to act and perform out of a spirit of spontaneous consensus. Noting that high-trust industrial relations are strategically important in both Eastern and Western cultures, Fox (1974) lamented the steady drain of these values and properties from workplace relations in Western industrial societies. Today, the principal custodians of trusting workplace relations are the "Oriental cultures such as China and Japan, [where] high trust underlying a high level of organisational commitment is ingrained in the traditional properties of these societies which emphasize altruistic orientation in economic and social life" (Kao & Ng, 1993, p. 47). The interesting implication of this transfer of custodianship is that ideas about work motivation may be fruitfully exchanged between East and West, across the so-called cultural divide.

The Japanese Case

IN Japanese society, the individual's approach to work and work organizations is still strongly influenced by traditional feudal values. Even within the large bureaucratic organizations of today, a myriad of particularistic and hierarchically oriented obligations in interpersonal relationships have persisted (Kao & Ng, 1993). It is believed that strict adherence to the letters of a contract may disrupt the harmonious cooperative relationships between various groups. Thus, enterprises purposively define the social roles of their employees in general and very flexible terms, in order that they can be modified whenever circumstances dictate (Kao & Ng, 1993; Yoshino, 1971).

This theme of trust is arguably the core factor behind the success of postwar Japanese industry. The best illustration of this argument is still Dore's (1973) benchmarking study of the Japanese factory-British factory. This exposition contrasted the workforce of Hitachi (Japan) with its counterpart in English

Electric (British). The study challenged basic Western assumptions about the logic of managing the workplace and motivating its workforce, notably the core notions of individualism, rationality, utilitarianism, and the contract. Contradicting these conventional assumptions, Dore found that the Hitachi workers were highly motivated and committed in their morale and discipline, despite *low* work satisfaction.

Underlying this surface contradiction is a distinction made by the Japanese worker, namely, between the immediate context of a measured fair deal today and the long-term perspective of a payoff from investment and commitment tomorrow. As Dore noted, "to be fully identified with the company family is not necessarily to love it. But it is doubtful whether the reservations which inhibited such affection were such as seriously to reduce efforts to make the firm prosper. For Hitachi workers, Hitachi is the best company they have got" (Dore, 1973, p. 219). There is, hence, an inner logic to the apparent contradiction between negative work satisfaction and a tenacious spirit of self-motivation in the Japanese context. This is the logic that is now better conserved and manifested in Eastern cultures than in the West.

The Hitachi case illustrates further the orientation of Oriental workers. They are motivated not only out of individualistic striving for self-interest but also by a collectivistic consciousness of the "commonwealth" that the work enterprise epitomizes. There is an altruistic belief in a durable job tenure, a degree of mutuality of trust, and a felt obligation shared by the individuals to contribute to company solidarity and survival: "His Hitachi workmates ... are more likely to form a Hitachi workers' reference group ... a Hitachi worker has no inhibitions about conflating his own individual pride in his company's achievements" (Dore, 1973, pp. 245-247).

The Chinese Case

THE Chinese style of motivating people to work is often considered analogous to the Japanese high-trust approach. This is by virtue of the two societies' shared heritage in the classic ethos of Confucian culture. Thus, for the Chinese, it has also been a normative ideal to associate motivation in the workplace with other moral dicta governing human relations. These include deferential subscription to the leader's authority and ability to lead, the altruistic web of role and relational obligations that sustains the competent exercise of such leadership, and the mutual sense of fidelity between the manager and the managed. The last is backed by the reciprocity of trust and the individual's ascetic beliefs in modesty, faith, harmony with nature, and affective altruism.

Such a Chinese prescription is enshrined heavily in the elaborate etiquette of Confucian ethical teaching. As such, it is widely subscribed to, and upheld, by mandarin entrepreneurs in Chinese business (Kao & Ng, 1995, August). Confucian philosophy does not address only this aristocracy, however. Over its history, the philosophy has also been devolved down the social hierarchy, perpetuating many Chinese values, customs, and indigenous norms at the grassroots level (Kao & Ng, 1988). Socialization and teaching commence in the family at adolescence. During this time, one notable feature is the cultivation of a consciousness about a moral obligation to discharge a series of duties. The duties are incumbent upon the individual by virtue of his or her socially ascribed familial role as the son or daughter to the parents, as the brother or sister to the siblings, or as kin to a number of relations of varied designated status.

The Chinese culture of familism has, in other words, been pervaded by the imperative assumption about the individual's natural yet particularistically defined duties. In whatever domain of secular life, whether in the family, the workplace (and the two sectors tended to converge in preindustrial days), or anywhere else, she or he is always motivated, foremost, to perform certain morally ordained duties and obligations implied by one's role relative to the context of activities: "The duties of the individual are the moral principles according to which one should act with regard to oneself and to others. In order to be a man or to be a sage, one must observe these moral principles in the cultivation and development of one's humanity" (Hsieh, 1967, p. 314). In the Chinese enterprise, the dynamics of motivation can therefore be more intrinsic, spiritually ingrained, and subtle. Its members are not induced to work purely because of calculative and instrumental considerations. Instead, propensity to act is associated with a conception of the moral sense and an awareness of the sacrosanct duties hence implied.

> The emergence of this dimension of the mind resulted from the internalization of sovereignty. It involved the transition from an original view of the sovereign as Heaven ... or the king, existing outside of the individual and sending down decrees (ming) to him, to the eventual view of a sovereign as also existing within the individual himself, issuing decrees to the individual ... that duty was like a command issued to the self. (Munro, 1977, p. 34)

Thus, the traditional attachment to the family and its business enterprise today spill over into the work arena. The twin notions of interrelatedness ("networking," in an instrumental-cum-affective sense) and reciprocity serve to instill in the Chinese mind a sensitivity to socialized security and mutual assistance. Such an altruistic perspective leads individuals to deflate the ego and to find security in the collective enterprise of the extended family or clanship. It also prepares the individual to endure sacrifices without haggling for immediate payoff (Kao & Ng, 1993).

This perhaps explains to a certain degree the mistrust of "the contract" in Oriental cultures like the Japanese and the Chinese, where the traditional ethos of the work enterprise has emphasized more the individual's holistic and solidaristic link to the group or the "clique" as the nexus of motivating and organizing human activities. Eastern cultures assume the togetherness of the collective conscience as natural and given; in the Western approach the group is not an axiomatic notion—for that reason, the individual's identity and solidarity with it can vary (Kao & Ng, 1993). This is why motivating a group by way of collectivized incentives has often proved volatile, divisive, unstable, and hazardous in the West.

In Chinese workplaces, by contrast, the general readiness of the parties to employment to assume away the exigencies of the contract has ironically nurtured a mutually accommodating, conciliatory, and pragmatic approach to technological and organizational change. As job security is safeguarded, workers have proved generally less recalcitrant in resisting changes, compared to their Western counterparts (Kao & Ng, 1993).

In the West, there has been a creeping awareness that the bureaucratic contract might be too rigid. Writers on organizational behavior have recast the concept of a contract into more human, psychological terms. The term *psychological contract* refers to the whole complex web of reciprocal rights and obligations between the managers and the managed—not contractual but tacitly understood as a bond of mutual faith that is largely independent of external sources of materialistic inducement or coercion. This is reminiscent of the classic Oriental appeal to trust, altruism, long-term extended reciprocity, and deferential benevolence under paternalistic values (Kao & Ng, 1992). Just how successful Western enterprises might be in assimilating Oriental features of binding and motivating their workforce using a high-trust psychological synergy has still to be tested. However, some clues may be contained in the case of Hong Kong.

The Hong Kong Case

ALTHOUGH more than 95 percent of Hong Kong's population is of Chinese ethnicity, its history is cosmopolitan. Having been exposed to Western cultural influence under British rule, Hong Kong's hybrid situation has been further compounded by an economy that is celebrated for its free enterprise and an administration that believes that it can best govern by following the logic of the "invisible hand." The latter means a restrained role of nonintervention except if necessary, so as to preserve Hong Kong as a resilient bastion of free-market capitalism. It has been argued that a high degree of instrumentalism and pragmatism is among the key features of the Hong Kong labor force and its psychology, contributing significantly to its adaptability, mobility, and efficiency. Such pragmatism has been associated with the predominantly refugee background of the territory's population in history; it has further been depicted as approximating the neoclassical economist's ideal state of free competition, where the worker can and does exploit because of normal conditions of full employment (Turner, 1980).

What, then, has helped sustain workplace motivation and, moreover, (Turner, 1980) commitment in industry, to the extent that human capital is now recognized as Hong Kong's most important resource (Patten, 1995)? Across the spectrum of different types of enterprise here (varying in size, ownership style, ethnicity, and so on) what is being practiced is a hybrid system. There is a diversity of pay and incentive arrangements, combining both Chinese and Western practices. There are further variations according to the size and location of the enterprise, whether it is in the public or subvented sector, whether it is a franchised type of service or industry, and according to individual factors such as a worker's occupational status, age, and skill/profession (Ng, Stewart, & Chan, 1995). Thus, work motivation in Hong Kong is characterized by organizational diversity and flexibility.

One common factor in workforce commitment, however, has been the so-called informality of practices, especially noticeable in the small-firm industry here, wherein relationships are characterized by trust. One study explored the impact of computerization, conducted in 1986 under the sponsorship of the Asian Productivity Organization. It found a general quiescent orientation on the part of the workforce toward computerization (Ng, Stewart, & Chan, 1995). One interpretation of this finding might simply posit a workforce that is characteristically docile, quiescent, and weakly organized, thanks to its refugee background and consequent aversion to "trouble." However, the Chinese preference for trust over the detailed specification of contractual obligation has been held to be an important cultural factor explaining the "immaturity" and sparse incidence of Western-style collectively bargained agreements in Hong Kong (Turner, Fosh, & Ng, 1991).

Thus, even in the best-developed example of collective bargaining in this Oriental society, the union concerned appears to have valued the spirit of the agreement more than its letters. What was enshrined in the ritual of entering into a collectively negotiated agreement was an understanding of mutual trust that each allow the other enough leeway to function, rather than a detailed concern for its substantive provisions. As a totem of pledging faith and a commitment to industrial partnership between the corporate employer and its organized labor, such a collective agreement was described by the union as less a contractual instrument than a set of guidelines for evolving harmonious industrial relations at the workplace (Leung, 1983).

Similarly, when the Hong Kong economy was trapped in doldrums during the last recession of 1974–1975, the workforce was motivated almost spontaneously (perhaps also with a prudent motive to help tide their employers over the difficulties of their businesses, closure of which would have otherwise threatened their job security more seriously) to remain committed to hard work in spite of the glut, while accepting voluntarily curtailed monetary compensation such as wage freezes, pay cuts, shorter hours, job sharing, and transfers between different job assignments. Even the trade unions were remarkably accommodative. They assumed a strategy of self-restraint that was perhaps more characteristic of Eastern cultural traits than Western collective bargaining (Kao & Ng, 1985).

In summary, the Hong Kong case seems to attest to the assertions that there is an alternative culture of work motivation in this territory, distinguishable not only from the Western mainstream but also from the newly popularized prescriptions of Japanese management. It has retained pervasive vestiges of the traditional Chinese heritage, such as informality and trust, yet is also capable of acclimatizing its organizations to a variety of Western management influences, such as individually negotiated pay and incentive packages. Moroever, it has applied these cross-cultural interfaces to form one of the world's most successful venues for "free enterprise" capitalism.

The Case of Mainland China

MAINLAND China has an even greater potential for developing hybrid models of motivation. Despite being seen as the orthodox custodian of classic Confucian culture, China's ideological system has changed, within the span of just one century, from the Manchu Imperial Dynasty, through the Nationalist Republic, to the Communist People's Republic. Now on the threshold of a liberalized and pluralistic form of market socialism, under a massive modernization and reconstruction program, the nation is seemingly at the crossroads of searching for a suitable mix of work motivation packages. In China today, it is widely believed that this mix will be critical in determining the future fate of its present enterprise reforms.

Prior to the present modernization reforms, motivation at the workplace inside socialist China was anchored in socialist ideology. That is, the role of materialistic incentives was minimized if not deemed irrelevant by the state. Instead, of prime importance in committing the workforce were the Party's indoctrination and socialization activities in the form of political education. This was doctrinal, puritanical, and collectivistic in nature. However, in spite of the official denunciation of the Confucian classics during the heydays in China of Leninist-style Marxism in the 1950s and 1960s, there is an implicit parallel between the Confucian and communist ethos. Each advocates the essentials of commonwealth rather than individualistic advancement, and each appeals accordingly to a moralistic self to work for the altruistic better-ment of the collectivity. In addition, these two ideological systems both inculcate trust and solidarity in the collectivity.

The two philosophies do of course diverge, however. For Confucianism, the collectivity is hierarchical, extending from the family to the state, with the primary focus upon the former, which engulfs the individual in a closely knit envelope of particularistic relations. For communism, the collectivity is polit-ical, extending from a centralized bureaucracy, with the primary focus not on personalized bonds of face-to-face trust but rather on shared awareness of common class interest.

It follows that the private property norm is sanctioned under Confucianism, although often collectivized under the auspices of family ownership. Concomitantly, in motivational terms, the role of the individual here is to help the family collective (or the family-like business) to prosper, thereby vicariously benefiting oneself. Conversely, ownership under commu-nism is public and socialist. Fraternal (i.e., brotherly) citizenship means egality of income and wealth. Thus, in post-1949 socialist China, there has been a centrally administered and rigidly structured wage system.

This wage system, however, has failed to motivate Chinese workers, a failure that has been the main reason for China's present enterprise reforms (Ng, 1995). According to the state architects of these reforms, the principle of egality in reward for work has inadvertently propagated an "iron rice bowl" mentality, whereby workers are not inspired beyond meeting their daily needs (Xue, 1981). Much of the thrust of the subsequent enterprise reform agenda has been consistently directed toward the issue of designing the appropriate dosage of incentives, utilitarian as well as spiritual, that will help to stimulate the morale and commitment of the laboring masses (Yu, 1994); it is hoped thereby to lift the state enterprises from their prolonged doldrums of low productivity and inefficiency (Ishihara, 1993). Although this includes borrowing heavily from Western-style technology, managerial, and organizational models

(Pearson, 1991), China has been steadfast in maintaining its socialist logic. This is evident in terms such as "market socialism," and "one country, two systems."

In summary, against its Confucian background, China has for the past forty years adopted egalitarianism as the main principle for allocating rewards to its socialist workers. The latest factor to enter the motivational equation is the notion of market force, a notion that enshrines competitiveness and self-excellence rather than solidarity. Just how these apparently incompatible properties are to be reconciled by the state and its enterprises in addressing the issue of workforce motivation is likely to remain central to the national agenda of workplace reform for the remaining years of this century.

Some Conclusions [and the Role of the Multinationals]

IN the two decades after the Second World War, many countries aspired to "catch up" with their advanced Western counterparts by emulating them. The postwar euphoria of decolonization (which witnessed the proliferation of newly independent nations in the Third World) and the consolidation of the Soviet bloc anxious to manage its huge industrial apparatus by adopting Western-style regulatory institutions further nurtured the assumption of institutional convergence among both industrialized and industrializing societies. Pragmatism would supposedly become universal, underwritten by the fundamentals of Western technology, institutions, ideas, and values.

Since the mid-1980s, however, the significant retreat of the Western industrial economies, alongside the rise in economic strength of Asian societies like Japan, Singapore, Taiwan, South Korea, Hong Kong, and even mainland China, has stimulated new interest in work motivation and economic success. Contrary to the notion of convergence, cultural explanations are now in the ascendant. These basically postulate that the Asian success stories are attributable to certain conducive cultural traits. If only they can be isolated, the "high-froth" syndromes of East Asia might be emulated elsewhere! This approach fails to recognize, though, that if any of these practices are owed entirely to the culture factor, then by definition they are not readily emulated (Kao, Sinha, & Ng, 1994). The dearth of a commensurate tradition may effectively prevent a Western enterprise from transplanting the same dosage of leadership and motivational strategy to commit its workforce as in the case of a Japanese and Chinese business, no matter how rigorously an organizational culture is being engineered (Kao, Sinha, & Ng, 1994). The historical abyss of tradition is potentially both an asset and a severe constraint.

It follows that the notion of a cultural divide has assumed increasing importance and attention. We have attempted to suggest that an East-versus-West demarcation may be overstated, or even illusory. Such an exaggerated watershed is often taken for granted, partly because of parochial sentiments and partly because of the conceptual difficulty of coming to grips analytically with the concept of "culture." Whatever skepticism we may harbor about its elusive nature, it is important, in any event, for us to appreciate culture meta-physically as a mental construct or classification and less as a property readily ascertainable in an empirical sense. This was elucidated when discussing, in the foregoing section, the three cases of an Oriental (or Confucian) approach to work motivation outside the mainstream of Western literature on the subject area. Hong Kong and mainland China are supposed to be more authentic Confucian societies than Japan because they are indigenously Chinese by ethnicity. Yet, neither today offers any "pure" illustrations of the type of high-trust, altruistic, and moralistic motives that are assumed to emanate from traditional Confucian/Chinese values, apart from sporadic instances of conservative Chinese management in Hong Kong. Japan's closer approximation to Confucian ideals may thus be due more to its relatively compressed historical span between feudal Japan and its modernization under the Meji reign than to culture per se.

In fact, Hong Kong is much more a genuinely cosmopolitan melting pot (or at least, meeting place) than a microcosm of the so-called East-West divide. The overriding or overarching imperative, held almost as the sacro-sanct logic of this city's economic survival, is that free-market competition should be given its maximum latitude to excel. It is hardly surprising that the sovereignty of the invisible hand breeds calculative values of instrumental pragmatism, flexible commitment, and cost-benefit rationality in the work-place, and that these are often at variance with the Confucian etiquette of moral discipline and social ethics. The same imperative may yet unite the apparently incompatible elements of Confucian, socialist, and Western-style incentives for building workplace commitment in mainland China.

When we adopt a cross-cultural perspective on work motivation, the boundary of the so-called culture divide is always shifting, elastic, and nego-tiable, in a way that is more liable to result in hybrid mixes than the conser-vation of pure types. This creates the possibility of fertilization across cultures. Western cultures were once not devoid of the paternalistic, high-trust, solidaristic, and personalized relationships now often seen as unique to Oriental societies today. The master-servant relationship, from which the modern contractual notion of formal waged employment was developed at the beginning of this century, was known for its affectivity, loyalty, and fidelity to a lifetime bond of mutuality between employer and employed (Fox, 1974). As late as the 1970s, civil service bureaucracies, as well as large corporate employers in the private sector, were accustomed to maintaining an internal labor market by conserving their human resources in an enclave, using commitment devices like lifetime career ladders, analogous to the Japanese system of lifetime employment (Galbraith, 1972).

In this postmodern era of trade globalization and internationalization of capital and human resources, the multinational corporation has become a strategic agency of transnational interface, exchange, and diffusion of cultural practices and philosophies. Multinationals are both flag bearers of their home practices and guests who are inevitably constrained to adapt to the local culture. Furthermore, the efficacy of managing an organizational culture will be anchored strategically in the fusion and harmonization between the culture prevailing at wider levels of society and that which is systematically nurtured within the organization itself (Kao & Ng, 1993; see also, Carr & MacLachlan, this volume). Foreign joint ventures in China may thus become the standard-bearers of new managerial methods and practices for a socialist society in the euphoria of economic reforms (Ng, 1994). In sum, the intercultural dynamics of work motivation look set to become increasingly important in the years to come.

References

Adams, J. S. (1965). Inequity in social exchange. *Advances in Experimental Social Psychology, 2,* 267–300.

Alderfer, C. P. (1972). *Existence, relatedness, and growth: Human needs in organizational settings.* New York: Free Press.

Boas, S. (1991). Meaning, self, and motivation in organizations. *Organization Studies, 12,* 405–424.

Brayfield, A. H., & Crockett, W. H. (1955). Employee attitudes and employee performance. *Psychological Bulletin, 52,* 394–424.

Dore, R. (1973). *British factory-Japanese factory.* London: Allen & Unwin.

Filey, A. C., House, R. J., & Kerr, S. (1976). *Managerial process and organizational behavior.* Glenview, IL: Scott Foresman.

Fox, A. (1974). *Beyond contract: Work, power, and trust relations.* London: Faber & Faber.

Galbraith, J. K. (1972). *The new industrial state,* 2nd ed. Harmondsworth, U.K.: Penguin.

Herbert, T. T. (1976). *Dimensions of organizational behavior.* New York: Collier Macmillan.

Herzberg, F., Mausner, B., Peterson, R. O., & Capwell, D. F. (1957). *Job attitudes: Review of research and opinion.* Pittsburgh: Psychological Service of Pittsburgh.

Hsieh, Y. W. (1967). The status of the individual in Chinese ethics. In C. A. Moore (Ed.), *The Chinese mind: Essentials of Chinese philosophy and culture* (pp. 307–322). Honolulu: East-West Center Press, University of Hawaii.

Ishihara, K. (1993). *China's conversion to a market economy.* Tokyo: Institute of Developing Economies.

Kao, H. S. R., & Ng, S. H. (1985). *Work and work organizations: East and West diversities.* Hong Kong: University of Hong Kong.

Kao, H. S. R., & Ng, S. H. (1988). Minimal "self" and Chinese work behavior: Psychology of the grass roots. In D. Sinha & H. S. R. Kao (Eds.), *Social values and development: Asian perspectives* (pp. 254-272). New Delhi: Sage.

Kao, H. S. R., & Ng, S. H. (1992). Organizational commitment and culture. In R. I. Westwood (Ed.), *Organizational behaviour: Southeast Asian perspectives* (pp. 173–198). Hong Kong: Longman.

Kao, H. S. R., & Ng, S. H. (1993). Organizational commitment: From trust to altruism at work. *Psychology and Developing Societies, 5,* 43–60.

Kao, H. S. R., & Ng, S. H. (1995, August). *Corporate statesmanship: A cursory note and implications.* Asian-Pacific Regional Conference of Psychology, Guangzhou, China.

Kao, H. S. R., Sinha, D., & Ng, S. H. (1994). Introduction: Social values and work organizations. In H. S. R. Kao, D. Sinha, & S. H. Ng (Eds.), *Effective organizations and social values* (pp. 11–27). New Delhi: Sage.

Kelly, J. E. (1992). Does job re-design theory explain job re-design outcomes? *Human Relations, 45,* 753–774.

Leung, S. H. (1983). Industrial relations in cable and wireless: A unionist's view. In S. H. Ng & D. A. Levin (Eds.), *Contemporary issues in Hong Kong labor relations* (pp. 123–133). Hong Kong: Centre of Asian Studies, University of Hong Kong.

Likert, R. (1961). *New patterns of management.* New York: McGraw-Hill.

Maslow, A. H. (1943). A dynamic theory of human motivation. *Psychological Review, 50,* 370–373.

Mayo, E. (1949). *The social problems of an industrial civilization.* New York: Routledge.

McClelland, D. C. (1961). *The achieving society.* Chicago: Van Nostrand.

Munro, D. J. (1977). *The concept of man in contemporary China.* Ann Arbor: University of Michigan Press.

Ng, S. H. (1994). Industrial relations in joint ventures in China. In S. Stewart (Ed.), *Joint ventures in the People's Republic of China* (pp. 13–28). Greenwich, CT: JAI Press.

Ng, S. H. (1995). Human resources in China at the dawn of "Market Socialism." Hong Kong: Department of Management Studies, University of Hong Kong.

Ng, S. H., Stewart, S., & Chan, F. T. (1995). Socio-cultural impact on productivity: The case of Hong Kong. In K. Hwang (Ed.), *Easternization: Socio-cultural impact on productivity* (pp. 47–96). Tokyo: Asian Productivity Organization.

Patten, C. (1995). *Hong Kong: Our work together.* Hong Kong: Government Press.

Pearson, M. M. (1991). *Joint ventures in the People's Republic of China: The control of foreign direct investment under Socialism.* Princeton: Princeton University Press.

Scott, W. G., & Mitchell, T. R. (1976). *Organization theory: A structural and behavorial analysis.* New York: Irwin.

Thurley, K., & Wirdenius, H. (1989). *Towards European management.* London: Pitman.

Turner, H. A. (1980). *The last colony: But whose?* Cambridge: Cambridge University Press.

Turner, H. A., Fosh, P., & Ng, S. H. (1991). *Between two societies: Hong Kong labor in transition.* Hong Kong: Center of Asian Studies, University of Hong Kong.

Vroom, V. H. (1964). *Work and motivation.* New York: Wiley.

Xue, M. Q. (1981). *China's socialist economy.* Beijing: Foreign Languages Press.

Yoshino, M. Y. (1971). *Japan's managerial system: Tradition and innovation.* Cambridge: MIT Press.

Yu, W. Z. (1994). Chinese motivation theory and application in China: An overview. In H. S. R. Kao, D. Sinha, & S. H. Ng (Eds.), *Effective organizations and social values* (pp. 147–131). New Delhi: Sage.

Chapter Nine

Motivational Gravity

STUART C. CARR *and* MALCOLM MACLACHLAN

Around the world today, the management of human resources is being linked increasingly to national development (Aktouf, 1994; Blunt & Jones, 1992; Karpin, 1995; Xu & Wang, 1991). The study of work motivation is recognized as fundamental to this enterprise (Kao & Ng, this volume; Munro, 1996). One particular motive that in a variety of ways has captured the attention and energy of psychologists is the desire to rise above others (Franken & Brown, 1995; Kasser & Ryan, 1993). The need for achievement, for example, is predicated on a drive to compete (McClelland, 1987), and a central tenet of intergroup theory is that in-groups will spontaneously strive to place themselves above out-groups (Tajfel, 1978). A great deal of contemporary psychology incorporates the received wisdom that people are naturally competitive (Carr, 1996b; Turner, 1991), an article of faith that appears to have been bolstered by the collapse of Soviet communism (Bookin-Weiner, 1995).

This chapter contends that such promotion, namely, of an unbridled unidirectional drive upward, is probably insensitive to many cultural contexts in the world today (Festinger, 1954). Although the general proposition of an interaction between modern and traditional cultural values (Schwartz, this volume) is certainly not new (e.g., Pataki-Schweizer, 1976), its applications to the workplace do seem to be relatively recent (Moghaddam, 1987; Montero & Sloan, 1988; Ong, 1991). Lately, it has been argued that neglecting the wider social context may help to explain the long-term failure of many organizational innovations (Blunt & Jones, 1992; Srinivas, 1995), and that, on the other hand, guarding respect for cultural traditions may partly account for the so-called high-froth syndrome of the Asian economic "Tigers" (Marsella & Choi, 1993).

The globalization of capitalism thereby leads us to consider the possibility of a dynamic interplay, at the psychological level, between the corporate advocation of self-promotion and the societal advocation of collective responsibility (for discussions of this social psychological level of analysis, see Hosking & Morley, 1991; Munro, this volume; Rousseau & House, 1994). Such intercultural dynamics may also be influenced by the sense of job insecurity that has tended to accompany the internationalization of market environments (Kao & Ng, this volume). As a result of these twin factors, upwardly mobile individuals may incur various social costs from those who work alongside them, and above them, in the organizational hierarchy.

To explicate this motivational gravity, we present two new theoretical axes; these are designed to express the degree of (dis)equilibrium in an organizational system. Quadrants on the resulting Motivational Gravity Grid are illustrated with preliminary empirical evidence from Africa, Asia, Australia, and the South Pacific. Using the grid, we also develop various context-sensitive hypotheses for enhancing motivation at work, thereby linking back to the broader, applied issue of national development (Allcorn, 1994).

The Pull-Down

FESTINGER (1954) cautioned against the possible culture-boundedness of unidirectional upward motivation. More recently, cross-cultural psychologists have shown some sensitivity to the possibility that a relatively pure self-orientation may be peculiar to mainstream cultural groups in the United States (e.g., Bond, 1988a; Triandis, 1988, 1989). Much of this critical awareness has derived from the realization that there are powerful collectivistic and (to a lesser extent) egalitarian norms in most societies (Hofstede, 1980). These societies include so-called developing and developed economies (Carr, 1994), as well as non-Western and Western countries (Feather & McKee, 1993).

In a widely respected review of this awareness, Markus and Kitayama (1991) have contrasted the independent view of self with the interdependent perspective. In the former, the self is seen as separate from others, as autonomous, as unique. In the latter, however, the emphasis is laid on belongingness;

occupying one's proper place; serving group goals; social achievement; reciprocity; and humility. Thus, face saving may be so important that managers are reluctant to employ individual criticism as a means of remotivating poor individual performance (Abdullah, 1992; Seddon, 1985).

For all its sensitivities, however, the cross-cultural approach still tends to regard collectivism and individualism as mutually exclusive. An essentially static view of cultural differences is adopted, ignoring the dynamics of any cultural interplay between collectivistic (or egalitarian) and individualistic values (Krewer & Jahoda, 1993). The existence of traditional collectivistic norms, for instance, creates a potential for intercultural conflict within U.S.-styled organizations (such as multinationals) operating in international settings. Conflicts of interest may thus arise between the demands of internal systems that propagate self-promoting behavior, and wider sociocultural systems of traditional collectivistic values that stress instead social obligation and sensitivity toward the needs of others.

One conceivable manifestation of such clashes between organizational and cultural norms would involve coworker peers collectively acting to curtail bestowal of too much reward on any one individual. As they might say in Malaŵi for instance, "Akufuna akhale ndani?!" (Who does he think he is?!). Would it be wise to embrace, resist, or attempt to modify an internal system that encourages the transgression of such traditional sociocultural norms? This important intercultural issue does not seem to have been explicitly or systematically addressed in the literature on work motivation (Carr, 1996a; Carr & MacLachlan, 1993; MacLachlan & Carr, 1994, July; Munro, 1996).

Some Australian and Japanese studies have recently recorded sentiments that high achievers should be cut down to size, termed "favor fall motives" (Feather, 1994; Feather & McKee, 1993). However, these studies have focused on interrelationships between student attributions, values, and attitudes toward socially prominent and therefore remote figures such as politicians. By definition, they have avoided tangible and deleterious behavior toward closer and therefore more comparable coworker peers.

In Southern and East Africa, however, Zambian, Malaŵian, and Kenyan employees reportedly may need to seek spells to protect them from the malevolent wishes of coworkers seeking promotion (Blunt, 1983; Bowa & MacLachlan, 1994; Carr, 1994; Carr & MacLachlan, 1993; MacLachlan & Carr, 1994, July, 1994). In West Africa, Yoruba advertisers in Nigeria carefully and sensitively avoid slogans that would provoke envy and destructive actions against them (Lawuyi, 1992).

In South and Southeast Asia, envy reportedly causes severe managerial problems in the workplaces of India (Nadkarni, 1994, June), and fear of success has been measured among ethnic Indians in Malaysia (Wan Rafaei, 1984). In Indonesia, newly qualified academics may sometimes be fearful of envy from less-well-qualified peers (Daroesman & Daroesman, 1992), and successful Balinese may be fearful of sorcery against them (Wikan, 1989). In Hong Kong, success may provoke the ill-feeling commonly referred to as "red-eye disease" (Bond, 1994). In South Korea, workplace envy is reported to be a problem (Lee, 1994).

In the South Pacific, successful and well-clad Papua New Guineans may attract the derisory label "Shoe-sock" (Carr, MacLachlan, & Schultz, 1995). Ango-Celtic Australians widely refer to the "tall poppy syndrome," namely, the common desire to see high achievers chopped down (Feather, 1994). Lazarevic (1992) found the term *Big Noting* being applied by Aboriginal Australians to derogate self-serving conspicuousness, and the Maoris use the term *Whakahihi* for the same purpose (Thomas, 1994, August).

On a more theoretical note, the original formulation of a unidirectional drive upward focused on individual social comparison (Festinger, 1954). However, people also compare themselves on an intergroup basis (Tajfel, 1978), particularly perhaps in more collectivist societies (Ghosh & Kumar, 1991; Hinkle & Brown, 1990; Lalonde & Silverman, 1994). In this regard, Munro (1986) warns that traditional collectivism in African contexts includes in-group loyalty and out-group diffidence, a point that has also been made in relation to the Middle East (Al-Zahrani & Kaplowitz, 1993) and Far East (Kim, 1994; Valentine, this volume). In China, for instance, Smith and Bond (1993) report, managers were relatively uncooperative with other managers who were felt to be part of an out-group rather than an in-group. A central characteristic of Chinese familism is a heightened distinction between in-group and out-group (Hui, 1990). According to Hui, Chinese in general are likely to be comparatively cooperative and helpful toward in-group members, and comparatively competitive and unhelpful toward out-group members. Thus, compared to Westerners, Chinese are more likely to sue a stranger and less likely to sue a friend (Leung & Wu, 1990).

The in-group—out-group distinction and in particular the question "Is a collectivist with *whom?*" may therefore be critical for understanding work motivation in collectivistic societies (Hui, 1990). Carr (1996b) has drawn an analogy between feelings toward the out-group and *inverse* resonance, discussing the extent to which employees in developing countries frequently originate from disparate social groups. Triandis (1984) has argued that economic growth in such countries may depend on inculcating an overriding sense of *in*-group into these workplaces. Our point is that without such an identity, unadulterated capitalist work practices may act as a catalyst for workplace conflict. Traditional norms preserve equilibrium in the wider society, but they may become corrupted in a capitalistic system that is predicated on individual competition.

On empirical and theoretical grounds, therefore, we envisage the operation of a pull-down motive. This term is chosen as a contrast to the terminology of unidirectional drive upward, not to insinuate that individual achievement is any better than social achievement. Indeed, just as gravity does not necessarily mean downward motion, the pull-down can be valenced as a centripetal force, pulling inward as a check on rampant individualism (Wober, 1993). Coming back down to earth is often a good thing! Nevertheless, in a purely organizational sense, workers who are restrained from climbing a corporate ladder are still brought *down* that ladder.

Just as it would be naive to stereotype collectivistic (or egalitarian) cultures, so it must be recognized that organizational cultures will vary greatly within the same national and historical context (Sampson, 1988). In the United States itself, Mayo (1949) observed strong egalitarian norms at the Hawthorne Plant of the Western Electric Company. In contemporary Sweden, an egalitarian norm of "royal Swedish envy" means that coworkers frequently resent colleagues' promotions, thereby causing demotivation (Schneider, 1991). Nonetheless, to the extent that collectivistic societies are less likely to separate working life from life outside work, societal norms concerning interindividual and intergroup conduct may exert proportionately more influence on workplace behavior (Templer, Beaty, & Hofmeyr, 1992).

The Push-Down

THE pull-down (as opposed to the push-up) can be considered as an attempt by coworker peers to restore "lateral" relations among themselves. Organizations are partly defined, however, by formal hierarchy, thereby introducing relations between superior on the one hand and subordinate on the other. Here, too, we envisage the possibility of motivational gravity. Just as coworker peers can work to restore lateral relations, superiors may sometimes feel the need to protect and defend their position from threats beneath them in the hierarchy. That is, superiors' reactions to subordinates' achievements may range from active encouragement, namely pull-up, to active *dis*couragement, or what we term push-down.

In East and West Africa, Tanzanian, Malaŵian, Kenyan, and Nigerian managers may sometimes resist sharing ideas or power with subordinates, despite reporting a comparatively high view of the latter's capacity for initiative (Jones, 1988, 1991; Seddon, 1985). In Malaŵi, Kenya, and Liberia, it has been reported that managers are often preoccupied with their own job security

(Blunt & Jones, 1986). These managers may ostensibly undervalue subordinate capacities in order to avoid threats to their own positions, making frequent transfers of personnel to preserve their positions (Kiggundu, 1991; Montgomery, 1987). Life in developing economies like Malaŵi is often an inherently insecure and uncertain business, even for relatively privileged managers (Jones, 1988, 1991). Munro (1996) has argued that such perpetual lack of security may in part motivate the relatively high levels of conformity recorded in cross-cultural social psychology (Smith & Bond, 1993). The same economically precarious conditions may also mean that subordinates' initiative sometimes becomes a liability to them, attracting push-down rather than pull-up.

On a more theoretical note, Machungwa and Schmitt (1983) found that tribalism, favoritism, and racial discrimination, immediately followed by poor relations between supervisors and subordinates, constituted the principal demotivators at work in Zambia. Kiggundu (1986) has described intergroup rivalry as characteristic of many organizations across Africa. These group-based accounts are consistent with the concept of inverse resonance (Carr, 1996b). The personal turmoil created by conflicting in-group and organizational loyalties is described by a former dean of Uganda's Makerere University as being "caught up between two moral worlds," with individual behavior "sometimes a function of competing moral systems within the same society" (Mazrui, 1980, p. 119). "Ethnic nepotism," Mazrui concludes (p. 119), had contributed to a state of crisis in African organizations. In gravitational terms, the benefits of pull-up (for in-groups) were outweighed by the costs of push-down.

In East Asia, Hui (1990) observes, Chinese superiors will tend to dominate subordinates who belong to out-groups, depriving them of information and scrutinizing them carefully compared to any in-group members. According to Hui, out-group members are frequently assumed to be lazy and unreliable, and delegation of authority is seen as synonymous with giving away power to an untrustworthy outsider. To maintain their positions further, it is reported that Chinese bosses frequently slight the contributions of nonfamilial subordinates (Hui, 1990). Meanwhile, Japanese expatriates in Hong Kong reportedly work as "shadow" managers, pushing down on, and resonating inversely with, their host counterparts (Wong, 1996).

In the South Pacific, Polynesian Tongan managers with chiefly rights (traditional power) may reportedly undermine the initiatives of unchiefly subordinates because they do not wish to see their own power eroded (Traynor & Watts, 1992). In Melanesian societies, "one talk" means that managers will sometimes fill positions below them with people from their own island or village, and "people from other groups who stand in the way of this process are treated badly" (p. 71). In Vanuatu, expatriates may jealously guard their managerial positions against indigenization programs (Traynor & Watts, 1992). In Australia, insecure managers reaching middle age may attack the new ideas of younger subordinates (Colling, 1992), and another study found that 50 percent of workplace bullying was occurring because a manager sought to consolidate power (McCarthy, 1996, January 27).

Thus, in a wide variety of settings, there is evidence to suggest the operation of a push-down motive. Again we choose our terminology in contradistinction to the existing notion of an unrestrained drive upward, not to insinuate that individual achievement and recognition should necessarily override group loyalty or respect for seniority. And just as it would be ridiculous to stereotype all "power-distant" cultures as prone to push-down (Hofstede, 1980), we also fully recognize that organizational cultures will overlap considerably across societal ones (Handy, 1985).

The advent of cross-cultural assignments alone may be sufficient to ensure this (Kao & Ng, this volume). In the context of sojourns in African countries, for instance, Western expatriates in senior positions sometimes disparage and discourage their local subordinates (Carr, McLoughlin, Hodgson, & MacLachlan, 1996; MacLachlan, 1993), a push-down tendency that extends to Western writers on African organizations (Munro, 1996). Cross-cultural psychologists themselves, working in Western universities, sometimes exploit their junior colleagues in developing countries by claiming raw data as their own (Moghaddam, 1993).

Blunt and Jones (1986) reported, however, that considered solely inside their home countries, Australian, American, and English managers were generally somewhat less preoccupied with security needs than their counterparts in Malaŵi, Kenya, and Liberia. In the long run, the comparative insecurity and uncertainty of employment in a developing economy may, possibly, render push-down more likely than in the industrialized countries.

The Grid

IT appears that in many societies personally successful individuals sometimes have to contend with forces from colleagues whom they would leave below (pulling such individuals back down), and forces from above (trying to stop their climbing up). The motivation to achieve cannot, therefore, be considered only at the individual level or only at the group level. Instead, achievement appears in many cultures to reflect a dynamic interaction between individualistic and collectivistic aspirations. This renders the possibility of a taxonomy of motivational cultures. Along one axis, coworkers may either

Figure 1: The Motivational Gravity Grid

NOTE: We are grateful to Matthew Hodgson of Newcastle University, Australia, for illustrating our ideas so vividly.

discourage or encourage their peers; on a second axis, superiors may either discourage or encourage their subordinates. Figure 1 illustrates how these gravitational forces may act on, and appear to, the individual in four distinctive combinations.

In quadrant one, the individual is working in a push-up–pull-up motivational culture, supported by both peers and superiors. In the opposing scenario (quadrant three), the individual is working in a pull-down–push-down motivational culture, that is, discouraged by both peers and superiors. The remaining two quadrants represent a clash of opposing forces. Whether the resulting gravity is experienced as motivating or demotivating may depend on a number of personality factors, as well as interpersonal and organizational ones. Being analogous to approach-avoidance situations, quadrants two and four may be indicative of the greatest conflict. However, quadrants one and three may also lead to intrapsychic conflict, specifically when organizational aspirations (of self, peers, or superiors) are not consonant with wider social expectations (personal, familial, or cultural).

In the remainder of this chapter, we explore such issues with emerging empirical evidence. Although this evidence is currently sparse and speculative, Feather (1994) reminds us that we do not yet possess any sophisticated theory of the *social* psychology of achievement, and taxonomies are widely recognized as providing a first step toward theory construction (Gould, 1994, March/April; Pryor, 1993, September). Nevertheless, we offer these examples as illustrations of what might happen, given particular combinations of societal and corporate norms. Insofar as organizational cultures are reflections of such contingencies, there may be a great deal of variability *within* countries (Bond, 1988b; Handy, 1985). Thus, a cross-cultural survey of work values among representatives from a variety of organizations warns that differences within countries often account for more of the variance than differences between them (Ralston, Gustafson, Elsass, Cheung, & Terpstra, 1992).

Pull-Down–Push-Down

IN the first African study explicitly addressing motivational gravity, a combination of seventy-eight Malaŵian managers and student managers were presented with brief written scenarios (Carr, MacLachlan, Zimba, & Bowa, 1995). These scenarios depicted a worker who was performing very well, for example, coming up with bright ideas or regularly earning a bonus. They were based on real events described by Malaŵian psychology lecturers who had themselves been managers. Using a graded scale, the respondents were asked to estimate which reaction—encouragement or discouragement—would prevail among fellow workers and from management. Such scenarios have been recommended for use in developing countries because they miminize tendencies to give socially acceptable rather than accurate responses (Blunt, 1983; Sinha, 1989).

Ninety-nine percent of the sample agreed with the statement "People in general want to do better than others." Against this unequivocal upward momentum, however, participants foresaw a sharp pull-down reaction by coworker peers, coupled with an equally sharp push-down reaction from superiors. Moreover, those with direct experience of the Malaŵian workplace anticipated these social consequences more frequently and more strongly. In response to the question "Should you encourage others to do better than your-self?" the experienced managers were significantly less likely to respond yes. This finding lends weight to an inference that some of Malaŵi's organizations are characterized by pull-down–push-down (Carr, MacLachlan, Zimba, & Bowa, 1995).

When the explanations for responses to the issue of encouraging others in the workplace were content analyzed, the predominant themes were fierce competition (e.g., "Everyone wants to be number 1!"), coupled with indications of both power distance and preoccupation with job security (e.g., threat to own position). The feeling that encouragement should be reserved for family and friends was also reported, thereby supporting the notion of inverse resonance. The overall pattern was consistent with individualistic motivation being bridled by both pull-down and push-down.

The possible long-term consequences of such high motivational gravity are suggested by a survey conducted at Malaŵi's major psychiatric facility (MacLachlan, Nyirenda, & Nyando, 1995). Forty percent of patients attributed their admission to explanations consistent with our concept of gravity, in the majority of cases stemming from perceived overachievement at work. As one patient remarked, "I was bewitched by my workmates because I work hard." Evidently, high gravity is capable of exacting a high toll on human resources. To the extent that the skills of human beings are particularly important in technologically and materially disadvantaged settings, motivational gravity may be more damaging to the development of less industrialized nations.

Push-Up–Pull-Up

HAVING positioned such organizational cultures on the grid, comparisons with companies wherein motivational gravity is absent, namely, push-up–pull-up, may under certain conditions reveal a discriminating and therefore critical difference in management practices between the two (Carr, 1994). A similar method has been applied cross-culturally to broaden our understanding of how to manage aid scholarships (Carr, 1996b), clinical depression (Schumaker, 1996), and interpersonal relations (Goodwin, this volume).

In the first Asian study explicitly addressing motivational gravity, fifty-eight Japanese middle managers were presented with two scenarios, involving a target figure's achievement and possible reactions by (1) coworker peers and (2) superiors (Carr, 1994). The Motivational Gravity Scenario Scale presents the target figure as being prominent in terms of (1) frequently receiving a bonus, being awarded a trip overseas, or being promoted ahead of time, and (2) putting forward bright ideas, taking a correspondence course, or being very keen. The subjects were then asked to estimate how many out of ten typical Japanese (1) coworker peers and (2) superiors would somehow offer encouragement (e.g., congratulations) or discouragement (e.g., ostracism, mockery). Each question also included a request to indicate how the respondent himself would react.

The overall tendency was clearly and consistently toward encouragement, a pattern that was repeated regarding subordinates. In terms of the grid, these organizations can be classified as push-up–pull-up. It is worth noting here that Japanese individuals may be relatively unsusceptible to self-serving biases (Kashima & Triandis, 1986; Smith & Bond, 1993) and have been found to be relatively high on favoring the fall of high achievers in a wider, social context (Feather & McKee, 1993). Indeed, a popular adage in Japanese society warns that "the nail that stands out gets pounded down" (Markus & Kitayama, 1991, p. 224). The encouragement in Carr's (1994) workplace study is therefore remarkable because the Japanese sample appear to have successfully managed a degree of motivational gravity.

Did any particular management practice stand out? When the Japanese managers were asked to explain their answers, a predominant theme did indeed emerge, namely, competition tempered by positive interdependence (Johnson & Johnson, 1991). This term normally refers to workers having a sense that each person's work (including achievements) benefits everyone else. It denotes the development of a working understanding or feeling among workers that individual achievement is to the mutual advantage of the collectivity (see Valentine, this volume, for a detailed perspective of what this might entail in the Japanese context). As one Japanese respondent succinctly remarked, "Competition is good. It leads to progress" (Carr, 1994, p. 44).

This finding of positive interdependence replicates much other research conducted in Japanese organizations over an extended period (e.g., from Clarke, 1979, to Kim, 1994). Hui (1990) observes that the slighting of out-group subordinates that is characteristic of many Chinese companies is noticeably absent from Japanese organizations. According to Hui, Japanese bosses recognize the mutual dependence between superior and subordinate, and are thereby motivated to develop a more supportive work atmosphere. In terms of relations between coworker peers, however, the Chinese have tended to view workplace self-promotion as divisive and therefore incongruent with the overarching goal of national development (Hui, 1990).

As these examples indicate, Asian societies may be sufficiently alike in certain cultural respects to enable meaningful comparisons on the grid. In turn, Asian societies may also to some extent resemble African ones, for example, by placing value on collectivism and on power distance (Hofstede, 1980). Blunt and Jones (1992), for instance, have argued that the demands placed on Asian and African managers often overlap. Perhaps, then, cases where motivational gravity is managed successfully in Asia will occasionally suggest solutions to managing gravity in African settings, particularly within the same multinational company.

The Japanese organization of work has been based on the traditional *ie*, or family metaphor, and not the machine metaphor of the West (Kashima & Callan, 1994). For instance, Japanese superiors have been overtly expected to fulfill a paternalistic function toward their subordinates. In such ways, company familism (*keiei-kazoku-shugi*), or a belief in the one-enterprise family (*kigyo-ikka*) has socially integrated employees into the firm (Kashima & Callan, 1994). Because such positive interdependent teamwork seems to harness motivational gravity well, then traditional family and group metaphors (e. g., Confucianism) may provide a key to initiatives for managing motivational gravity (Carr, 1994). Thus, in Kenya for instance, recruitment from family networks has already proved to be an effective method of generating company loyalty (see, Blunt, 1983).

Cross-fertilization might also be possible regarding the notion of centripetal motives. In China, volitional emulation consisted of emulating rather than grounding outstanding achievers in one's work group, and redefining achievement as action from the center of the group (Sheridan, 1976). Emulation was also prominent in Carr's (1994) study of encouragement of achievement in Japan. In Malaŵi, Bowa and MacLachlan (1994) have argued, the concept of collective ascension, namely, all improving together, should be socially marketed in order to counteract pull-down–push-down behavior. Indeed, team incentives have previously proved effective both in India and in Tanzania (see, Blunt, 1983; Blunt & Jones, 1992).

In theoretical terms, the Japanese and other success stories in relation to managing motivational gravity might be attributable to the creation of suitable superordinate goals (Sherif, 1956). In a variety of cultural and cross-cultural contexts, this concept has been efficacious in creating a sense of positive inter-dependence (Smith & Bond, 1993). The jigsaw technique, for example, involves giving each worker in a group one particular task to do toward a mutually valued (superordinate) goal. Each person depends on every other person in the group for solving parts of the puzzle (Aronson, Blaney, Stephan, Sikes, & Snapp, 1978). Such strategies might be particularly relevant in an organizational culture involving both individual competitiveness and collective restraint (Carr, 1994). This is because jigsaw techniques afford the simultaneous expression of both individualism (each worker has his or her own particular project) and collectivism (interlocking team roles).

Pull-Down-Pull-Up

SUCH conflicts of interest between individual expression and collective good might also apply in pull-up–pull-down settings. We have seen that motivational gravity in Australia is popularly referred to as the "tall poppy syndrome." The term originates from an ancient Roman analogy between decapitating tall poppies and the removal of chiefs who posed a threat to the state, an image that connotes pull-down from below (or alongside) rather than push-down from above. Indeed, Australians popularly apply the term to prominent, literally high-profile politicians and business tycoons. Historically, development of the "tall poppy syndrome" has been attributed to reactance against Australia's former status as a penal colony of Britain (Conway, 1971). That is, it symbolized rejection of the old colonial hierarchy in favor of an egalitarian mateship, wherein Jack was as good as his master and there were "no bars to achievement except a man's own will and determination" (Colling, 1992, p. 11).

Hofstede (1980) may have captured traces of such individualism in his 1970s survey of IBM. Today, however, there is an increasing recognition that "tall-poppy" attitudes might also be smothering workplace innovation (Anderson & Alexander, 1995, October; Brewer, 1995; Karpin, 1995; Robbins, Waters-Marsh, & Cacioppe, 1994). They may both stifle individual coworkers' motivation to achieve (Orpen, 1990) and clash with the value that superiors place on achievement (Orpen, 1993). From Figure 1, Australian workers may sometimes find themselves caught between pull-down and pull-up.

This dilemma is nicely encapsulated in the expression "quiet achiever," which frequently appears in Australian recruitment notices. The apparent paradox of the term led Carr (1994) to suggest, in contrast to existing theories of impression formation, that employees with many personal achievements may be regarded as "loud" achievers, thereby creating a motivational gravity dip in the impression they create—particularly on those with stronger pull-down attitudes (p. 49). These predictions have recently been supported in an experimental study in which more than three hundred participants were asked to rate potential coworkers on the basis of the number of their achievements (Smith & Carr, in press).

A motivational gravity dip may also occur, of course, among superiors selecting and placing subordinates. This could represent either direct push-down (motivated by insecurity perhaps) or indirect pull-down, motivated by concern over potential pull-down from coworker peers. An American-owned restaurant complex in Australia recently became unmanageable following the promotion by senior managers of achieving individuals (former workmates) to management positions. As a result of the tension created between pull-up from bosses and pull-down from former coworker peers, it took just a few months for this complex to close down completely (McLoughlin & Carr, 1994). Such dramas would go some way toward explaining why Australian managers may sometimes be reluctant to praise individuals for their personal achievements (Carnegie & Butlin, 1993; Vecchio, Hearn, & Southey, 1992). Workers commonly refer to the "mushroom syndrome" (being kept in the dark and fed bullshit), while the government vainly exhorts managers to nurture a clever country.

Chidgey (1995) has suggested that the preventive application of a traditional Australian (sporting-team) metaphor may have averted the kind of management disaster that took place in the restaurant complex, a suggestion given credence in a recent government report contrasting reactions to the captains of industry versus those in sport (Karpin, 1995). Preliminary results of a first study on the viability of a sporting metaphor support Chidgey's hypothesis. Australians from a variety of organizations perceived that personal achievements are much more likely to receive encouragement within a sporting versus factory (or indeed familial) schema (Chidgey, 1995).

Wober (1993) has suggested that group discussion might reverse motivational gravity, and Feather (1994) has found that Australians' attitudes toward high achievers consist of two distinctive factors: favor fall and favor reward. Given this duality, the tendency toward reward may (upon measurement) prove to be stronger than the tendency toward fall. In that event, the likelihood for group discussion to polarize group norms (Lamm & Myers, 1978) may produce a clearer dominance of support for high achievers over hostility against them (Carr, 1996a, b). Indeed, Carr's net-gain hypothesis has recently been corroborated in a polarization experiment involving pull-down attitudes (Carr, Pearson, & Provost, 1966).

Conway (1971) has traced Australian ambivalence to identification with authority coupled to a historical rejection by (and therefore of) that very authority. Making a more general (and supporting) observation, Reeve (1992) reminds us that individual success often attracts an ambivalent combination of both admiration and hatred, that is, envy. If some kind of intercultural tension often exists inside organizations, then small-group, net-gain techniques might have relatively wide applications to counteracting motivational gravity (Carr, 1996a, b).

Push-Up-Push-down

ANOTHER possibility, more generic perhaps, concerns discrimination against women. In Australia, for example, when outstanding work was attributed to Australian women rather than men, it tended to attract downgrading from men (Ellerman & Smith, 1983). Australian bosses may similarly downgrade female subordinates' achievements in the workplace, namely, by attributing them to luck rather than to ability or superior effort (Ashkanasy, 1994). Women are underrepresented in Australian management generally (Karpin, 1995).

Newly qualified women leaving Australia and returning home to Asia are less likely to be fully recognized for their achievements, and some will not even complete their studies for fear of superseding their husbands (Daroesman & Daroesman, 1992). In Malaysia (Nasir & Ismail, 1994, August) and in Singapore (Kaur & Ward, 1992), women have already been found to be fearful of success in the male-dominated workplace. Melamed (1995) found that more than 55 percent of a gender gap in career success was attributable to sex discrimination. A search of the database Psychlit for the period 1987–1994 revealed that 68 percent of all studies of fear of success were concerned with women, and women score in general more highly than men on fear of success (e.g., Santucci, Terzian, & Kayson, 1989). Across Oriental and Occidental cultures, socialist and capitalist systems, and developed versus developing economies, women are grossly underrepresented in management—despite their interest in attaining management positions (Adler, 1993).

We suspect that women generally will not have to ascend in organizational terms as far as men before they become overconspicuous to male superiors, thereby attracting push-down. Consistent with this glass-ceiling prediction, Smith and Carr (in press) found that it took fewer achievements before female (versus male) job applicants became susceptible to a motivational gravity dip, particularly when the judge was male.

At the same time, from peers (i.e., the majority of other women), the continuing strength of the feminine movements such as Women in Development would lead one to hope for a social norm of support from other women, namely, push-up. The empirical evidence is rather more equivocal, however. Although one of the hallmarks of female development may be intimacy with friends of the same gender (Schultz, 1991), women described as seeking traditionally masculine occupations are also least preferred as friends both by men and by women (Pfost & Fiore, 1990). Festinger (1954) suggested that people may prefer to compete against those whom they more closely resemble, raising the theoretical possibility that women may sometimes exert gravitational pull on their women peers. Power (1994, October) reports from Australia that women subordinates frequently withhold support from prospective female managers, but preliminary analyses from Singapore indicate that women there are likely to be supportive of achieving women (Carr, Ng, Hong, Singh, & Bishop, 1995).

New Directions

ONE possible framework for exploring such issues empirically may be the narrative typology (see Kashima, this volume). Both the glass ceiling and the myth of women's lack of interest in management are widely discussed themes in the literature (e.g., Adler, 1993; Melamed, 1995). Similarly, our understanding of pull-down–pull-up may be partly imbedded in, and thereby partly motivated by, a New World narrative in which an oppressive colonial hierarchy is replaced by a radical egalitarianism (Carr, 1996a, b). Colling (1992) discusses how the "level playing field" of sport, through teamwork, provides a sense of heroic achievement in contemporary Australia. In societies where hierarchy is traditionally valued, as in many collectivistic countries (Hofstede, 1980), the narrative of resistance to neocolonialism may partly account for various so-called demotivating features of work (Carr, 1996a, b). Among the "tigers" of Southeast Asia, a Confucian or family narrative may be a significant motivating force (see Kao & Ng, this volume; Kashima & Callan, 1994).

A further possible vehicle for future research is catastrophe theory (Bigelow, 1982). To return to our opening observations regarding the unidirectional drive upward, a widespread assumption seems to be that performance is linearly related to "achievement" motivation. Our analysis suggests that additional forces may be acting on that relationship. As portrayed in Figure 1, those impinging forces may create a discontinuity in the presupposed linear function, as the latter passes through the centroid of the grid and encounters motivational gravity and its attractors. In such an event, the relationship between intermediate levels of achievement motivation and workplace performance could become nonlinear and even perhaps "chaotic," e. g., through some employees experiencing resonance while others with identical levels of achievement motivation, or indeed themselves in another work relationship, experience *inverse* resonance. Evidence on this issue could eventually prove useful to managers working in multinational settings.

Throughout this chapter, we have suggested that the situation of multinationals lends itself particularly well to an analysis in terms of motivational gravity (see also Kao & Ng, this volume). Future research might seek to compare multinationals with Western and non-Western orientations in developing versus developed countries, in terms of motivational gravity, work motivation, and productivity. We hope that such research will indeed take place, and that it will be aided in measurable terms by the use of our grid.

Acknowledgments

For many stimulating conversations, we thank our former students and colleagues at the University of Malaŵi. The Japanese project reported in this paper was funded by grant no. 45/280/340, awarded by the Research Management Committee at the University of Newcastle, Australia.

References

Abdullah, A. (1992). *Understanding the Malaysian workforce.* Kuala Lumpur: Malaysian Institute of Management.

Adler, N. J. (1993). An international perspective on the barriers to the advancement of women managers. *Applied Psychology: An International Review, 42,* 289–300.

Aktouf, O. (1994). *Le management entre tradition et renouvellement.* Casablanca, Morocco: Gaetan Morin.

Allcorn, S. (1994). *Anger in the workplace.* Chicago: Quorum Books.

Al-Zahrani, S. S., & Kaplowitz, S. A. (1993). Attributional biases in individualistic and collectivistic cultures: A comparison of Americans with Saudis. *Social Psychology Quarterly, 56,* 223–233.

Anderson, R. S., & Alexander, R. (1995, October). Innovate to grow. *Management: The Magazine of the Australian Institute of Management,* 8–10.

Aronson, E., Blaney, N., Stephan, C., Sikes, J., & Snapp, M. (1978). *The jigsaw classroom.* Beverly Hills, CA: Sage.

Ashkanasy, N. M. (1994). Automatic categorisation and causal attribution: The effect of gender bias in supervisor responses to subordinate performance. *Australian Journal of Psychology, 46,* 177–182.

Bigelow, J. (1982). A catastrophe model of organizational change. *Behavioral Science, 27,* 26–42.

Blunt, P. (1983). *Organizational theory and behaviour: An African perspective.* New York: Longman.

Blunt, P., & Jones, M. L. (1986). Managerial motivation in Kenya and Malaŵi: A cross-cultural comparison. *Journal of Modern African Studies, 24,* 165–175.

Blunt, P., & Jones, M. L. (1992). *Managing organisations in Africa.* Berlin: De Gruyter.

Bond, M. H. (Ed.) (1988a). *The cross-cultural challenge to social psychology.* Beverly Hills, CA: Sage.

Bond, M. H. (1988b). Finding universal dimensions of individual variation in multicultural studies of values: The Rokeach and Chinese Value Surveys. *Journal of Personality and Social Psychology, 55,* 1009–1015.

Bond, M. H. (1994). Personal correspondence, April 1.

Bookin-Weiner, J. (1995). Building business and management programs in the post-communist world. In S. Aroni & T. Adams (Eds.), *Proceedings,* Vol. 1: *The Fourth International Symposium on the Role of Developing Countries in Developing Areas* (pp. 1–15). Melbourne, Australia: UNESCO/INRUDA/IDTC/RMIT.

Bowa, M., & MacLachlan, M. (1994). "No congratulations in Chichewa": Deterring achievement motivation in Malaŵi. In S. S. Chiotha (Ed.), *Research and development III.* Zomba: University of Malaŵi.

Brewer, A. M. (1995). *Change management: Strategies for Australian organisations.* Sydney: Allen & Unwin.

Carnegie, R., & Butlin, M. (1993). *Managing the innovating enterprise.* Melbourne: Business Council of Australia.

Carr, S. C. (1994). Generating the velocity for overcoming motivational gravity in LDC business organizations. *Journal of Transnational Management Development, 1,* 33–56.

Carr, S. C. (1996a). Social psychology and culture: Reminders from Africa and Asia. In H. Grad, A. Blanco, & J. Georgas (Eds.), *Key issues in cross-cultural psychology* (pp. 68–85). Lisse, The Netherlands: Swets & Zeitlinger.

Carr, S. C. (1996b). Social psychology and the management of aid. In S. C. Carr & J. F. Schumaker (Eds.), *Psychology and the developing world* (pp. 103–118). Westport, CT: Praeger.

Carr, S. C., & MacLachlan, M. (1993). Asserting psychology in Malaŵi. *Psychologist, 6,* 413–419.

Carr, S. C., MacLachlan, M., & Schultz, R. (1995). Pacific Asia psychology: Ideas for development? *South Pacific Journal of Psychology, 8,* 1–18.

Carr, S. C., MacLachlan, M., Zimba, C., & Bowa, M. (1995). Managing motivational gravity in Malaŵi. *Journal of Social Psychology, 135,* 659–662.

Carr, S. C., McLoughlin, D., Hodgson, M., & MacLachlan, M. (1996). Effects of unreasonable pay discrepancies for under- and overpayment on double demotivation. *Genetic, Social, and General Psychology Monographs, 122,* 477–494.

Carr, S. C., Ng, A. K., Hong, E. L., Singh, R., & Bishop, G. D. (1995). *Motivational gravity in Singapore? A question of gender.* Singapore: National Productivity Board/National University of Singapore.

Carr, S. C., Pearson, S. A., & Provost, S. C. (1996). Learning to manage motivational gravity: An application of group polarization. *Journal of Social Psychology, 136,* 251-254.

Chidgey, J. (1995). *Managing motivational gravity using a sporting metaphor in Australia.* Ph.D. thesis. University of Newcastle, Australia.

Clarke, R. (1979). *The Japanese company.* New Haven: Yale University Press.

Colling, T. (1992). *Beyond mateship: Understanding Australian men.* Sydney: Simon & Schuster.

Conway, R. (1971). *The great Australian stupor.* Melbourne, Australia: Sun Books Pty.

Daroesman, I. P., & Daroesman, R. (1992). *Degrees of success: A tracer study of Australian government sponsored Indonesian fellowships 1970–1989.* Canberra: AIDAB/IDP.

Ellerman, D. A., & Smith, E. P. (1983). Generalised and individual bias in the evaluation of the work of women: Sexism in Australia. *Australian Journal of Psychology, 35,* 71–79.

Feather, N. T. (1994). Attitudes toward high achievers and reactions to their fall: Theory and research concerning tall poppies. *Advances in Experimental Social Psychology, 26,* 1–73.

Feather, N. T., & McKee, I. R. (1993). Global self-esteem and attitudes toward the high achiever for Australian and Japanese students. *Social Psychology Quarterly, 56,* 65–76.

Festinger, L. (1954). A theory of social comparison processes. *Human Relations, 1,* 117–140.

Franken, R. E., & Brown, D. J. (1995). Why do people like competition? The motivation for winning, putting forth effort, improving one's performance, performing well, being instrumental, and expressing forceful/aggressive behavior. *Personality and Individual Differences, 19,* 175–184.

Ghosh, E. S., & Kumar, R. (1991). Hindu-Muslim intergroup relations in India: Applying socio-psychological perspectives. *Psychology and Developing Societies, 3,* 93–112.

Gould, S. J. (1994, March/April). Pride of place: Science without taxonomy is blind. *Sciences,* 38–39.

Handy, C. B. (1985). *Understanding organizations.* London: Penguin.

Hinkle, S., & Brown, R. J. (1990). Intergroup comparisons and social identity: Some links and lacunae. In D. Abrams & M. A. Hogg (Eds.), *Social identity theory: Constructive and critical advances* (pp. 48–70). Hemel Hempstead, U.K.: Harvester-Wheatsheaf.

Hofstede, G. (1980). *Culture's consequences: International differences in work related values.* Beverly Hills, CA: Sage.

Hosking, D. M., & Morley, I. E. (1991). *A social psychology of organizing.* Hemel Hempstead, U.K.: Harvester-Wheatsheaf.

Hui, C. H. (1990). Work attitudes, leadership styles, and managerial behaviors in different cultures. In R. W. Brislin (Ed.), *Applied cross-cultural psychology* (pp. 186–208). Newbury Park, CA: Sage.

Johnson, D. W., & Johnson, F. P. (1991). *Joining together: Group theory and group skills.* Englewood Cliffs, NJ: Prentice-Hall.

Jones, M. (1988). Managerial thinking: An African perspective. *Journal of Management Studies, 25,* 481–505.

Jones, M. L. (1991). Management development: An African focus. In M. Mendenhall & G. Oddou (Eds.), *Readings and cases in human resource management* (pp. 231–244). Boston: PWS Kent.

Karpin, D. (1995). *Enterprising nation: Renewing Australia's managers to meet the challenges of the Asia-Pacific century.* Canberra: Australian Government Publishing Services.

Kashima, Y., & Callan, V. J. (1994). The Japanese work group. In H. C. Triandis, M. D. Dunnette, & L. M. Hough (Eds.), *Handbook of Industrial and Organizational Psychology,* Vol. 4 (pp. 609–646). Palo Alto, CA: Consulting Psychologists Press.

Kashima, Y., & Triandis, H. C. (1986). The self-serving bias in attributions as a coping strategy:

A cross-cultural study. *Journal of Cross-Cultural Psychology, 17,* 83–97.

Kasser, T., & Ryan, R. M. (1993). A dark side of the American dream: Correlates of financial success as a central life aspiration. *Journal of Personality and Social Psychology, 65,* 410–422.

Kaur, R., & Ward, C. (1992). Cross-cultural construct validity study of "fear of success": A Singaporean case study. In S. Iwawaki, Y. Kashima, & K. Leung (Eds.), *Innovations in cross-cultural psychology* (pp. 214–222). Lisse, The Netherlands: Swets & Zeitlinger.

Kiggundu, M. N. (1986). Limitations to the application of sociotechnical systems in developing countries. *Journal of Applied Behavioural Science, 22,* 341–353.

Kiggundu, M. N. (1991). The challenge of management development in Sub-Saharan Africa. *Journal of Management Development, 10,* 32–47.

Kim, U. (1994). *Rediscovering the human mind: The indigenous psychologies approach with specific focus on East Asian cultures.* Kuala Lumpur: Universiti Kebangsaan Malaysia.

Krewer, B., & Jahoda, G. (1993). Psychologie et culture: Vers une solution du "Babel"? *International Journal of Psychology, 28,* 367–375.

Lalonde, R. N., & Silverman, R. A. (1994). Behavioral preferences in response to social injustice: The effects of group permeability and social identity salience. *Journal of Personality and Social Psychology, 66,* 78–85.

Lamm, H., & Myers, D. G. (1978). Group induced polarization of attitudes and behavior. *Advances in Experimental Social Psychology, 11,* 145–187.

Lawuyi, O. B. (1992). Vehicle slogans as personal and social thought: A perspective on self development in Nigeria. *New Directions for Educational Reform, 1,* 91–98.

Lazarevic, R. (1992). *The self-esteem of rural and urban Aboriginal students in New South Wales.* Master's thesis, University of Newcastle, Australia.

Lee, J. K. (1994). Personal correspondence, June 17.

Leung, K., & Wu, P. G. (1990). Dispute processing: A cross-cultural analysis. In R. W. Brislin (Ed.), *Applied cross-cultural psychology* (pp. 209–231). Newbury Park, CA: Sage.

Machungwa, P., & Schmitt, N. (1983). Work motivation in a developing country. *Journal of Applied Psychology, 68,* 31–42.

MacLachlan, M. (1993). Sustaining human resource development in Africa: The influence of expatriates. *Management Education and Development, 24,* 153–157.

MacLachlan, M., & Carr, S. C. (1994). Pathways to a psychology for development: Reconstituting, restating, refuting and realising. *Psychology and Developing Societies, 6,* 21–28.

MacLachlan, M., & Carr, S. C. (1994, July). *Motivational gravity.* 23rd International Congress of Applied Psychology, Madrid.

MacLachlan, M., Nyirenda, T., & Nyando, M. C. (1995). Attributions for admission to Zomba Mental Hospital: Implications for the development of mental health services in Malaŵi. *International Journal of Social Psychiatry, 41,* 79–87.

Markus, H. R., & Kitayama, S. (1991). Culture and the self: Implications for cognition, emotion and motivation. *Psychological Review, 98,* 224–253.

Marsella, A. J., & Choi, S. C. (1993). Psychosocial aspects of modernization and economic development in East Asian nations. *Psychologia: An International Journal of Psychology in the Orient, 36,* 201–213.

Mayo, E. (1949). *The social problems of an industrial civilization.* New York: Routledge.

Mazrui, A. A. (1980). *The African condition.* London: Heinemann.

McClelland, D. C. (1987). Characteristics of successful entrepreneurs. *Journal of Creative Behaviour, 21,* 219–233.

McCarthy, P. (1996, January 27). Bullying rife in the workplace: A study. *Newcastle Herald,* p. 3.

McLoughlin, D., & Carr, S. C. (1994). *The Buick Bar & Grill.* Melbourne, Australia: University of Melbourne Case Study Services.

Melamed, T. (1995). Barriers to women's career success: Human capital, career choices, structural determinants, or simply sex discrimination? *Applied Psychology: An International Review, 44,* 295–314.

Moghaddam, F. M. (1987). Psychology in the three worlds. *American Psychologist, 42,* 912–920.

Moghaddam, F. M. (1993). Traditional and modern psychology in competing cultural systems: Lessons from Iran, 1978–1981. In U. Kim & J. W. Berry (Eds.), *Indigenous psychologies* (pp. 118–132). London: Sage.

Montero, M., & Sloan, T. S. (1988). Understanding behavior in conditions of economic and cultural dependency. *International Journal of Psychology, 23,* 597–617.

Montgomery, J. D. (1987). Probing managerial behaviour: Image and reality in Southern Africa. *World Development, 15,* 911–929.

Munro, D. (1986). Work motivation and values: Problems in and out of Africa. *Australian Journal of Psychology, 38,* 285–296.

Munro, D. (1996). Work motivation and developing nations: A systems approach. In S. C. Carr & J. F. Schumaker (Eds.), *Psychology and the developing world* (pp. 130–139). Westport, CT: Praeger.

Nadkarni, R. P. (1994, June). *Use of music for transforming the work culture.* Third World Business Congress, Penang, Malaysia.

Nasir, R., & Ismail, N. (1994, August). *Attitude toward women managers and its relationship with fear of success among female students.* Third Afro-Asian Psychological Congress: Kuala Lumpur.

Ong, C. N. (1991). Ergonomics, technology transfer, and developing countries. *Ergonomics, 34,* 799–814.

Orpen, C. (1990). Measuring support for organizational innovation: A validity study. *Psychological Reports, 67,* 417–418.

Orpen, C. (1993). The Multifactorial Achievement Scale as a predictor of salary growth and motivation among middle managers. *Psychological Studies, 38,* 79–81.

Pataki-Schweizer, K. J. (1976). Meth drinkers and lotus eaters: Some educational aspects of transcultural psychiatry in Papua New Guinea. *Australian and New Zealand Journal of*

Psychiatry, 10, 129–131.

Pfost, K. S., & Fiore, M. (1990). Pursuit of nontraditional occupations: Fear of success or fear of not being chosen. *Sex Roles, 23,* 15–24.

Power, V. (1994, October). *Gender bias and the "glass ceiling."* 29th Annual Conference of the Australian Psychological Society, Wollongong.

Pryor, R. G. L. (1993, September). Returning from the wilderness. *Australian Journal of Career Development,* pp. 13–17.

Ralston, D. A., Gustafson, D. J., Elsass, P. M., Cheung, F., & Terpstra, R. H. (1992). Eastern values: A comparison of managers in the United States, Hong Kong, and the People's Republic of China. *Journal of Applied Psychology, 77,* 664–671.

Reeve, J. M. (1992). *Understanding motivation and emotion.* Fort Worth, TX: Harcourt Brace Jovanovich.

Robbins, S. P., Waters-Marsh, T., & Cacioppe, R. (1994). *Organisational behaviour: Concepts, controversies, and applications.* Sydney: Prentice-Hall.

Rousseau, D. M., & House, R. J. (1994). Meso organizational behavior: Avoiding three fundamental biases. In C. L. Cooper & D. M. Rousseau (Eds.), *Trends in organizational behavior,* Vol. 1 (pp. 13–30). Chichester, U.K.: Wiley.

Sampson, E. E. (1988). The debate on individualism: Indigenous psychologies of the individual and their role in personal and societal functioning. *American Psychologist, 43,* 15–22.

Santucci, R., Terzian, D., & Kayson, W. A. (1989). Fear of success: Influence of sex, year, and program in college. *Psychological Reports, 64,* 551–555.

Schneider, S. C. (1991). National vs. corporate culture: Implications for human resource management. In M. Mendenhall & G. Oddou (Eds.), *Readings and cases in international human resource management* (pp. 13–27). Boston: PWS Kent.

Schultz, K. (1991). Women's adult development: The importance of friendship. *Journal of Independent Social Work, 5,* 19–30.

Schumaker, J. F. (1996). Understanding psychopathology: Lessons from the developing world. In S. C. Carr & J. F. Schumaker (Eds.), *Psychology and the developing world* (pp. 180–190). Westport, CT: Praeger.

Seddon, J. (1985). The development and indigenisation of Third World business: African values in the workplace. In V. Hammond (Ed.), *Current research in management* (pp. 98–109). London: Pinter.

Sheridan, M. (1976). Young women leaders in China. *Signs: Journal of Women in Culture and Society, 2,* 59–89.

Sherif, M. (1956). Experiments in group conflict. *Scientific American, 195,* 54–58.

Sinha, D. (1989). Cross-cultural psychology and the process of indigenisation: A second view from the Third World. In D. M. Keats, D. Munro, & L. Mann. *Heterogeneity in cross-cultural psychology* (pp. 24–40). Lisse, The Netherlands: Swets & Zeitlinger.

Smith, B., & Carr, S. C. (in press). Number of achievements and impression formation: The motivational gravity dip. *South Pacific Journal of Psychology.*

Smith, P. B., & Bond, M. H. (1993). *Social psychology across cultures.* Hemel Hempstead, U.K.:

Harvester Wheatsheaf.

Srinivas, K. M. (1995). Organization development for national development: A review of evidence. In D. Saunders & R. N. Kanungo (Eds.), *Employee management in developing countries* (pp. 197–223). Greenwich, CT: JAI Press.

Tajfel, H. (1978). *Differentiation between social groups.* London: Academic Press.

Templer, A., Beaty, D., & Hofmeyr, K. (1992). The challenge of management development in S. Africa: So little time and so much to do. *Journal of Management Development, 11,* 32–41.

Thomas, D. R. (1994, August). *Developing community and social psychology for Aotearoa: Experience from a New Zealand programme of indigenization.* Third Afro-Asian Psychological Congress, Kuala Lumpur.

Traynor, W. J., & Watts, W. R. (1992). Management development in the Pacific during the 1990s. *Journal of Management Development, 11,* 67–79.

Triandis, H. C. (1984). Toward a psychological theory of economic growth. *International Journal of Psychology, 19,* 79–95.

Triandis, H. C. (1988). Collectivism vs. individualism: A reconceptualization of a basic concept in cross-cultural social psychology. In G. K. Verma & C. Bagley (Eds.), *Cross-cultural studies of personality, attitudes, and cognition* (pp. 60–95). Hong Kong: Macmillan.

Triandis, H. C. (1989). Cross-cultural studies of individualism and collectivism. In J. J. Berman (Ed.), *Nebraska Symposium on Motivation, 1989,* Vol. 37 (pp. 41–133). Lincoln: University of Nebraska Press.

Turner, J. C. (1991). *Social influence.* Milton Keynes, U.K.: Open University Press.

Vecchio, R. P., Hearn, G., & Southey, G. (1992). *Organisational behaviour: Life at work in Australia.* Marrickville, Australia: Harcourt Brace Jovanovich.

Wan Rafaei, A. R. (1984). Achievement motivation and attribution of success in urban Malaysian ethnic groups. In Y. C. Leong, H. K. Chiam, & L. S. M. Chew (Eds.), *Preparation for adulthood: Proceedings of Third Asian Workshop on Child and Adolescent Development* (pp. 266–267). Kuala Lumpur: University of Malaya.

Wikan, U. (1989). Managing the heart to brighten face and soul: Emotions in Balinese morality and health care. *American Ethnologist, 16,* 294–312.

Wong, M. M. L. (1996). Shadow management in Japanese companies in Hong Kong. *Asia Pacific Journal of Human Resources, 34,* 95–110.

Wober, M. (1993). Personal communication, September 9.

Xu, L., & Wang, Z. (1991). New developments in organisational psychology in China. *Applied Psychology: An International Review, 40,* 3–14.

Intrapsychic Processes

Chapter Ten

Unconscious Motivation and Culture

WILLIAM WEDENOJA *and* ELISA J. SOBO

We have been asked to discuss the relationship between unconscious motivation and culture, two subjects that academic psychology has until recently ignored. Anthropology, on the other hand, has been investigating the relationship between psyche and culture for about seventy-five years now. This effort occupied center stage in American anthropology in the 1930s, '40s, and '50s in the school of "culture and personality," which relied heavily on psychoanalytic theory and the idea of unconscious motivation. A new direction was taken in the 1960s with the appearance of "cognitive anthropology." An eclectic marriage of the two was made in the 1970s, under the heading of "psychological anthropology." And in the 1980s a more interdisciplinary reconceptualization called "cultural psychology" began to take shape.

The Concept of the Unconscious

THE unconscious refers to "mental processes of which the subject is not aware" (Rycroft, 1972, p. 172). The concept is most closely associated with Sigmund Freud, although the idea existed before him. Freud identified two kinds of unconscious thoughts, the *latent unconscious* or preconscious, which can be brought to consciousness, and the *dynamic unconscious,* which is inaccessible to consciousness. The dynamic unconscious includes instinctual wishes or drives, particularly sexual ones, that have been repressed because they are unacceptable or threatening. Nonetheless, they continually press for discharge or fulfillment, resulting in intrapsychic conflict and possibly neurotic behavior.

Freud's erstwhile colleague Carl Jung referred to the unconscious of the individual, including the latent and the dynamic unconscious, as the *personal unconscious.* He also proposed that human beings are born with innate and universal predispositions to perceive and organize experiences according to images called archetypes. These archetypes, which come from the evolutionary past of our species, make up the *collective unconscious.* They are expressed particularly in dreams, visions, and symbols.

To experimental psychologists, the unconscious has been a wildly speculative idea. In part, this was due to its uncomfortable association with Freud and psychoanalysis. Another problem has been the difficulty of testing the idea convincingly in the laboratory. A growing body of experimental evidence, however, is now confirming the existence of unconscious mental processes.

Current research focuses on the *cognitive unconscious,* defined as "mental structures and processes that, operating outside phenomenal awareness, nevertheless influence conscious experience, thought, and action" (Kihlstrom, 1987, p. 1445). This includes subliminal perception; automatized skills; unconscious rules, strategies, heuristics, and algorithms; and implicit memories (i.e., prior experiences that are not consciously remembered).

Recent reviews have referred to the idea of unconscious processes as "no longer questionable" (Loftus & Klinger, 1992, p. 764) and "solidly established" (Greenwald, 1992, p. 766). Unconscious influences are said to be very common: "People sometimes consciously plan and then act, but more often behavior is influenced by unconscious processes" (Jacoby, Lindsay, & Toth, 1992, p. 802). They "encompass a large portion of mental life" (Kihlstrom, 1987, p. 1446).

How does the cognitive unconscious compare with Freud's dynamic unconscious? *U.S. News and World Report* (October 22, 1990) remarked that "the realm of the unconscious is at once much vaster and far more prosaic than Freud imagined" (p. 60). Kihlstrom, Barnhardt, and Tataryn (1992) said Freud's unconscious "was hot and wet; it seethed with lust and anger; it was hallucinatory, primitive, and irrational," whereas "the unconscious of contemporary psychology is kinder and gentler than that and more reality bound and rational" (p. 789).

Freud's unconscious was a clever one. Some psychologists think the cognitive unconscious is "intellectually much simpler than the sophisticated agency portrayed in psychoanalytic theory" (Greenwald, 1992, p. 766); others say it is "incomparably more able to process formally complex knowledge structures, faster, and 'smarter' overall, than our ability to think and identify meanings of stimuli in a consciously controlled manner" (Lewicki, Hill, & Czyzewska, 1992, p. 801).

Motivation and Culture

MOTIVATION refers to "why people initiate, terminate, and persist in specific actions in particular situations" (Markus & Kitayama, 1991, p. 239). Psychologists generally assume a universal set of needs and drives. Freud reduced behavior to two instincts; Henry Murray identified a large number of human needs such as achievement, affiliation, and dependence; and Abraham Maslow proposed a hierarchy of needs. Anthropologists, on the other hand, generally believe that motivation is crafted largely by culture.

Psychologists also generally assume that motivation is internal and part of the unique self of an individual. This assumption could be ethnocentric because it is based on an "independent construal of the self" that may be uniquely Western. Markus and Kitayama (1991) argued that non-Western societies have an "interdependent construal of the self," which is "more connected and less differentiated from others" (p. 227) and more social in its motivation.

Cognitive anthropologist Claudia Strauss (1992) has emphasized that human motivation is "the product of interaction between events and things in the social world and interpretations of those events and things in peoples' psyches" (p. 1). These interpretations usually if not always involve cultural knowledge. During the course of ethnographic research in Jamaica, for instance, one of us knew a young man from a humble background who had become a bank teller, a relatively "respectable" and important position in the town. He was, however, chronically fearful that others, especially his own relatives, were envious of his success and would try to "bring him down" by paying an "obeahman" (sorcerer) to work magic against him. Over the course of several years, he consulted a number of traditional healers and obeahmen to confirm his suspicions and to gain their protection, but eventually he took his own life. The point of this story, which is not atypical, is that his morbid state of mind took the form of, and was supported by, popular beliefs. Can we ignore these cultural constructions of reality when striving to explain behavior?

The Concept of Culture

CULTURE is the key concept of anthropology, which is concerned primarily with the origin and evolution of culture and an understanding of cultural variation. Culture is often confused with society, but they are distinctly different, albeit related, ideas. A society is a group of individuals who live and work together. Many animals, as well as humans, live in societies. Every society has a social structure, made up of patterns of relationships between individuals and groups. Every human society also has a culture, perhaps more than one, although animal societies generally have little if any culture.

The definition of culture is continually negotiated in anthropology, but some ideas are widely accepted. For instance, culture is knowledge that is shared or public. It includes language, symbols, values, beliefs, attitudes, ideals, norms (rules and standards of behavior), skills, customs, and world-view (basic assumptions about the nature of the world). That is, virtually everything we think or do involves culture. And culture is essential for human survival. Perhaps most important, it provides expectations for behavior, which make social interaction predictable and enhance cooperation.

Culture is based on the human capacity to symbolize (White, 1940). To symbolic anthropology, which took shape in the 1970s, it is primarily a system of symbols and meanings. Clifford Geertz (1973), for example, wrote that "culture consists of socially established structures of meaning in terms of which people do ... things" (p. 181).

Culture is traditional or received knowledge in that it is passed on from generation to generation by means of learning. Over the generations, the amount of culture will accumulate, becoming ever larger and more complex. To be cultural, knowledge must be shared. But there is more culture in a society than any one person can know. Therefore, cultural knowledge is "distributed" (Schwartz, 1978). Some knowledge may be exclusive to a group within a society, or restricted largely to an occupation, or to one sex, or to one social class.

In the past decade, anthropologists have focused increasingly on how culture is "negotiated" by individuals and groups. As we write, for example, the World Series has started, and the appropriateness of calling baseball teams "Indians" and "Braves" is a source of public debate. To Daniel Linger (1994), culture is "a set of conceptual and emotional chunks temporarily shared and continually refashioned" (p. 286).

The concept of culture as outlined above is quite psychological. In fact, Philip Bock's (1988) brief historical survey of psychological anthropology begins with the argument that "all anthropology is psychological" (p. 1) and ends with the conclusion that "all psychology is cultural" (p. 211).

Ethnopsychology of the Unconscious

CULTURAL beliefs about mental activity are referred to as folk psychologies or ethnopsychologies. Jamaicans, for example, locate the mind in the chest. For them, the mind is the seat of volition and has certain emotional functions. Computational thinking takes place in the head, where facts are stored. Psychological problems are attributed mostly to biological shortcomings, therefore they are generally cured with physical treatments, such as tonics for strengthening or restoring the "nerves" (Sobo, in press).

According to Roy D'Andrade (1987), the ethnopsychology of Western culture emphasizes cognition, conscious awareness, self-control, and deliberate intention. Both psychoanalysis and academic psychology developed out of this folk model but diverged in different directions from it. Freud's model focuses on unconscious motivation and conflict, whereas academic psychology emphasizes "what can be described physically—hours of deprivation, the neural pathways, peripheral responses and so on" (D'Andrade, 1987, p. 140).

The idea of unconscious motivation was a part of Western ethnopsychology before Freud (Ellenberger, 1970), but is it strictly a Western concept? Obeyesekere (1990, p.253) remarked:

> The idea of unconscious and preconscious motivation and "thought" is, in my view, consonant with forms of thought in many non-Western societies.... Both Buddhism and Hinduism clearly recognize unconscious motivation, and indeed delve more deeply into such processes than Freudianism.... I also think that shamanism, spirit possession, and other kinds of hypnomantic states are widespread forms of life that recognize implicitly the centrality of unconscious motivation.

A key word in Obeyesekere's argument is "implicitly." Cultural relativists argue that "native" explanations should be taken at face value. For example, Rosaldo (1984) was reluctant to attribute certain violent acts between Ilongot brothers to repressed anger because the Ilongot did not see them that way. But Spiro (1984) interpreted Rosaldo's data according to psychoanalysis, using the psychodynamic processes of denial and displacement to explain why the Ilongot fail to recognize angry resentment and hostility in this situation.

Non-Western ethnopsychologies do not seem to explicitly recognize unconscious motivation, particularly in the Freudian sense of repressed material, but this does not mean that every thought, feeling, or act is attributed to conscious intent. Mind and behavior are also understood to be influenced by the body, other people, society, and spiritual agents.

Lienhardt (1985) pointed out that in Africa witches "may not always be thought conscious of being so" (p. 146). Among the Azande, for instance, witchery was said to be inborn. A physical substance inherited from parents and located under the sternum drove them to bewitch others. It was understood to be an impersonal force, not an unconscious desire.

Some behavior in every culture is attributed to extrahuman influence. For example, in Zion Revival, an African-Christian religion in Jamaica, followers are often "led by the Spirit to move in mysterious ways." In one service that Wedenoja observed, the leader, a healer, was spontaneously "led" to a person in need and washed her soul with a bouquet of flowers. Thoughts, feelings, and actions can also be influenced by the magic of sorcerers, by amoral forces such as ghosts, and by malevolent forces such as Satan and fallen angels (Wedenoja, 1989).

The Azande witchcraft substance and "the Spirit" in Jamaica may be metaphors for unconscious motivation, but that is a psychoanalytic *interpretation* of the data, not what people explicitly say they believe. Unconscious motivation is most likely to be recognized as such in societies that are secularized and individualistic. People in religious and sociocentric (or interdependent) societies may not have the same need to claim sole authorship for everything they say and do as people in the dis-enchanted states of Europe and North America.

Interpretations of Dreams

WHAT we make of our dreams depends largely on the ethnopsychology of our culture. As Edgar (1994) has remarked: "dream imagery is both socially constructed and socially interpreted by means of cultural symbolism" (p. 103).

Freud thought that dreams were the royal road to the unconscious. If so, then cross-cultural differences in dreams could provide insight into psychological differences between societies. LeVine (1966), for example, discovered different levels of achievement motivation in the dreams of male Ibo, Yoruba, and Hausa students in Nigeria. Herr (1981) found that nightmares are very common in Fiji, where men's nightmares focus on changes in tradition and women's nightmares are threateningly erotic. Gregor (1985) identified "deeply seated conflicts and fears" about sexuality in the dreams of Mehinaku Indians in the Amazon (p. 160).

Rational thought is highly favored in Western culture, where dreams and emotions are regarded as mysterious and irrational. Some Western psychologists believe that dreams are merely the meaningless product of random firing of neurons in the brain. Aside from followers of the New Age movement, Westerners would think it unseemly and nonsensical to make important decisions on the basis of dreams. Some societies are, however, much more attentive to dreams. The Mohave Indians of California were called a "dream culture" because they "habitually *wish* to dream, *do* dream and *think* over their dreams in great detail" (Devereux, 1961, p. 494). And the Mehinaku often tell their dreams to members of their household in the morning (Gregor, 1981, p. 354).

Westerners generally assume a dream is a psychological phenomenon that says something about our hidden self, but in many non-Western societies, it is a supernatural experience. The Mehinaku say that "dreams occur when the soul ... leaves its home in the iris of the eye to wander about through a nocturnal world peopled by spirits, monsters, and the souls of other sleeping villagers" (Gregor, 1981, p. 354).

Dreams are sometimes believed to be messages from deities. In ancient Egypt gods communicated with royal figures through dreams. Jamaican Revivalists receive "orders" from angels in dreams, which must be obeyed or they will be punished (Wedenoja, 1990). The seventeenth-century Iroquois acted out dreams in public, with the aid of the community, in order to satisfy the wishes of the soul, a guardian spirit, or a supernatural being because they believed the wish, if frustrated, could bring about the death of the dreamer or even a national disaster (Wallace, 1958).

Dreams are also believed to be prophetic. The Mehinaku say they "are symbols ... of events to come" (Gregor, 1981, p. 354). To the Quiche Maya of Guatemala, a dream might be a direct representation of a future event or the reverse (Tedlock, 1981). Prophetic dreams in Fiji almost always portend death or affliction rather than positive events (Herr, 1981).

Among many North American Indian tribes, such as the Ojibwa, young boys sought power and guidance from "other-than-human-persons" during a lonely vigil of fasting and prayer. The supplicant became obligated to the other-than-human-person and had to follow certain taboos or restrictions revealed in a dream or a vision (Hallowell, 1966).

Sometimes a dream or a vision is interpreted as a calling to adopt a special role, such as that of a shaman. Certain dreams could, for example, drive a Sioux Indian man to become a *berdache* by renouncing his manhood, dressing like a woman, and taking on female roles (Kilborne, 1981a).

Often cultural beliefs and practices such as dances and rituals are acquired or validated through dreams or visions. The Mohave, for example, believed that shamans could return to the mythical time of creation in dreams and learn from the creators themselves (Devereux, 1961). In 1800 the Iroquois chief Handsome Lake fell into a trance for seven hours and was taken on a journey through the sky by a spirit guide who taught him a moral plan. This plan became the code for a new religion, and a new way of life (Wallace, 1972).

Many societies have specialists in dream interpretation. In the Quiche Maya village of Momostenango, with a population of 45,000, there were approximately 10,000 interpreters! (Tedlock, 1981, p. 314). Devereux (1961) reported that the Mohave shaman diagnosed disease primarily on the basis of his patient's dreams and had an "unusually great ability to observe and to understand neurotics and psychotics" (p. 495). Kilborne (1981b) argued that the cognitive and affective salience of dream interpretation in Morocco depends on "shared fantasies and unconscious feelings and motivations" (p. 299).

The Dynamic Unconscious and Culture

ANTHROPOLOGISTS have used psychoanalytic theory far more than any other psychological theory, mainly because it has more to say about symbolism, the basis of culture. In addition, Freud had a keen interest in culture, which has been lacking among academic psychologists. There is today a vigorous subfield of psychoanalytic anthropology, based on the assumption "that human life is meaningfully influenced by unconscious thoughts, affects, and motives" (Paul, 1989, p. 177).

Sexuality and Culture

ALL human behavior, according to Freud (1923), is motivated by only two instincts: sex and aggression. One of his most controversial ideas is that infants and children are sexual beings. Freud maintained that the sexual development of boys culminates in the Oedipus complex, which involves intense love for the mother and hostile rivalry toward the father. This situation is normally resolved by repression (and ultimately displacement) of love for the mother and unconscious identification with the father.

The universality of the Oedipus complex was challenged by Bronislaw Malinowski, who studied the Trobriand Islanders in Melanesia. Malinowski (1927) argued that Freud's theory was culturally biased and applied only to the bourgeois patriarchal nuclear family of Western Europe. Descent is matrilineal in the Trobriands, and the main authority figure for a boy is his mother's brother. Malinowski argued that an "avuncular complex" developed, with the boy directing his hostility toward his mother's brother and his incestuous interest toward his sister.

Fifty-five years later, Spiro (1982) reopened the case and argued on the basis of Malinowski's data that there was in fact an unusually strong and classic complex in the Trobriands. He reaffirmed the universality of the Oedipus complex and added that it is not merely a debate "about a passing episode in the psychological development of the child" but "a psychological constellation which ... has pervasive cultural, social, and psychological consequences" (pp. 173–174). In societies where the complex is particularly strong or poorly repressed, he suggested, there are two institutionalized ways of dealing with it. One is extrusion: the boy is sent off to live somewhere else—another household, a dormitory, a boarding school, even a children's village (Spiro, 1982, p. 92). The other is through painful initiation rites.

In many tribal societies, boys are subjected to painful rituals involving isolation, hazing, taboos, torture, ordeals, and genital mutilation, which mark the transition to adulthood. The psychoanalyst Bruno Bettelheim (1954) argued that male initiation rites are symbolic expressions of male envy of female anatomy and reproductive power and are means by which males appropriate that power. Australian aborigines, for example, performed subincision of the penis, calling the incision the "vulva" and the blood that ran from it "menses" (p. 105). In other rituals, men symbolically asserted that they could bear children just as women do or even better. Such rituals may help initiates to master their ambivalence toward women.

An alternative explanation for initiation rites is that they are an institutionalized means by which societies deal with an "unresolved" Oedipus complex. In all cases, boys are removed from their mothers' care, often forcibly, and subjected to the stern discipline of their fathers' peers. A classic cross-cultural study (Whiting, Kluckhohn, & Anthony, 1958) supported this theory by identifying a relationship between a long postpartum sex taboo and exclusive mother-son sleeping arrangements (which presumably create strong maternal identification) and the presence of male puberty rites.

Initiation rites are a major focus of some tribal societies in New Guinea. Among the Sambia, who have been studied by Herdt (1987), there is a strong division between women and men. Boys spend childhood in the women's world, but at the age of seven to ten they begin the first of six initiations leading to manhood. Herdt agreed with the Oedipal interpretation of initiation rites. He also provided evidence for male envy of women's ability to give birth and breast-feed. Herdt added another component to his explanation: protest masculinity. In this hypermasculine culture, men constantly proclaim, ritually and symbolically, "I am a man, not a woman" (p. 50), evidently to deny an unconscious feminine identity.

Heald (1994) noted that the circumcision ritual of the Gisu of Uganda, which is undergone at the age of seventeen to twenty-five to validate manhood, actually highlights rather than resolves father-son rivalry. This may be to heighten the emotional intensity of the rite, and the symbolic messages it communicates.

Heald's approach draws on the work of Victor Turner, who wrote much about ritual symbolism among the Ndembu of Zambia. Turner (1973) noted that ritual symbols have multiple meanings and condense many ideas, actions, and relationships. For example, the key symbol of the N'kanga puberty ritual, which takes place when a girl begins to develop breasts, is the mudyi tree, which exudes white latex when the bark is scratched. According to Turner (1967), this "milk tree" carries many meanings in Ndembu culture, which can be separated into two semantic poles: the "sensory" or "orectic" pole (breast milk, a woman's breasts, breast-feeding, dependence, nurturing) and the "ideological" or "normative" pole (maternal ancestors, matrilineal kinship, tribal custom, Ndembu society, and the unity and continuity of Ndembu society). The sensory meanings appeal to the unconscious and generate powerful emotions, which are then transferred to the normative meanings, giving emotive force to the norms, values, beliefs, and structure of society.

The Social Unconscious

ONE of the central concerns of psychological anthropology has been the relationship between the psychology of the individual and that of society. Freud (1930) addressed this issue in *Civilization and Its Discontents,* in which he argued that civilization is based on guilt, deferral of gratification, repression, and the sublimation of instinctual drives to the needs of society.

According to the "ontogenetic theory of culture" of the Freudian anthropologist Geza Roheim (1941), the main characteristic of humans is prolonged infancy. Culture develops from sublimations and reaction formations to infantile conflicts, and its main function is to relieve anxieties and provide security. Different cultures are responses to different infantile traumas and conflicts.

In 1934 anthropologist Ruth Benedict published a popular book, *Patterns of Culture,* which set the agenda for psychological anthropology for decades to come. She proposed that a culture might have a "configuration" or personality such as "Apollonian," or "paranoid," and she worried about the fate of an individual born into a culture with an opposing personality type.

Psychoanalytic and anthropological ideas such as these came together in the culture and personality school of anthropology, which was particularly interested in the personality characteristics of a people. The paradigm for this school was developed by Abram Kardiner (1939, 1945), a psychoanalyst who led a very productive interdisciplinary seminar in New York from 1933 to 1955. Kardiner referred to elements of a society that have a direct influence on childhood, such as family structure and the mode of subsistence, as "primary institutions." He proposed that children who are exposed to the same institutions and have similar experiences will develop a "basic personality structure" of common personality traits, including unconscious drives, conflicts, and anxieties that stem from early traumatic experiences. This repressed material makes up the "projective system" of the basic personality, which finds expression and compensation in "secondary institutions" such as art, play, mythology, folklore, and religion.

Subsequent research in culture and personality has for the most part continued to assume some relationship between childhood experiences and culture, and between the dynamic unconscious and culture. One popular application of Kardiner's model has been the analysis of *projective culture* to uncover the dynamic unconscious of a people, which could be called their *social unconscious.*

Anthropologist Alan Dundes (1984) is a prolific author of psychoanalytic interpretations of folklore, including the anal emphasis in Germanic culture. He suggested that the widespread Earth Diver creation myths of North American Indians reflect unconscious male envy of women's natural ability to give birth (Dundes, 1962). And he analyzed American football as a male masculinity ritual that is replete with homosexual metaphors (Dundes, 1978).

Religion is the most examined form of projective culture. Freud (1918) proposed that religion, along with ethics, society, and art, stems from the Oedipus complex (p. 202) and that "god at bottom is nothing but an exalted father" (p. 190). LaBarre (1972) attributed the universality of religion to prolonged childhood in a nuclear family. He traced magic to the omnipotence of thought of infants and dependence on the mother in the oral stage and associated religion with the later Oedipal relation with the father.

Cultural Psychology

PSYCHOLOGICAL anthropologists have not been content to simply interpret folklore and religion as if they were Rorschach responses. The emerging field of cultural psychology seeks to understand "the way cultural traditions and social practices regulate, express, and transform the human psyche" (Shweder, 1991, p. 73).

Possession by deities is a common element of worship in many societies, and illnesses often involve possession by malevolent spirits too. Possession, Kakar (1982) noted, is possibly "the single most widespread psychotherapeutic technique in the world today" (p. 105) in that it serves as a cultural vehicle for the expression of normally repressed needs and feelings. Mischel and Mischel (1958), for example, described how Shango worshippers in Trinidad use ritual possession to meet needs for dominance, attention, intimacy, and aggression, as well as to engage in sex-role reversals and regressive behavior.

Spiro (1965) discovered serious emotional conflicts in a study of Burmese Buddhist monks that he believed could have led to psychosis. He argued that their mental stability was preserved because monastic roles served as a *culturally constituted defense mechanism,* permitting the gratification of repressed drives and the reduction of anxieties in a disguised and socially approved manner.

Culturally constituted defense mechanisms are widespread. Kluckhohn (1944) argued that the Navaho Indians of the American Southwest avoided intrafamily aggression by channeling or displacing hostile affect into accusations of witchcraft. Spiro (1952) proposed that aggressive impulses on the Pacific atoll of Ifaluk were projected in the belief in malevolent ghosts. Kilborne (1981b) noted that dream interpretation in Morocco encourages the projection of hostile and aggressive wishes onto malicious spirits. Wedenoja (1989) observed that the relationship between traditional healers and patients in Jamaica is patterned on the mother-child bond and meets the dependency needs of clients. Hutchins (1987) suggested that myth in the Trobriand Islands of Melanesia "provides a way of thinking about things that are too painful or too threatening to address directly" (p. 288).

Obeyesekere (1981) has suggested that individuals turn cultural symbols into *personal symbols* when they use them to objectify and externalize idiosyncratic conflicts. Thus, the psychological significance of a cultural symbol will vary from one individual to another. More recently, Obeyesekere (1990) has emphasized that there is more to religion than regressive symptom-formation and defense mechanisms. In some cases, culture can also help people resolve or progress and move away from conflicts.

The Cognitive Unconscious and Culture

THE Soviet psychologist Lev Vygotsky (1978) wrote that "the internalization of socially rooted and historically developed activities is the distinguishing feature of human psychology, the basis of the qualitative leap from animal to human psychology" (p. 57). That is, the internalization of culture transforms our native psychological structures and processes. Consequently, Vygotsky divided cognition into *elementary structures,* the basic and largely biological capacities of all humans, and *higher structures,* which are culturally constituted and socially produced. Following Vygotsky, we divide the cognitive unconscious into two forms. Current research in psychology deals largely with the *elementary unconscious,* which is innate and universal. The *constructive unconscious* involves higher structures that are learned, including norms, beliefs, values, schemas, models, and worldview.

The Elementary Unconscious

JUNG'S notion of archetypes can be subsumed under the category of the elementary unconscious because they are defined as innate and universal mental images. Anthropologists have seldom employed this concept in the study of culture, but Jungian analysts have proposed that archetypes are manifested in myths, rituals, and symbols that are widespread if not universal.

The work of the anthropologist Claude Lévi-Strauss bears some similarities to that of Jung. Lévi-Strauss has studied the mythology of Native Americans in the Amazon and in North America for decades, concentrating on the structure of myths rather than their content. The structure is implicit; people are not consciously aware of it. He also maintains that the same structural principles are found in every culture. The ultimate goal of his research is to identify innate, universal, and largely unconscious principles of human thought that underlie the diversity of cultures.

Lévi-Strauss has argued that the structure of myth and the universal mytho-logic underlying it are dialectical. Nature and society are divided into "binary oppositions" such as left and right, male and female, clean and dirty, life and death, good and evil, heaven and hell, and sacred and profane. The function of myth is to provide models for the resolution of contradictions of life. One way this is accomplished is through a mediating figure. Other elements of mytho-logic include analogy, metaphor, metonymy, and metamorphosis (Leach, 1970).

The Constructive Unconscious

FRANZ BOAS, a founder of American anthropology, believed that many elements of culture were unconscious (Stocking, 1992, p. 316). This idea was pursued by his student Edward Sapir (1928), who proposed that "normal human beings ... [react] in accordance with deep-seated cultural patterns ... [that] are not so much known as felt, not so much capable of conscious description as of naive practice" (p. 121).

Sapir's main example of unconscious patterning was language. It takes painstaking research by a linguist to identify the intricate rules of a language, yet "even a child may speak the most difficult language with idiomatic ease" (p. 123). The speaker does not even have conscious knowledge of these rules: "He is the unconscious and magnificently loyal adherent of thoroughly socialized phonetic patterns" (p. 134).

Sapir (1921) and Whorf (1941) developed the controversial thesis that language can shape the way people think about the world. A recent review by Hunt and Agnoli (1991) ascribed "a great deal of truth" to the Sapir-Whorf hypothesis. For example, a message in one language can require more memory or more processing time than in another language. Languages also force speakers to describe events in different ways or adopt different styles of reasoning. Furthermore, language can influence the schemas people use to order their experiences.

Although some linguistic structures may be basic to all humans, the rules of a particular language are learned and unconscious. They are, therefore, part of the constructive unconscious. Even more important, part are cognitive *schemas,* which Strauss (1992) defined as "learned, internalized patterns of thought-feeling that mediate both the interpretation of ongoing experience and the reconstruction of memories" (p. 3). Schemas are acquired through experience and, to the extent that an experience is socially patterned, the resulting schema is likely to be shared or cultural, in which case it is referred to by cognitive anthropologists as a *cultural model* (D'Andrade, 1987).

Cultural models are "presupposed, taken-for-granted models of the world that are widely shared ... by the members of a society and ... play an enormous role in their understanding of that world and their behavior in it" (Quinn & Holland, 1987, p. 4). They are apparently based on protypical events or sequences of events set in idealized and simplified worlds. Some North American examples are "attending a lecture," "meeting friends," "being a breadwinner," and "becoming a success" (D'Andrade, 1992). A culture will apparently have a few very general-purpose or upper-level models, which are incorporated into a vast number of special-purpose or lower-level models.

Cultural models fuse disparate elements of culture such as symbols, beliefs, norms, and values. As D'Andrade (1981) has noted, they also fuse facts and ideas with emotions, giving them directive or motivational force. This is particularly true when a model is used to understand oneself and one's life (Quinn & Holland, 1987). Therefore, as Strauss (1992) has stated: "To understand why people do what they do, we have to understand the cultural constructs by which they interpret the world" and "to show how actors internalize those constructs" (p. 4).

Cultural models are unconscious or at least transparent in that people interpret the world through them without usually being aware of them (D'Andrade, 1992). The social psychologist Serge Moscovici (1993) suggested this is "probably the most pervasive phenomenon in common life" (p. 47). When people interpret the world unconsciously, they experience it as undeniably real rather than as an interpretation (D'Andrade, 1992; Jacoby, Lindsay, & Toth, 1992). Moscovici (1993) has referred to this kind of cultural influence as an "irresistible belief," which is relatively fixed or difficult to change, compulsive, directive, and, he proposed, most likely to come to the fore when people are in groups.

Review

THE idea that behavior is influenced by unconscious psychological forces is apparently a Western idea. In many non-Western societies, however, behavior is often attributed to "other-than-human" forces, such as spirits and deities, which could be interpreted as cultural metaphors for unconscious motives.

Discussing the relationship between unconscious motivation and culture is complicated by the fact that there are several different meanings of the word *unconscious*. We have tried to remedy this situation by using several terms.

Psychoanalysts focus on the dynamic unconscious of individuals. Psychoanalytic anthropologists have investigated the possibility that unconscious motives may be shared by members of a society, which we referred to as the social unconscious, and vary from one society to another. They also agree that expressive and symbolic elements of culture such as symbols, myths, and rituals are psychodynamically related to repressed motives, feelings, and experiences.

We divided the cognitive unconscious into two forms: elementary and constructive. The elementary unconscious involves purely psychological, innate, and universal cognitive processes, which can give shape to the structure of myths and other forms of culture. The constructive unconscious includes learned schemata through which individuals actively interpret their experiences. Culture includes schemata that are shared by members of a society. Therefore, some and probably much of a culture is unconscious or at least transparent to those who have internalized it. This transparency may give cultural models much motivational force.

References

Benedict, R. (1934). *Patterns of culture.* Boston: Houghton Mifflin.

Bettelheim, B. (1954). *Symbolic wounds: Puberty rites and the envious male.* Reprint, New York: Collier Books, 1962.

Bock, P. K. (1988). *Rethinking psychological anthropology.* New York: W. H. Freeman.

D'Andrade, R. G. (1981). The cultural part of cognition. *Cognitive Science, 5,* 179–195.

D'Andrade, R. G. (1987). A folk model of the mind. In D. Holland & N. Quinn (Eds.), *Cultural models in language and thought* (pp. 112–148). New York: Cambridge University Press.

D'Andrade, R. G. (1992). Schemas and motivation. In R. G. D'Andrade and C. Strauss (Eds.), *Human motives and cultural models* (pp. 23–44). New York: Cambridge University Press.

Devereux, G. (1961). *Mohave ethnopsychiatry: The psychic disturbances of an Indian tribe.* Reprint, Washington, DC: Smithsonian Institution Press, 1969.

Dundes, A. (1962). Earth-diver: Creation of the mythopoeic male. *American Anthropologist, 64,* 1032–1051.

Dundes, A. (1978). Into the endzone for a touchdown: A psychoanalytic consideration of American football. *Western Folklore, 37,* 75–88.

Dundes, A. (1984). *Life is like a chicken coop ladder: A portrait of German culture through folklore.* New York: Columbia University Press.

Edgar, I. (1994). Dream imagery becomes social experience. In S. Heald and A. Deluz (Eds.), *Anthropology and psychoanalysis: An encounter through culture* (pp. 99–113). London: Routledge.

Ellenberger, H. F. (1970). *The discovery of the unconscious: The history and evolution of dynamic psychiatry.* New York: Basic Books.

Freud, S. (1918). *Totem and taboo.* Reprint, New York: Vintage Books, 1946.

Freud, S. (1923). *The ego and the id.* Reprint, New York: Norton, 1962.

Freud, S. (1930). *Civilization and its discontents.* Reprint, New York: Norton, 1962.

Geertz, C. (1973). *The interpretation of cultures.* New York: Basic Books.

Greenwald, G. A. (1992). New look 3: Unconscious cognition reclaimed. *American Psychologist, 47,* 766–769.

Gregor, T. (1981). A content analysis of Mehinaku dreams. *Ethos, 9,* 353–390.

Gregor, T. (1985). *Anxious pleasures: The sexual lives of an Amazonian people.* Chicago: University of Chicago Press.

Hallowell, A. I. (1966). The role of dreams in Ojibwa culture. In V. Grunebaum and R. Caillois (Eds.), *The dream and human societies* (pp. 267–292). Berkeley: University of California Press.

Heald, S. (1994). Everyman a hero: Oedipal themes in Gisu circumcision. In S. Heald and A. Deluz (Eds.), *Anthropology and psychoanalysis* (pp. 184–209). New York: Routledge.

Herdt, G. (1987). *The Sambia: Ritual and gender in New Guinea.* New York: Holt, Rinehart & Winston.

Herr, B. (1981). The expressive character of Fijian dream and nightmare experiences. *Ethos, 9,* 331–352.

Hunt, E., & Agnoli, F. (1991). The Whorfian hypothesis: A cognitive psychology perspective. *Psychological Review, 98,* 377–389.

Hutchins, E. (1987). Myth and experience in the Trobriand Islands. In D. Holland & N. Quinn (Eds.), *Cultural models in language and thought* (pp. 269–289). Cambridge: Cambridge University Press.

Jacoby, L. L., Lindsay, D. S., & Toth, J. P. (1992). Unconscious influences revealed: Attention, awareness, and control. *American Psychologist, 47,* 802–809.

Kakar, S. (1982). *Shamans, mystics and doctors: A psychological inquiry into India and its healing traditions.* Boston: Beacon Press.

Kardiner, A. (1939). *The individual and his society.* New York: Columbia University Press.

Kardiner, A. (1945). *The psychological frontiers of society.* New York: Columbia University Press.

Kihlstrom, J. F. (1987). The cognitive unconscious. *Science, 237,* 1445–1452.

Kihlstrom, J. F., Barnhardt, T. M., & Tataryn, D. J. (1992). The psychological unconscious: Found, lost, and regained. *American Psychologist, 47,* 788–791.

Kilborne, B. J. (1981a). Pattern, structure, and style in anthropological studies of dreams. *Ethos, 9,* 165–185.

Kilborne, B. J. (1981b). Moroccan dream interpretation and culturally constituted defense mechanisms. *Ethos, 9,* 291–312.

Kluckhohn, C. (1944). *Navaho witchcraft.* Reprint, Boston: Beacon Press, 1989.

LaBarre, W. (1972). *The ghost dance: The origins of religion.* New York: Dell.

Leach, E. (1970). *Lévi-Strauss.* London: Fontana.

LeVine, R. A. (1966). *Dreams and deeds: Achievement motivation in Nigeria.* Chicago: University of Chicago Press.

Lewicki, P. Hill, T., & Czyzewska, M. (1992). Nonconscious acquisition of information. *American Psychologist, 47,* 796–801.

Lienhardt, G. (1985). Self: Public, private. Some African representations. In M. Carrithers, S. Collins, & S. Lukes (Eds.), *The category of the person: Anthropology, philosophy, history* (pp. 141–155). Cambridge: Cambridge University Press.

Linger, D. (1994). Has culture theory lost its minds? *Ethos, 22,* 284–315.

Loftus, E. F., & Klinger, M. R. (1992). Is the unconscious smart or dumb? *American Psychologist, 47,* 761–765.

Malinowski, B. (1927). *Sex and repression in savage society.* Reprint, Cleveland: Meridian Books, 1969.

Markus, H. R., and Kitayama, S. (1991). Culture and the self: Implications for cognition, emotion, and motivation. *Psychological Review, 98,* 224–253.

Mischel, W., and Mischel, F. (1958). Psychological aspects of spirit possession. *American Anthropologist, 60,* 249–260.

Moscovici, S. (1993). The return of the unconscious. *Social Research, 60,* 39–93.

Obeyesekere, G. (1981). *Medusa's hair: An essay on personal symbols and religious experience.* Chicago: University of Chicago Press.

Obeyesekere, G. (1990). *The work of culture: Symbolic transformations in psychoanalysis and anthropology.* Chicago: University of Chicago Press.

Paul, R. A. (1989). Psychoanalytic anthropology. *Annual review of anthropology, 18,* 177–202.

Quinn, N., & Holland, D. (1987). Culture and cognition. In D. Holland & N. Quinn (Eds.), *Cultural models in language and thought* (pp. 3–40). Cambridge: Cambridge University Press.

Roheim, G. (1941). The psychoanalytic interpretation of culture. Reprint in W. Muensterberger (Ed.), *Man and his culture: Psychoanalytic anthropology after "Totem and Taboo"* (pp. 31–51). New York: Taplinger, 1970.

Rosaldo, M. (1984). Toward an anthropology of self and feeling. In R. Shweder and R. LeVine (Eds.), *Culture theory: Essays on mind, self, and emotion* (pp. 137–157). Cambridge: Cambridge University Press.

Rycroft, C. (1972). *A critical dictionary of psychoanalysis.* Harmondsworth, U.K.: Penguin.

Sapir, E. (1921). *Language.* New York: Harcourt Brace.

Sapir, E. (1928). The unconscious patterning of behavior in society. Reprint, in C. M. Child et al., *The unconscious: A symposium* (pp. 114–142). Freeport, NY: Books for Libraries Press, 1966.

Schwartz, T. (1978). Where is the culture? Personality as the distributive locus of culture. In G. D. Spindler (Ed.), *The making of psychological anthropology* (pp. 419–441). Berkeley: University of California Press.

Shweder, R. (1991). *Thinking through cultures: Expeditions in cultural psychology.* Cambridge: Harvard University Press.

Sobo, E. J. (in press). The Jamaican body's role in emotional experience and sense perception. *Culture, Medicine and Psychiatry.*

Spiro, M. E. (1952). Ghosts, Ifaluk, and teleological functionalism. *American Anthropologist, 54,* 497–503.

Spiro, M. E. (1965). Religious systems as culturally constituted defense mechanisms. Reprint, in B. Kilborne and L. L. Langness (Eds.), *Culture and human nature: Theoretical papers of Melford E. Spiro* (pp. 145–160). Chicago: University of Chicago Press, 1987.

Spiro, M. E. (1982) *Oedipus in the Trobriands.* Chicago: University of Chicago Press.

Spiro, M. E. (1984). Some reflections on cultural determinism and relativism with special reference to emotions and reason. In R. Shweder and R. LeVine (Eds.), *Culture theory: Essays on mind, self, and emotion* (pp. 323–346). Cambridge: Cambridge University Press.

Stocking, G. (1992). Polarity and plurality: Franz Boas as psychological anthropologist. In T. Schwartz, G. M. White, & C. A. Lutz (Eds.), *New directions in psychological anthropology.* (pp. 311–323). Cambridge: Cambridge University Press.

Strauss, C. (1992). Models and motives. In R. G. D'Andrade and C. Strauss (Eds.), *Human motives and cultural models* (pp. 1–20). New York: Cambridge University Press.

Tedlock, B. (1981). Quiche Maya dream interpretation. *Ethos, 9,* 313–330.

Turner, V. (1967). Symbols in Ndembu ritual. In V. Turner, *The forest of symbols: Aspects of Ndembu ritual* (pp. 19–47). Ithaca, NY: Cornell University Press.

Turner, V. W. (1973). Symbols in African ritual. *Science, 179,* 1100–1105.

Vygotsky, L. S. (1978). *Mind in society: The development of higher psychological processes* (M. Cole, V. John-Steiner, S. Scribner, & E. Souberman (Eds.). Cambridge: Harvard University Press.

Wallace, A. F. C. (1958). Dreams and the wishes of the soul: A type of psychoanalytic theory among the seventeenth century Iroquois. *American Anthropologist, 60,* 234–248.

Wallace, A. F. C. (1972). *The death and rebirth of the Seneca.* New York: Vintage Books.

Wedenoja, W. (1989). Mothering and the practice of "Balm" in Jamaica. In C. S. McClain (Ed.), *Women as healers: Cross-cultural perspectives* (pp. 76–97). New Brunswick, NJ: Rutgers University Press.

Wedenoja, W. (1990). Ritual trance and catharsis: A psychobiological and evolutionary perspective. In D. K. Jordan & M. J. Swartz (Eds.), *Personality and the cultural construction of society* (pp. 275–307). Tuscaloosa: University of Alabama Press.

White, L. (1940). The symbol: The origin and basis of human behavior. *Philosophy of Science, 7,* 451–463.

Whiting, J. W. M., Kluckhohn, R., and Anthony, A. (1958). The function of male initiation ceremonies at puberty. In E. Maccoby, T. Newcomb, and E. Hartley (Eds.), *Readings in social psychology* (3rd ed., pp. 359–370). New York: Holt.

Whorf, B. (1941). The relation of habitual thought and behavior to language. In L. Spier (Ed.), *Language, culture and personality* (pp. 75–93). Menasha, WI: Sapir Memorial Publication Fund.

Chapter Eleven

Cultural Conceptions of Duty

Implications for Motivation and Morality

JOAN G. MILLER

The concept of duty carries predominately negative connotations in modern Western cultures, as well as in psychological theories that have arisen largely in modern Western cultural contexts. In this view, duty is associated primarily with constraint and is seen as coming into play in compelling individuals to perform behaviors that they would not be inclined to undertake spontaneously. The ideal is seen as achieved when social constraints have been internalized so that individuals feel that their behavior is freely given rather than undertaken in conformity to social pressures.

The present chapter makes the argument that this view of duty and its implications for psychological functioning need to be seen as culturally specific, with qualitatively distinct views of duty and divergent implications for psychological functioning recognized as existing in cultures maintaining less individualistic views of self. The first section presents a contrast between this modern Western cultural approach and that emphasized in Hindu Indian culture. In the next sections, major psychological theories of motivation and morality are analyzed to highlight respects in which they embody this modern Western cultural viewpoint. Cross-cultural research is presented to demonstrate the need for divergent theories of motivation and morality to account for psychological functioning among Hindu Indians and other cultural populations emphasizing more sociocentric cultural views of self. In conclusion, arguments are made regarding the need to recognize biases in present psychological characterizations of agency. Agency is defined as the carrying out of action under the control of intentional states (Bruner, 1990). Although agency represents a universal, its form may be seen to be patterned, in part, by culturally variable beliefs, desires, and moral commitments maintained by individuals.

Cultural Conceptions of the Self and Social Duty

THE present discussion will focus on global differences in the cultural views of self and of social duty emphasized in European-American culture as compared with Hindu Indian culture. The purpose is to highlight major differences in cultural conceptions that may be expected to impact on psychological aspects of motivation and morality in each cultural population. The contrasts drawn here are at a broad level, linked generally to the individualism/collectivism distinction (e.g., Markus & Kitayama, 1991; Shweder & Bourne, 1982; Triandis, 1989), and do not address the considerable heterogeneity in each cultural viewpoint (e.g., Murray, 1993).

As theorists have noted, the modern Western cultural conceptions found among European-American populations are premised on dualistic assumptions that pit the solitary individual against the collective and that draw a sharp distinction between self/other, nature/culture, and duty/desire (Lutz & White, 1986). Within this cultural perspective, the core self is conceptualized as a source of intentionality and consciousness that exists behind the constrained self that appears in everyday social role performances:

> The basic conception of self in the Western culture can be very briefly outlined thus: in each human being, there obtains an inner core which is separable and different from everything else. In such a culture, when one speaks of finding oneself, one means that one should look inside oneself and peel everything away that surrounds this core. To such a self, even its own actions can appear strange. (Balagangadhara, 1988, p. 100)

It is only this perceived internal self that is identified as the true self and that is regarded as free and agentic:

> An analytic framework that equates "self/individual" with such things as spontaneity, genuine feeling, privacy, uniqueness, constancy, the "inner life" and then opposes these to mask, role, rule or context is a reflection of dichotomies that constitute the modern Western self. (Rosaldo, 1985, p. 146)

This modern Western cultural viewpoint portrays the self not only as separate from but in opposition to the surround. Social duties, other than those associated with preserving individual rights, tend to be conceptualized as artificial:

> Liberalism teaches that there is something natural, fundamental and inescapable about people's right to liberty. Consequently, the duty to respect others' liberties (though derivative) is equally natural and inescapable. But an obligation to work for the benefit of others is seen as artificial rather than natural. (Becker, 1980, p. 39)

In contrast to this modern Western perspective, traditional Hindu Indian conceptions of self are premised on monistic assumptions (Kakar, 1978). No sharp distinction is drawn between the self and the role, much less between material and spiritual nature or between the person and the surround:

> The assumption of the easy, proper separability of action from actor, of code from substance (similar to the assumption of the separability of law from nature, norm from behavior, mind from body, spirit or energy from matter), that pervades both Western philosophy and Western common sense ... is generally absent. (Marriott, 1976, pp. 109-110)

The self is seen as embodied in, and as inseparable from, his/her social actions or, as Balagangadhara argues, "... a distinction is not made between an agent who performs the action and the actions that the agent performs" (Balagangadhara, 1988, p. 102). Agency, then, is seen as originating within, rather than outside role-based action.

Central to this Hindu Indian view of self is the concept of dharma, which denotes simultaneously moral duty, code for conduct, right action, and inherent character (Kakar, 1978; Marriott, 1990; Weightman & Pandey, 1978). It is assumed that dharma inheres in all living things. Acting in accord with dharma not only ensures the smooth functioning of the social and natural order but also represents the means for realizing individual nature. Unlike Western conceptions, which tend to portray persons as naturally autonomous and duty as a restriction on this freedom, Hindu Indian conceptions tend to portray persons as naturally social and duty as congruent with individual nature:

> Traditional India regards duty as emanating from one's nature—one can't help doing it—while the Western idea of duty requires a struggle against oneself, and the idea of "glad concurrence" is far less prominent in Western attitudes to duty than is the image of bitter medicine. (O'Flaherty & Derrett, 1978, p. xix)

Internalization Processes
Self-Determination Theory

The present discussion will examine ways in which the various modern Western cultural assumptions about the self discussed above are reflected in internalization theories of motivation that have been developed within psychology. Suggestions will be made about the need for alternative theories of motivation to account for internalization processes within Hindu Indian cultural populations and other cultural groups emphasizing more social views of the self.

Internalization processes are seen as implicated in all cases in which behavior is undertaken in conformity to social expectations. They describe the mechanisms through which such expectations come to have motivational force for individuals. Theories of internalization, then, are informative regarding ways in which social duties both are integrated by individuals in their conceptions of self and affect individuals' behavioral motivation.

Attention here centers on the self-determination theory of motivation developed by Deci and Ryan (1985, 1990; Ryan, 1991). This model offers one of the most fully elaborated accounts of internalization, has been subject to extensive empirical research, and shares many of its tenets with other related motivational approaches (e.g., Kelman, 1958; Lepper, 1983; Schafer, 1968).

In this view, individual motivation is portrayed as developing in the direction of greater perceived self-determination. Four levels of internalization are distinguished: (1) external regulation, in which the individual is seen as motivated by external authority, fear of punishment, or rule compliance; (2) introjected regulation, in which the individual is seen as motivated by internally controlling imperatives, such as avoidance of guilt or shame or concerns about self-approval and other-approval; (3) identified regulation, in which the individual is seen as valuing or identifying with extrinsic regulations; and (4) integrated regulation, in which the individual is seen as not only identifying with extrinsic regulations but as integrating them into his or her needs, values, and behavioral commitments.

In this view, self-determination is assumed to be characterized by a phenomenological experience of freedom, authenticity, and responsibility:

> When an action is endorsed by its "author," the experience is that of integrity and cohesion—the experience is one of being true to one's self. Authenticity is thus self-determination. (Deci & Ryan, 1990, p. 277)
>
> It is these descriptors—freedom, choice, agency, responsibility and commitment—that capture and define the self in the organismic perspective. (Ryan, 1991, p. 218)

Importantly, maintaining interdependent relationships with others is seen as compatible with self-determination to the extent that individuals are responsive to others' expectations in a way that is fully voluntaristic:

> [O]ne is likely to feel most secure and satisfied in interdependent relationships when one feels autonomously involved and similarly experiences the other as being involved by choice. (Deci & Ryan, 1990, p. 273)

Among the key propositions that follow from self-determination theory are (1) that social environments that are experienced as controlling lead to the development of less-self-determined forms of motivation; and (2) that the most adaptive modes of functioning are associated with perceived self-determined as compared with perceived controlled forms of motivation.

Extensive evidence exists supporting these claims (for reviews see, e.g., Deci & Ryan, 1990; Pittman & Heller, 1987). It has been demonstrated that greater perceived control is associated not only with lesser enjoyment and satisfaction in behavioral activities but also with more negative behavioral outcomes. For example, perceived motivation to be responsive to the needs of others diminishes when helping is undertaken in the presence as contrasted with absence of a reward (Batson, Coke, Jasnoski, & Hanson, 1978; Kunda & Schwartz, 1983), with the quality of helping degraded in the former as contrasted with latter case (Garbarino, 1975). It has also been shown that self-determined reasons for behavior are associated with greater behavioral satisfaction.

A Cultural Perspective

EMPIRICALLY, a limitation of work in this tradition is its neglect of social aspects of motivation. The vast majority of studies conducted to date have focused on behaviors involving individual mastery or play activity rather than on behaviors involving helping or other forms of interpersonal responsiveness. Also, in most of the studies, the controlling nature of behavioral contexts has been varied through the use of impersonal manipulations (e.g., use of rewards, deadlines, surveillance), with few studies undertaken to examine the impact of role expectations or other interpersonal norms on motivation.

Arguably, this neglect of the social aspects of motivation has arisen, at least in part, from the tendency of research in this tradition to be premised on the Western cultural assumption that the social order is fundamentally artificial rather than natural in character. Thus, theorists appear implicitly to have assumed that to observe self-determined modes of motivation, focus should center on behaviors that involve an individual's acting on the world, in play, exploration, or mastery activity, and not an individual's acting to meet social role expectations.

On a conceptual level, the internalization models under consideration may be seen to embody Western cultural assumptions. The emphasis on the individual's experience of a "true" and "authentic" underlying self, for example, reflects the Western cultural tendency to draw a sharp distinction between the self and the surround and between nature and culture. Equally, the assumption that agency is linked to a phenomenological sense of freedom and choice embodies a Western cultural viewpoint that links agency with autonomous individual control of behavior.

To formulate an internalization model that would be more sensitive to Hindu Indian and other relational cultural views of self, theories would need to embody more monistic premises. It cannot be assumed that perceived exogenous sources of motivation are antithetical to perceived endogenous sources of motivation, that is, individuals act from a sense of either duty or desire but not from both simultaneously. Rather, in India for example, it would be expected that acts governed by dharma would be regarded simultaneously as endogenously and exogenously motivated. Such behaviors would be experienced in endogenous terms, in being regarded as expressive of individual nature and giving rise to behavioral satisfaction. Simultaneously, such behaviors would be experienced in exogenous terms, in being perceived as based on an objective order in the universe and as congruent with social expectations.

Alternative predictions follow more from this monistic view of motivation than from self-determination theory. Specifically, it would be expected that among Hindu Indians and other cultural populations maintaining these more monistic views, social expectations that are experienced as controlling may be associated both with behavioral satisfaction and with more adaptive behavioral outcomes.

The limited available cultural research that has addressed these issues provides support for the present predictions. For example, research by Rohner and Pettengill (1985) demonstrates that Korean adolescents associate greater perceived parental control with greater perceived parental warmth. Also, parents who are regarded by their adolescent offspring as stricter tend to be seen as less behaviorally neglecting and indifferent than are more permissive parents. These trends contrast sharply with the negative relationship documented to exist among European-Americans between perceived social control and positive adaptive outcomes. Attributional research that we have conducted also indicates that in contrast to European-Americans, Hindu Indians consider self-determined forms of motivation to be positively related to a perceived sense of obligation (Miller & Bersoff, 1994). We have found that both Americans and Indians regard behavior as controlled more by social expectations when an agent is helping someone in response to reciprocity norms, compared with helping spontaneously. However, whereas Americans judge agents to be less altruistically oriented and to derive less satisfaction in cases involving reciprocal as contrasted with spontaneous helping, Indians judge agents to be equally altruistic and to derive the same levels of satisfaction in the two cases.

In sum, attention to the cultural grounding of views of self and of social duty suggests certain biases in theory and research on internalization. The view of internalization as a process leading to a perceived autonomy from social expectations appears to be grounded in a Western cultural view of self that may not capture the ways that internalization proceeds in various non-Western cultural populations. There also appears to have been culturally based skewing in research undertaken in this tradition, with little attention to motivation in fulfilling role expectations.

Interpersonal Morality
The Morality of Caring

In this section, attention will be directed to ways in which psychological theories of interpersonal morality embody Western cultural views of self and social duty. Interpersonal morality refers to the commitments that individuals feel to be responsive to the needs of family, friends, and others in special relationships. It then bears on the present question of the types of interdependent ties that individuals establish with others and on the extent to which these ties are based on social expectations.

For many years, the domain of morality was identified in psychology exclusively with issues of justice and individual rights (e.g. Kohlberg, 1981; Turiel, 1983). It was assumed that interpersonal relationships involve affective bonds that are egoistic and fleeting in nature and thus provide an unreliable basis for moral commitments.

Perhaps the most influential challenge to this viewpoint has been the morality-of-caring framework developed by Gilligan (1982). As described in Gilligan's model, the morality of caring represents an orientation in which individuals feel a responsibility to care for others in special relationships when they become aware of the others' needs and are able to help. This sense of moral responsibility is seen as based on individuals' developing a connected view of self, in which they consider meeting others' needs as integral to their personal identity (Gilligan, Ward, & Taylor, 1988). Responsibilities of caring are assumed to be enduring in time, far-reaching in scope, and noncontingent on purely egoistic considerations, such as the trivial tastes and preferences of the agent. They are also assumed to be emphasized particularly by females.

Although there has been little empirical support for the claim that the morality of caring is gender-specific (see review by Walker, 1984), there is considerable empirical evidence for its existence. Most of this evidence is based on in-depth interpretive analyses of individuals' conceptions of self and processes of personal decision making (e.g., Gilligan, Ward, & Taylor, 1988; Lyons, 1983).

A striking feature of the morality-of-caring framework is the widespread interest and enthusiasm that it has generated. Beyond its impact on the field of moral development, Gilligan's theory has stimulated the interest of feminist theorists, has been embraced as a cultural critique of psychology, and has informed anthropological research, as well as provided impetus for educational reform. The model has also been well received by the lay public, as evidenced, for example, in the widespread interest in Gilligan's (1982) book, *In a Different Voice: Psychological Theory and Women's Development*.

Gilligan's model has been successful in broadening present conceptions of the content of morality and in sensitizing researchers to possible subgroup diversity in moral orientations. Despite the framework's major challenges to present psychological theories of morality, however, it stays well within Western cultural conceptions of the self. It may be argued that this is one reason why the model has been so widely embraced by modern Western audiences. These audiences may find in Gilligan's theory a view of community that is both familiar and acceptable.

Gilligan's framework is premised on the same types of modern Western dualistic views of the self that are evident in self-determination theory. It is assumed in Gilligan's viewpoint that the true self exists apart from and behind role performances. Embodying Western assumptions, social role expectations are regarded as in tension with this true self and with agency.

From the perspective of Gilligan's theory, a morality that is based on conventional definitions of interpersonal commitments is seen as coercive in its oppression of the self and as flawed in leading to the absence of personal responsibility for conduct. As Gilligan (1982, pp. 67-68) argues:

> The essence of moral decision is the exercise of choice and the willingness to accept responsibility for that choice. To the extent that women perceive themselves as having no choice, they correspondingly excuse themselves from the responsibility that decision entails.

It is also assumed that individuals who base their sense of morality on conventional role expectations lack a viable sense of self. As interviewed by Gilligan, a college senior who bases her morality on role expectations reports experiencing a perceived absence of self:

> "I see myself as an onion, as a block of different layers. The external layers are for people that I don't know that well, the agreeable, the social, and as you go inward, there are more sides for people I know that I show. I am not sure about the innermost, whether there is a core, or whether I have just picked up everything as I was growing up, these different influences." (Gilligan, 1982, pp. 67-68)

In contrast, a fully mature morality of caring is portrayed as one in which commitments to others are balanced against commitments to self and, thus, avoids the pitfalls of an overly selfless stance. Reflecting the same types of assumptions as made in self-determination theory, the most mature form of a morality of caring is portrayed as one in which commitments to others are given in a way that allows for both choice and personal responsibility. Gilligan, for example, portrays one of her adult subjects who has obtained this mature form of caring as no longer acting in conformity to social expectations but, rather, in a voluntaristic and fully agentic way:

> Examining the assumptions underlying the conventions of female self-abnegation and moral self-sacrifice, she rejects these conventions as immoral in their power to hurt.... Care then becomes a universal injunction, a self-chosen ethic, which, freed from its conventional interpretation, leads to a recasting of the dilemma in a way that allows the assumption of responsibility for choice. (Gilligan, 1982, p. 90)

Empirically, there has been limited attention to possible subgroup or cultural variation in the morality of caring, because most studies conducted to date have been based on European-American cultural populations. Also, in cases in which studies have been undertaken with minority cultural populations in the United States or with non-U.S. cultural populations, there has been limited attention to the contrasting cultural assumptions that may be underlying their responses and, thus, that may possibly lead to qualitative differences in their caring orientations (for exceptions, see Stack, 1986).

Conceptually, the morality-of-caring framework may be criticized for its inattention to aspects of culture other than those associated with gender differentiation (Miller, 1994). Whereas it is acknowledged that conceptions of justice are influenced by Western individualistic meanings and practices, caring orientations that develop among modern Western populations are portrayed as developing in a way that it is unaffected by these aspects of the culture.

A program of research that my colleagues and I have undertaken among European-American and Hindu Indian populations highlights the implicit individualistic cultural grounding of the type of interpersonal moral orientation that develops among European-Americans and that is captured, at least in part, in the morality-of-caring framework. The research also demonstrates that a qualitatively distinct approach to interpersonal morality is found among Hindu Indians and possibly among other collectivist cultural populations that reflects the contrasting views of self and associated practices emphasized in these cultures. We have demonstrated, for example, that whereas Americans tend to treat their responsibilities of caring in voluntaristic terms as matters for personal decision making, Indians tend to treat them in more duty-based terms as socially enforceable obligations (Miller & Luthar, 1989; Miller, Bersoff, & Harwood, 1990; Miller & Bersoff, 1992). We have also found that, compared with Indians, Americans tend to view their interpersonal responsibilities as more delimited in scope and as more contingent on self-serving considerations, such as personal tastes and interests (Miller & Bersoff, 1996).

Focus here will briefly center on what we have observed to be the qualitatively distinct approaches to duty emphasized in the two views of interpersonal morality. Consonant with the claims of Gilligan's model, Americans appear to be concerned with balancing commitments to self against commitments to others, and they judge that oppression of the self results if the requirements of the group or of social duties become too great. In contrast, Indians tend to view the inclinations of the self as more naturally congruent with the requirements of the group and to regard the fulfillment of social duties not as a source of oppression of the self but as a means of individual satisfaction.

These cultural differences may be seen, for example, in an investigation that examined Americans' and Indians' conceptions of everyday family responsibilities (Miller & Bersoff, 1995). Asked to generate examples of family behaviors that they considered exemplary, Americans emphasized incidents that involved the expression of affection and psychological support (e.g., a grown daughter's communicating her love for her mother in a note). These types of behaviors were valued as a voluntaristic means that proceeds independently of role expectations of solidifying social bonds and of reassuring others that they can expect social support. In contrast, Indians emphasized incidents that involved selflessness (e.g., a son's resigning from his career as an air force officer in order to settle nearby and to personally look after his elderly parents). The latter types of behaviors were valued for their agentic qualities in demonstrating that individuals are able to master personal strivings that could otherwise lead them to neglect social duties and that they are able to display the accommodation and equanimity necessary to function well as part of a social whole.

Americans' and Indians' contrasting interpretations of the meaning of social obligations may be illustrated in responses given in a follow-up investigation, in which subjects were asked to reason about a subset of the behaviors generated in the first study. Subjects were asked to reason about the following real-life case involving selfless behavior:

> A year after their marriage, a woman's husband was injured in a motorcycle accident and became paralyzed from the waist down. The wife found that many of her expectations for marriage were disappointed. For the rest of his life, her husband would require a lot of care and would be depressed and inactive. But even though the wife felt very unfulfilled by her marriage, she decided not to leave him because she felt that if she did, his life would be even worse.

An Indian subject who judged this type of behavior to be highly desirable focused on the satisfaction that the woman would experience in being responsive to her husband's welfare and fulfilling her duties as a wife:

> She will have the satisfaction of having fulfilled her duty. She helped her husband during difficulty. If difficulties and happiness are both viewed as equal, only then will the family life be smooth.

In contrast, in appraising this behavior as highly undesirable, an American subject focused on the dissatisfaction that she expected the woman would experience in giving insufficient weight to her personal feelings and desires:

> She is acting out of obligation—not other reasons like love. She has a sense of duty, but little satisfaction for her own happiness. (Miller & Bersoff, 1995, p. 275)

In sum, the present evidence implies that the notion of duty and of self assumed in the morality-of-caring framework is culturally specific. It has been seen that despite its communal focus, the morality-of-caring framework is premised on relatively asocial and individualistic assumptions about the self that are grounded in modern Western cultural viewpoints. It has been seen that the type of approach to interpersonal morality found in Hindu India and possibly in other collectivist cultures embodies a culturally based view that not only places greater weight on social duties than does the morality-of-caring framework but treats these duties in more endogenous terms.

Conclusions

THE theory and research discussed in this chapter have highlighted respects in which psychological theories of motivation and morality have been informed by Western cultural premises about the nature of duty. The discussion has also pointed to the need for qualitatively distinct theories to account for forms of motivation and morality that develop in cultures emphasizing individualistic as compared with collectivist meanings and practices. More broadly, the present considerations underscore the need to recognize that agency is expressed in diverse culturally grounded forms rather than in a form that is universal and culture-free.

Many perspectives within psychology treat individual agency as necessarily linked to individualistic cultural systems and as incompatible with collectivist cultural systems. The latter type of system is portrayed as requiring that individuals passively conform to social expectations, with individual agency having little or no place. This type of characterization may be seen, for example, in arguments made by social critics that collectivism invariably oppresses the individual and that it is only individualistic cultural systems that promote individual volition (e.g., Guisinger & Blatt, 1994; Sampson, 1988). It also underlies the resistance shown in cognitive developmental and related viewpoints to treating enculturation processes as a source of patterning of psychological development (Piaget, 1966; Turiel, 1983). Drawing links between "individuality and agency," Nucci (in press) concludes that the "exercise of choice within the personal ... serves as the instantiation of oneself as agent rather than scripted martinet."

The theory and evidence discussed in the present chapter, however, implies that the expression of agency needs to be recognized as culturally variable, with qualitatively distinct forms of agency arising in cultural contexts emphasizing contrasting views of the self. Thus, it was seen, that social duties that are interpreted by European-Americans as oppressing the self are interpreted by Hindu Indians as congruent with the self. Equally, whereas European-Americans tend to regard selfless behavior as indicative of a lack of agency, Hindu Indians view the control over self-serving strivings embodied in such behavior as agentic, although not in an individualistic way.

In conclusion, it may be argued that there is a need to de-parochialize the conceptions of agency in psychological theory. Psychological theories must take into account individual differences in behavior and the processes through which cultural expectations are resisted and transformed (Miller, 1996). With this active view of the agent, however, must also come an active view of the culture as qualitatively impacting on individual motivation.

References

Balagangadhara, S. N. (1988). Comparative anthropology and moral domains: An essay on self-less morality and the moral self. *Cultural Dynamics, 1,* 98–128.

Batson, C. D., Coke, J. S., Jasnoski, M. L., & Hanson, M. (1978). Buying kindness: Effect of an extrinsic incentive for helping on perceived altruism. *Personality and Social Psychology Bulletin, 4,* 86–91.

Becker, L. C. (1980). The obligation to work. *Ethics, 91,* 35–49.

Bruner, J. (1990). *Acts of meaning.* Cambridge: Harvard University Press.

Deci, E. L., & Ryan, R. M. (1985). *Intrinsic motivation and self-determination in human behavior.* New York: Plenum Press.

Deci, E. L., & Ryan, R. M. (1990). A motivational approach to self: Integration in personality. In R. A. Dienstbier (Ed.), *Nebraska Symposium on Motivation,* Vol. 38, *Perspectives on Motivation,* pp. 237–238. Lincoln: University of Nebraska Press.

Garbarino, J. (1975). The impact of anticipated reward upon cross-age tutoring. *Journal of Personality and Social Psychology, 32,* 421–428.

Gilligan, C. (1982). *In a different voice: Psychological theory and women's development* (pp. 183–222). Hillsdale, NJ: Erlbaum.

Gilligan, C., Ward, J. V., & Taylor, J. M. (Eds.). (1988). *Mapping the moral domain: A contribution of women's thinking to psychological theory and education.* Cambridge: Harvard University Press.

Guisinger, S., & Blatt, S. J. (1994). Individuality and relatedness: Evolution of a fundamental debate. *American Psychologist, 49,* 104–111.

Kakar, S. (1978). *The inner world: A psychoanalytic study of childhood and society in India.* Oxford: Oxford University Press.

Kelman, H. C. (1958). Compliance, identification, and internalization: Three processes of opinion change. *Journal of Conflict Resolution, 2,* 51–60.

Kohlberg, L. (1981). *The philosophy of moral development: Moral stages and the idea of justice,* Vol. 1, *Essays on moral development.* New York: Harper & Row.

Kunda, Z., & Schwartz, S. (1983). Undermining intrinsic moral motivation: External reward and self-presentation. *Journal of Social Psychology, 45,* 763–771.

Lepper, M. R. (1983). Social-control processes and the internalization of social values: An attributional perspective. In E. T. Higgins, D. N. Ruble, and W. W. Hartup (Eds.), *Social cognition and social development* (pp. 294–330). New York: Cambridge University Press.

Lutz, C. & White, G. M. (1986). The anthropology of emotions. *Annual Review of Anthropology, 15,* 405–436.

Lyons, N. (1983). Two perspectives: On self, morality and relationships. *Harvard Educational Review, 53,* 125–146.

Markus, H., & Kitayama, S. (1991). Culture and the self: Implications for cognition, emotion and motivation. *Psychological Review, 98,* 224–253.

Marriott, M. (1976). Hindu transactions: Diversity without dualism. In B. Kapferer (Ed.), *Transaction and meaning* (pp. 109–142). Philadelphia: Institute for Study of Human Issues.

Marriott, M. (Ed.) (1990). *India through Hindu categories.* New Delhi: Sage.

Miller, J. G. (1994). Cultural diversity in the morality of caring: Individually oriented versus duty-based interpersonal moral codes. *Cross-cultural Research, 28,* 3–39.

Miller, J. G. (1996). Theoretical issues in cultural psychology. In J. W. Berry, Y. Poortinga, & J. Pandey (Eds.), *Handbook of cross-cultural psychology: Theoretical and methodological perspectives* (rev. ed.), Vol. 1. Boston: Allyn & Bacon.

Miller, J. G., & Bersoff, D. B. (1992). Culture and moral judgment: How are conflicts between justice and interpersonal responsibilities resolved? *Journal of Personality and Social Psychology, 62,* 541–554.

Miller, J. G., & Bersoff, D. M. (1994). Cultural influences on the moral status of reciprocity and the discounting of endogenous motivation. In *Personality and Social Psychology Bulletin, 20.* The self and the collective: Groups within individuals [special issue].

Miller, J. G., & Bersoff, D. M. (1995). Development in the context of everyday family relationships: Culture, interpersonal morality and adaptation. In M. Killen & D. Hart (Eds.), *Morality in everyday life: Developmental perspectives* (pp. 259–282). New York: Cambridge University Press.

Miller, J. G., & Bersoff, D. B. (1996). *Culture and the role of personal affinity and liking in perceptions of interpersonal responsibilities.* New Haven, CT: Yale University.

Miller, J. G., Bersoff, D. M., & Harwood, R. L. (1990). Perceptions of social responsibilities in India and in the United States: Moral imperatives or personal decisions? *Journal of Personality and Social Psychology, 58,* 33–47.

Miller, J. G., & Luthar, S. (1989). Issues of interpersonal responsibility and accountability: A comparison of Indians' and Americans' moral judgments. *Social Cognition, 3,* 237–261.

Murray, D. W. (1993). What is the Western concept of the self? On forgetting David Hume. *Ethos, 21,* 3–23.

Nucci, L. P. (in press). Morality and personal freedom. In E. Reed & E. Turiel (Eds.), *Values and cognition.* Hillsdale, NJ: Erlbaum.

O'Flaherty, W. D., & Derrett, J. D. (1978). Introduction. In W. D. O'Flaherty & J. D. Derrett (Eds.), *The concept of duty in South Asia* (pp. xiii–xix). New Dehli, India: School of Oriental and Asian Studies.

Piaget, J. (1966). Need and significance of cross-cultural studies in genetic psychology. *International Journal of Psychology, 1,* 3–13.

Pittman, T. S., & Heller, J. F. (1987). Social motivation. *Annual Review of Psychology, 38,* 461–489.

Rohner, R. P., & Pettengill, S. M. (1985). Perceived parental acceptance-rejection and parental control among Korean adolescents. *Child Development, 56,* 524–528.

Rosaldo, M. Z. (1985). Toward an anthropology of self and feeling. In R. A. Shweder & R. A. Levine (Eds.), *Culture theory: Essays on mind, self, and emotion* (pp. 137–157). Cambridge: Cambridge University Press.

Ryan, R. M. (1991). The nature of the self in autonomy and relatedness. In J. Strauss and G. R. Goethals (Eds.), *The self: Interdisciplinary approaches* (pp. 208–238). New York: Springer-Verlag.

Sampson, E. E. (1988). The debate on individualism: Indigenous psychologies of the individual and their role in personal and societal functioning. *American Psychologist, 43,* 15–22.

Schafer, R. (1968). *Aspects of internalization.* New York: International Universities Press.

Shweder, R. A., & Bourne, E. J. (1982). Does the concept of the person vary cross-culturally? In A. J. Marsella & G. M. White (Eds.), *Cultural conceptions of mental health and therapy* (pp. 97–137). London: Reidel.

Stack, C. B. (1986). The culture of gender: Women and men of color. *Signs, 11,* 321–324.

Triandis, H. C. (1989). The self and social behavior in differing cultural contexts. *Psychological Review, 96,* 506–520.

Turiel, E. (1983). *The development of social knowledge: Morality and convention.* Cambridge: Cambridge University Press.

Walker, L. J. (1984). Sex differences in the development of moral reasoning: A critical review. *Child Development, 55,* 677–691.

Weightman, S., & Pandey, S. M. (1978). The semantic fields of Dharm and Kartavy in modern Hindi. In W. D. O'Flaherty & J. D. Derrett (Eds.), *The concept of duty in South Asia* (pp. 217–227). India: School of Oriental and African Studies.

Chapter Twelve

Religious Motivation Across Cultures

John F. Schumaker

Religion is an important motivational system that interacts closely with the workings of culture. The definition of *religion* offered by Geertz (1966) makes reference to the cultural motivations that are generated by religion:

> A religion is a system of symbols which acts to establish powerful, pervasive and long-lasting moods and motivations by formulating conceptions of a general order of existence and clothing these conceptions with such an aura of factuality that the moods and motivations seem uniquely realistic. (p. 4)

A more common approach has been to understand religion as the end product of individual motivations that find expression in various cultural religious systems.

Some Sources of Religious Motivation

RELIGION has been understood by many as a response to motivation states operating at the existential level. In this regard, Royce (1973) argued that existential anxiety is the primary motivation underlying religion. Religion then imposes the semblance of order on a chaotic world while also providing "solutions" to such matters as death, meaninglessness, and aloneness. Accordingly, culture is frequently viewed as "the locus of our confrontation with reality" (Bellah, 1970, p. 201). Steeman (1977) observes that human beings are driven by necessity to escape the perception that life leads nowhere. Religion, he adds, is a solution to "the ultimate problem of human life" (p. 315). In a related way, Erich Fromm (1947) wrote about the inevitable dilemma in which hyperaware human beings find themselves as a result of being "thrown" into a world that makes no apparent sense and lacks all apparent meaning. This "thrownness" led Fromm to introduce *the need for transcendence* as one of his so-called existential needs that are part of our human nature. For Fromm, it is this particular need that propels the human being in a predictable way toward religion and related modes of reality transcendence.

De Vos and Sofue (1984) elaborate on religion as an expression of human motivation, while speculating that religion begins with a "panhuman sense of helplessness" (p. 12) and a deep-seated need for nurturance. They summarize their "psychocultural" model of religious motivation by saying that "religious beliefs and practices represent dependency and a need for nurturance and protection, the seeking of affiliation, the assuagement of isolation, a need for harmony versus discord and violence, a need for self-acceptance versus debasement, and a basic need to give meaning to suffering and to seek forms of release from human afflictions" (p. 12). As an example, De Vos and Sofue mention the belief in divine benevolence as a method whereby people are able to achieve deep emotional comfort and a sense of security. In their opinion, the full range of religious beliefs and practices stem from the motivation to enhance the sense of well-being and safety while reducing anxiety and the experience of helplessness.

Dobzhansky (1965) accounts for religion in terms of evolutionary developments that resulted in greatly elevated levels of awareness and self-consciousness, and in particular the emergence of death awareness. Ultimately, this motivates the human being to escape certain unsavory facts of human existence, something that can be accomplished by other-world tenets of group-sanctioned religion. In this view, Schumaker (1990) traces the motivational origin of religion to "the collision of amplified consciousness and reality," (1995, p. 16) that is usually absorbed at the cultural level.

Certain other theories make specific reference to fear and other emotions as the motivational basis of religion. Evans-Pritchard (1965) regarded religious rituals and taboos as cultural mechanisms designed to manage the fears associated with those beliefs. In Freud's (1927) view, fears about the harsh reality of adulthood cause people to seek the psychological comfort of religions, most of which entail an omnipotent "father" who protects and reassures them. Still others have explained the religious motive as an attempt to establish control over natural processes (Frazer, 1925; Harris, 1974). In this way, religion has been likened to a form of magic that can bring positive outcomes through certain ritual practices.

The human motivation toward religion can be understood by additional benefits that are forthcoming from religion. Schumaker (1992a) summarizes some of these, which include religion's capacity to (1) provide a reassuring fatalism that enables people to deal better with pain and suffering; (2) offer solutions to a myriad of situational and emotional conflicts; (3) give a sense of power and effectiveness through association with an all-powerful being; (4) establish self-serving and other-serving moral guidelines that promote social cohesion and reduce self-destructive practices; (5) provide the basis for a clearly focused social identity that satisfies the need for belongingness; and (6) offer a foundation for cathartic ritual. Of course, religion does not always respond effectively or entirely to the motivations that seem to demand religion, but this does not alter the fact that such needs exist.

Some theorists are so impressed by the deeply rooted nature of the religious motive that they have described religion as an "instinct," or at least as a process that can be understood at the brain level. Jastrow (1902) wrote that religion is both innate and instinctive. In fact, in the early part of this century, the instinctual explanation of religion was widely held. In the preface to Cogley's (1968) book *Religion in a Secular Age,* Arnold Toynbee wrote that "religion is one of those distinctively human characteristics that differentiate us from our non-human fellows on this planet" (p. vi). He then made the controversial statement that *every* human being has religion, and that one cannot be human without having religion in *some* form. Without doubt, such a point of view could be supported only if a very broad definition of *religion* was employed.

At the turn of the century, LeBon (1903) argued that religion was an actual instinct. He labeled this the "religious sentiment." Since then, others have been struck by the all-pervasive nature of religion and tempted to think in terms of biological predispositions toward religion. For example, Ostow and Scharfstein (1954) proposed a *need* to believe that is as important as the need for food and drink. Without such a belief, they argued, the human being is unable to function properly and unable to reach its fullest potential. Of course, the idea that "instinct" underlies religious behavior has fallen out of favor. Likewise, it is unpopular to suggest that religion can be explained in part by biological predispositions. Doubt is even cast on suggestions that religion is somehow linked inextricably to human nature or to the conditions of human existence. Few scholars today refer to the inevitability of religion, largely because the world appears more and more to be "secular" in nature. However, before we dismiss altogether the prospect that human beings are motivated *naturally* toward religion, it is worthwhile to consider the *extent* of religion in human life and culture. A cross-cultural analysis of religious belief and involvement can cast considerable light on the topic of religious motivation.

Religious Motivation: Cross-Cultural Comparisons

IN contemporary Western society, it is common to encounter people with an *apparent* absence of religious motivation. But it has been said that this is a historical aberration and that religion was *a total way of life* in premodern culture (Turner, 1985; Schumaker, 1992b; Wijeyewardene, 1986). Unfortunately, there is no way to test such speculation in an empirical way. Even if it is the case that religious motivation was inevitable and strong in premodern times, the question of modern irreligion would still need to be answered.

A study of current cross-cultural variations can aid our understanding of religious motivation. Frequently, such variations (or lack thereof) can answer questions about the motivational origins of specific behaviors (Schumaker, 1996). If little or no variation is found across all cultures, one can conclude that the behavior is motivated at a fairly "deep" level; that is, the behavior is linked either to biological processes or to some fundamental aspect of the human makeup. By contrast, large amounts of cross-cultural variation lead to the opposite conclusion, namely, that individual or sociocultural factors underlie the behavior. In the case of religion, there is general consensus that religion exists in *all* cultures of the world. Giddens (1989) writes that "there are no known societies in which there is no form of religion" (p. 478). Luckmann (1967) refers to religion as a "universal anthropological phenomenon" (p. 34), while cautioning social scientists about understanding religion primarily in relation to today's apparent decline of religion.

The inevitability of religion at the cultural level is also addressed by Byrne (1989). He makes the case that, because religion is one of the few truly universal categories of human behavior, we must also speak of "a natural human religiousness" (p. 206). Byrne describes culture as the principal mediator between religion and human nature. In the view of De Vos and Sofue (1984), such a "human nature" would consist in part of the motives that propel people in the direction of religion. Once again, these include the urge for meaning, a sense of order and security, relief from existential anxiety, and so forth. Geertz (1966) reiterates that there is no human society that lacks religion under the present definition, which again tempts one to comprehend religious motivation as a very "natural" outcome among human beings. However, he goes on to say that it is surely not the case that everyone in all societies is religious according to those same definitions. So let us now turn to the research examining the actual variations in religious motivation across cultures.

Barrett (1982) compared 200 cultures in relation to the percentage of people who were either atheistic or altogether irreligious. In 36 of those cultures, he found no evidence whatsoever of irreligion. That is, no one studied in those cultures could be identified as lacking entirely in religious motivation. In another 87 cultures, less than 1 percent of the population were found to be irreligious. Irreligion rates between 1 percent and 3 percent were found in 33 cultures. Only 22 of the cultures had irreligion rates in excess of 10 percent, and 13 of those had Marxist governments that suppressed religion. Five of the remaining 9 were in Western Europe (France, Sweden, Germany, the Netherlands, Italy). Japan and Hong Kong, which are two of the most Westernized countries in East Asia, also had irreligion rates of 10 percent or more. The two remaining countries were Australia and Uruguay. Although Uruguay seems to stand out as an exception to the "Westernization" explanation of higher rates of irreligion, it is considered the most Westernized and most modern country in South America.

Barrett's findings revealed that except in those countries that remained "entirely" religious, the number of irreligious people has increased since 1900 in all societies. The three religions that have been most resistant to decline are Islam, Buddhism, and Hinduism (Duke & Johnson, 1989). Islam is growing in some parts of the world; for example, it is the fastest-growing religion among Black Americans. However, regardless of all that has been said about the so-called Secular Age, the fact remains that most people in most societies have a certain degree of religious motivation. It may even be more the case that Spiro (1965) is still correct in labeling the human being *homo religiosus*. On this subject, Barrett (1982) concludes generally that despite some religious weakening, religion remains alive and well in the minds of people.

In one of the most sophisticated studies of its kind, Campbell and Curtis (1994) compared religiosity across twenty-two Western countries. The greatest levels of overall religious involvement were found in the United States, Northern Ireland, South Africa, Canada, and Mexico. The lowest overall religious involvement was seen in Europe, most notably Sweden, Denmark, Finland, France, and Iceland. Japan also stood out because of comparatively low religious involvement. Ireland had the highest rate of weekly church attendance (82 percent), followed by Mexico (54 percent), Northern Ireland (52 percent), South Africa (43 percent), and the United

States (43 percent). The lowest rates of weekly church attendance were in Iceland (2 percent), Denmark (3 percent), Finland (3 percent), Norway (5 percent), and Sweden (5 percent). Belief in God was highest in Mexico (97 percent), the United States (95 percent), Ireland (95 percent), Northern Ireland (91 percent), and Canada (90 percent). Lowest rates of belief in God were found in Japan (39 percent), Hungary (44 percent), Sweden (52 percent), Denmark (53 percent), and France (59 percent). The countries with the highest percentages of people who reported "feeling religious" were the United States (81 percent), Italy (80 percent), Mexico (74 percent), Canada (74 percent), South Africa (69 percent), and Belgium (69 percent). The lowest percentages of people who reported "feeling religious" were in Japan (24 percent), Sweden (32 percent), Hungary (42 percent), Norway (43 percent), and France (48 percent).

The Campbell and Curtis (1994) survey shows that a large discrepancy exists across societies in relation to some religious variables. With weekly church attendance, for example, a large difference can be seen between countries like Iceland (2 percent) and Ireland (82 percent). Very importantly, however, this particular variable (which measures the outward social expression of religion) is not necessarily a good predictor of subjective religious *experience*. In fact, a higher percentage of people in Iceland (67 percent) reported "feeling religious" than in Ireland (63 percent). In Denmark, only 3 percent of people attend church weekly, but 56 percent report "feeling religious." In Spain, weekly church attendance is much higher (40 percent), but the rate of "feeling religious" is only slightly higher at 61 percent. With the exception of Japan (and possibly Sweden), the various societies studied by Campbell and Curtis do not vary greatly in terms of the percentage of people who experience themselves as "religious." To some extent, the same is true with regard to belief in God. For instance, 56 percent of Danes believe in God, whereas only 3 percent attend church regularly. In Iceland, 77 percent believe in God, even though only 2 percent are regular church attenders. In Belgium, more than 30 percent attend church regularly, but their percentage of belief in God (76 percent) is actually slightly lower than Iceland's. Also, despite their exceptionally low church attendance, 75 percent of Icelanders believe in life after death. But the Belgians, who are much better church attenders, have a much lower rate (37 percent) of belief in life after death. Such discrepancies show the need to distinguish between objective and subjective measures of religiosity (Levin, Taylor, & Chatters, 1995). Cross-cultural research seems to indicate that objective measures (e.g., church attendance) vary more than subjective measures.

Campbell and Curtis (1994) provide a fifteen-year comparison (1968–1983) of religious belief and involvement for ten Western countries. They conclude that "there has been little change in attitudinal response to religion across the nations" (p. 225). But weekly church attendance showed significant decline in all countries except the United States. In France, the rate of weekly church attendance fell from 25 percent in 1968 to 11 percent in 1983; in Norway, the rate fell from 14 percent to 5 percent. The rate stayed the same at 43 percent in the United States. Great Britain stood out as an exception in the temporal comparison with substantial *increases* in all categories of religious belief from 1968 to 1983. This contrasts with church attendance rates that have been declining steadily since the middle of the nineteenth century (Giddens, 1989).

Because of seven decades of religious suppression, the states of the former Soviet Union are of special interest to those studying religious motivation. Fletcher, Egorov, and Pavlov (1987) reported that 60 percent of people were "religious" in the non-Russian areas of the former Soviet Union. They argued that this represented a renewal of religious life, made possible by a more mature Communist Party that recognized the failure of earlier antireligious campaigns. Greeley (1994) presented an in-depth analysis of the remarkable religious revival taking place in Russia. He cites data indicating that between 1986 and 1991, 20 percent of the population shifted from a rejection of religion to an acceptance of it. One-third of self-admitted atheists have now returned to theism. Greeley's research shows that 48 percent of Russians now identify themselves as "theists." Belief in God is now endorsed by 74 percent of the population, and 75 percent report having "a great deal of confidence in the church." Quite remarkably, as Greeley notes, Russia (along with Poland) leads the rest of the world on this latter variable. With regard to belief in God, Russia has surpassed half of the twenty-two countries surveyed by Campbell and Curtis (1994). Greeley (1994) suggests that not since the early Middle Ages has the world witnessed mass conversion on the scale of Russia today. Greeley mentions still more recent data, showing that religious momentum is continuing to build at a rapid rate in Russia. Data gathered in 1993 show that between 1989 and 1993, the percentage of Russian "unbelievers" dropped from 65 percent to 40 percent. In that same time, the percentage who never go to church fell from 65 percent to 45 percent. Greeley concludes, "It is not too early to say that antireligious Socialism failed completely to crush out the Russian religious heritage" (p. 272).

Greeley (1994) supports his conclusion by offering data from Hungary, which is also undergoing a powerful revival of religion. Only 25 percent of people surveyed in 1986 reported attending church *ever*. But by 1991, that had increased threefold to 75 percent. The same was found for people attending church on a regular basis ("several times a month or more"). Only 6 percent of Hungarians attended church regularly in 1986, but this rose sharply to 19 percent by 1991, an increase that was evenly distributed across age groups.

Now, as Greeley observes, Hungary is on par with New Zealand in terms of regular church attendance. Of course, part of the recent changes in places such as Russia and Hungary are probably due to a greater willingness to admit religious beliefs and to engage openly in religious behavior. The religious revival in East Germany and Slovenia has been slower than in Russia, according to Greeley (1994). Future research will need to determine if religion there is as resilient as in Russia.

Cross-cultural research reveals some sex differences with regard to religious motivation variables. Women in a large percentage of societies are more likely than men to participate in organized religion (Argyle, 1958; Giddens, 1989; Gee & Veevers, 1989). Veevers and Cousineau (1980), for example, reported that 5.65 percent of Canadians had "no religion"; the same was the case for only 3.25 percent of women. Vernon and Caldwell (1972) summarized sixty studies of sex differences in religion and found that with the exception of Mormons and Jews, women were higher than men on the full range of religiosity measures. Moberg (1962) explains the male-female difference in terms of women's traditional role as "culture bearers"; Bibby (1987) blames this difference on women's social inequality and social deprivation. Gee and Veevers (1989) comment on the lack of attention that has been paid to the higher degree of religiosity in women, while calling for more research.

Explaining Cross-Cultural Variations

ONE explanation for the cross-cultural variations observed in religious motivation revolves around the overlapping issues of cultural complexity, differentiation, and "centrality" of culture. Berger (1969) argues that complex urban industrialized societies affect people's consciousness in such a way that traditional religious beliefs are certain to wane. Irreligion on a mass scale was nonexistent prior to the Industrial Revolution (Campbell, 1971). But churches today find it difficult to influence people with their ideological and moral directives because the directives lack applicability and relevance to modern work situations and bureaucratic institutions. In Berger's view, the modern industrial world does not lend itself to a single dominant religion that can achieve an agreed-upon interpretation of reality. As Turner (1985) wrote "[O]ur culture now lacks a center" (p. 264), which makes an *agreed-upon* religion very difficult. The result is that religion has become *subcultural.* Turner sees large numbers of people today turning to religious "surrogates," such as nature, art, and humanity itself.

Berger (1969) describes how individuals today find themselves in a competitive religious marketplace, in a position of selecting a "private" religion that suits their needs. This, according to Berger (1969), reflects a larger process of "individualization" wherein religion becomes a matter of choice and preference. But he adds that "private religiosity cannot any longer fulfill the classical task of religion, that of constructing a common world within which all of social life receives ultimate meaning binding on everybody" (pp. 132-133). Bellah (1970) elaborates the theme of "religious individualism" (p. 16) and explains it in terms of the concept of cultural differentiation. In "undifferentiated" societies, the world, self, and society are united, and usually fused by a single religious system that possesses great explanatory power. However, as a society becomes more differentiated, its institutions (e.g., art, science, religion) become separated from one another. Within a relatively differentiated society, Bellah postulates, more demand is placed on the *individual* with regard to commitment and decision. Not only does religion lose its central role but members find themselves with much more personal responsibility to meet their religious needs. This does not mean that people have less of a need for religion; rather, in the modern age, solutions to religious yearnings are more personal than social. This may create the outward appearance that religious motivation is declining when, in fact, it has become more inward and "private." On this matter, Bellah (1971) prefers the term *civic religion* to describe modern privatized patterns of religiosity, while arguing that religion never disappears. His views correspond to those of Luckmann (1967), who proposed that "invisible religion" fills the void created by the disappearance of conventional organized religion.

Another common explanation for variations in religious motivation across cultures concerns the so-called rationality that has infiltrated some parts of the world, especially the West. Campbell (1971) traces the history of irreligion in some European countries (e.g., France and England) to patterns of intellectual dissent whereby irreligion gained certain respectability within the framework of radical politics. Wilson (1971) observes that "rational organization is a prominent feature in societies that have a culture of unbelief" (p. 267), and concludes that religious belief has lost its centrality in our rational contemporary Western world. This common line of reasoning maintains that science is at odds with religion and that religion eventually succumbs to the "facts" of science. Yet, Bellah (1971) argues convincingly that a completely "literal" world is ultimately unbearable and that people cannot tolerate an unrelenting diet of the rational. They will achieve some type of transcendence, even if it must be accomplished in a "private" fashion. Thus, we are left with the task of identifying religion's new garbs.

Religious Motivation as a Possible Constant

FROM the above discussion, a key question emerges concerning the issue of religious motivation as it seems to vary across cultural settings. That is, does religious motivation remain *constant* despite apparent variations within and across cultures? Phrased differently, is it possible that the motivating forces underlying religion are an inevitable consequence of "human nature" and that these motives seek an outlet regardless of environmental or cultural circumstances? After all, if religion stems from a basic need to find meaning and hope, to combat one's insignificance, and to transcend the limits of empirical reality, then it makes little sense that this need vanishes once organized religion recedes. It seems more likely that the religious motives remain intact, and that the expression of these needs takes other forms (e.g., "civic religion," "invisible religion").

If religion is a universal need, we would expect religion to remain alive in one form or another under conditions of religious suppression. Then, once the suppression was lifted, we would expect religion to rebound quite quickly rather than remain dead. As mentioned earlier, this is exactly what we see in countries like Russia and Hungary. In this regard, Bellah (1970) argues that our definition of religion should be broad enough to include the "idiosyncratic" expressions of "religion" that substitute for conventional religion at certain times. Bocock (1985) describes some of the "civic religion" and "socialist liturgy" that prevailed in the Soviet Union, which compensated in part for religious deprivation. Communism is often described as a political religion. For Machovec (1971), what seems to be an absence of religious belief is actually "other belief." The underlying motives remain essentially the same.

Vernon (1968) casts light on the religious "belief" of supposedly irreligious people. He reports on people who declare that they have "no religion." Only 23 percent of religious "nones," as Vernon calls them, are atheistic, and only 19 percent have no personal God. It seems that a great deal of religion remains, even when "no religion" is indicated.

Again, if religion represents a universal need, we would expect genuine deficits in religion to be filled by something that can mimic the function of religion. Emmons and Sobal (1981) researched the possibility that nonreligious paranormal beliefs (e.g., witches, ghosts, UFOs, ESP, astrology) can serve as functional alternatives to mainstream religion in people who lack traditional religion. As predicted, they found that nonreligious individuals endorsed significantly greater numbers of paranormal beliefs than their religious counterparts. They conclude that increased nonreligious paranormal belief represents an example of "invisible religion" (Luckmann, 1967) that compensates for deficits in conventional organized religion. Bainbridge and Stark (1980a) obtained the same results, once again concluding that nonreligious beliefs tend to compensate for a lack of traditional religion. Bainbridge and Stark (1980b) also tested the hypothesis that cults would be more common in less religious parts of the United States (e.g., the Pacific and mountain states), and less prevalent in the most religious areas (e.g., southern and central states). Their hypothesis was confirmed, providing still more evidence that deficits in mainstream religion find compensation in less "visible" modes of belief and experience.

Stark (1993) provides additional support for the prospect that religious motivation will find alternative expression when it is not obtainable by way of dominant cultural religions. He calculated the number of cult movements per million people in the United States and eighteen European countries. In general, he found that the least religious countries had the greatest number of cult movements. Relatively irreligious Europe had twice as many cult movements as the more religious United States. Iceland, which has an exceptionally low level of religious involvement, had five times the rate of cult movements when compared to the United States. Switzerland had nearly ten times the United States rate, whereas the United Kingdom had seven times the United States rate. Sweden, which was shown earlier to have one of the lowest levels of religiosity in the world, had four times the rate of cult movements in the United States. Stark found the same trend with regard to the growth of the Jehovah's Witness movement, with a faster rate of growth found in Europe than the United States.

Grimmer (1992) summarized the various New Age movements, which he argues can serve as functional equivalents of religion. Support for such a prospect was provided by Greer and Roof (1992), who showed that the highest rates of "private religion" (e.g., New Age movements, men's movements, "12-step programs") were significantly higher in geographical areas characterized by weak conventional religion. Pantic (1987) describes the way in which low levels of organized religion in the former Yugoslavia were followed by an increase in "secular religiosity" involving "religiosity" in sports and politics, as well as the increased "worship" and overvaluing of ideas, persons, institutions, symbols, and events. It was concluded that this secular religiosity serves the same function as religion.

If religious energy shifts *directions,* rather than changing in magnitude, one should see a compensatory process at work in societies experiencing declines in their mainstream religions. Duke and Johnson (1989) analyzed patterns of religious transformation in two hundred societies and found that declining dominant religions are usually replaced by several minority religions; in a small number of societies, a single religion replaced the declining dominant one. They conclude that secularization theory is not supported by these data, and offer an alternative model that views religious transformation as a cyclical process. That is, religion in all viable cultures will revitalize itself following periods of decline.

In light of these and similar findings, secularization theory has been largely abandoned in recent years (Bruce, 1992; Dobbelaere & Voye, 1990; Hervieu-Leger, 1990). Stark (1993) also argues for the need to rethink the notion of "secularization" in light of research showing that people and entire societies remain "religious" despite outward appearances to the contrary. He even states that it is inaccurate to describe the seemingly irreligious Scandinavians as somehow deficient in religious motivation: "Their lack of church attendance does not reflect a lack of *demand* for religion, but merely the lack of motivated and effective *suppliers....* Scandinavians are indifferent to the lazy monopoly state churches that confront them with a subsidized and regulated religious economy, but their level of individual, subjective religiousness remains high" (p. 396). Rather than search for variations in religious motivation at the level of the individual, Stark maintains that it is more fruitful to study variations in the ability of organized religions to respond to the ever-present demand for religion.

Another worthwhile topic for future study concerns the actual cultural conditions that keep religion "visible" as compared with "invisible." For instance, Campbell and Curtis (1994) demonstrate that this phenomenon is not the result of demographic or socioeconomic factors; rather, explanations have centered on national values such as individualism. Lipset (1990) theorizes that individualistic values incline Americans toward *social* participation in many areas, including religious activities. On this subject, Sasaki (1993) reports on research showing that so-called secularization is the result of deteriorating community rather than deteriorating beliefs. Another factor might be the aggressive "marketing" of religion that takes place in the United States (Bibby, 1987).

Wagar (1982) remarks that the new revised model of secularization holds that we can "live without this or that particular variety of religious belief and practice, but not without religion of any kind" (p. 4). That is, secularization does not mean doing without religion but, rather, *transforming* religion and shifting the focus of one's "ultimate concern." In a much different way, Miller (1992) accounts for the unique social expressions of religion in Japan in terms of a "service industry perspective" that views religion as something that is consumed on an "as-needed" basis. Miller (1995) refers to the ultra-pragmatic nature of the Japanese, while showing that their "consumer mentality" leads them to pick and choose elements from different religions, again as they are needed. One effect of this pattern may be to create the false impression of low religious commitment. Additional studies of this nature will illuminate the cultural processes that cause religious motivation to assume different appearances.

Conclusions

RELIGION is one of the most powerful and all-pervasive forms of human motivation. Not only does it exist in all cultures of the world but the majority of people in most cultures display some degree of religious motivation. The small number of exceptions are limited to Western settings and to ones with repressive Marxist regimes. Furthermore, as we see clearly with Russia, religion bounces back once freedom of expression is restored. Even today, half or more of world cultures have little or no evidence of irreligion.

Although religion represents a prominent feature of human life, recent decades have seen a decline in the outward expression of conventional religion. This is true of most but not all cultures. Some religions (e.g., Hinduism, Buddhism, Islam) have been relatively resistant to decline. Declines in a culture's dominant religion tend to be followed by the emergence of other religions, suggesting that cultures attempt to revive themselves in terms of religion. The magnitude of decline in personal modes of religion has been less than the declines in group traditional religion. In this regard, a high percentage of people continue to feel religious or "spiritual," even though they may not have an obvious outlet for those feelings. Research suggests that low levels of traditional religiosity find compensation in "private" religion, or quasi-religious movements and belief systems that mimic religion. Even in the most "irreligious" cultures, the demand for religion remains high. As Stark (1993) noted, the appearance of low religious motivation may actually reflect a lack of motivated "suppliers" of religion. All considered, the recent abandonment of the notion of "secularization" seems to be justified.

A great deal remains to be learned about all facets of religious motivation. But the remarkable resilience of religion seems to speak on behalf of a deep-seated "need" of some sort. This may be tied in an existential way to the human urge to transcend the constraints of this-world reality and to locate sources of meaning, significance, and explanation. Because religion is a cultural universal, it is reasonable to propose that culture inevitably recognizes and responds to this need. One could even raise the possibility that "individual" modes of religion manifest themselves only in cultures that are somehow out of form (see Campbell, 1973; Schumaker, 1995).

The exact extent to which religion ever disappears, or even declines, within a culture is a matter for future investigation. Research studies need to look more closely at potential ways in which people compensate for deficits in traditional religion. It is also important to compare the religious *techniques* that operate within highly religious cultures with ones that have faltering traditional religions. This may cast much-needed new light on the breakdowns in religion that cause people to embark on a course of "private" or "invisible" religion.

References

Argyle, M. (1958). *Religious behavior.* London: Routledge & Kegan Paul.

Bainbridge, W. S., & Stark, R. (1980a). Superstitions: Old and new. *Skeptical Inquirer, 4,* 18–31.

Bainbridge, W. S., & Stark, R. (1980b). Client and audience cults in America. *Sociological Analysis, 41,* 199–214.

Barrett, D. B. (1982). *World Christian encyclopedia.* Nairobi: Oxford University Press.

Bellah, R. N. (1970). *Beyond belief: Essays on religion in a post-traditional world.* New York: Harper & Row.

Bellah, R. N. (1971). The historical background of unbelief. In R. Caporale & A. Grumelli (Eds.), *The culture of unbelief* (pp. 39–52). Berkeley: University of California Press.

Berger, P. L. (1969). *The social reality of religion.* London: Faber & Faber.

Bibby, R. W. (1987). *Fragmented gods: The poverty and potential of religion in Canada.* Toronto: Irwin.

Bocock, R. (1985). Religion in modern Britain. In R. Bocock & K. Thompson (Eds.), *Religion and ideology* (pp. 207–233). Manchester, U.K.: Manchester University Press.

Bruce, S. (1992). *Religion and modernization.* Oxford, U.K.: Clarendon Press.

Burhoe, R. W. (1975). *Genetic, neurophysiological, and other determinants of religious ritual and belief.* Paper presented for The Society for the Scientific Study of Religion. Milwaukee, Wisconsin, October, 1975.

Byrne, P. (1989). *Natural religion and the nature of religion.* London: Routledge.

Campbell, C. (1971). *Toward a sociology of irreligion.* London: Macmillan.

Campbell, C. (1977). Analysing the rejection of religion. *Social Compass, 4,* 339–346.

Campbell, J. (1973). *Myths to live by.* London: Souvenir Press.

Campbell, R. A., & Curtis, J. E. (1994). Religious involvement across societies: Analyses for alternative measures in national surveys. *Journal for the Scientific Study of Religion, 33,* 215–229.

Cogley, J. (1968). *Religion in a secular age.* London: Pall Mall Press.

De Vos, G. A., & Sofue, T. (1984). *Religion and the family in East Asia.* Berkeley: University of California Press.

Dobbelaere, K., & Voye, L. (1990). From pillar to postmodernity: The changing situation of religion in Belgium. *Sociological Analysis, 51,* 1–13.

Dobzhansky, T. (1965). Religion, death, and evolutionary adaptation. In M. E. Spiro (Ed.), *Context and meaning in cultural anthropology* (pp. 61–73). New York: Free Press.

Duke, J. T., & Johnson, B. L. (1989). The stages of religious transformation: A study of 200 nations. *Review of Religious Research, 30,* 209–224.

Emmons, C., & Sobal, J. (1981). Paranormal beliefs: Functional alternatives to mainstream religion. *Review of Religious Research, 22,* 301–312.

Evans-Pritchard, E. E. (1965). *Theories of primitive religion.* New York: Oxford University Press.

Fletcher, W., Egorov, N. A., & Pavlov, P. S. (1987). Soviet believers. *Sotsiologicheskie, 14,* 28–35.

Frazer, J. G. (1925). *The golden bough.* New York: Macmillan.

Freud, S. (1927). The future of an illusion. In J. Strachey (Ed. & Trans.), *The standard edition of the complete works of Sigmund Freud,* Vol. 21. London: Hogarth.

Fromm, E. (1947). *Man for himself: An inquiry into the psychology of ethics.* New York: Holt, Rinehart & Winston.

Gee, E. M., & Veevers, J. E. (1989). Religiously unaffiliated Canadians: Sex, age, and regional variations. *Social Indicators Research, 21,* 611–627.

Geertz, C. (1966). Religion as a cultural system. In M. Banton (Ed.), *Anthropological approaches to the study of religion,* ASA Monographs, Vol. 3. London: Tavistock.

Giddens, A. (1989). *Sociology.* Cambridge: Polity Press.

Greeley, A. (1994). A religious revival in Russia? *Journal for the Scientific Study of Religion, 33,* 253–272.

Greer, B. A., & Roof, W. C. (1992). Desperately seeking Sheila: Locating religious privatism in American society. *Journal for the Scientific Study of Religion, 31,* 346–352.

Grimmer, M. R. (1992). Searching for security in the mystical: The function of paranormal beliefs. *Skeptical Inquirer, 16,* 173–176.

Harris, M. (1974). *Cows, pigs, wars, and witches: The riddles of culture.* New York: Random House.

Hervieu-Leger, D. (1990). Religion and modernity in the French context: For a new approach to secularization. *Sociological Analysis, 51,* 15–25.

Jastrow, M. (1902). *A study of religion.* New York: Scribner.

LeBon, G. (1903). *The crowd.* London: T. Fisher Unwin.

Levin, J. S., Taylor, R. J., & Chatters, L. M. (1995). A multidimensional measure of religious involvement for African Americans. *Sociological Quarterly, 36,* 157–173.

Lipset, S. M. (1990). *Continental divide: The values and institutions of Canada and the United States.* New York: Routledge.

Luckmann, T. (1967). *The invisible religion.* London: Collier Macmillan.

Luckmann, T. (1971). Belief, unbelief, and religion. In R. Caporale & A. Grumelli (Eds.), *The culture of unbelief* (pp. 21–51). Berkeley: University of California Press.

Machovec, M. (1971). Round table discussion. In R. Caporale & A. Grumelli (Eds.), *The culture of unbelief* (pp. 91–105). Berkeley: University of California Press.

Miller, A. S. (1992). Conventional religious behavior in modern Japan: A service industry perspective. *Journal for the Scientific Study of Religion, 31,* 207–214.

Miller, A. S. (1995). A rational choice model of religious behavior in Japan. *Journal for the Scientific Study of Religion, 34,* 234–244.

Moberg, D. O. (1962). *The church as a social institution.* Englewood Cliffs, NJ: Prentice-Hall.

Ostow, M., & Scharfstein, B. A. (1954). *The need to believe.* New York: International Universities Press.

Pantic, D. (1987). Secular religiosity: An empirical inquiry. *Kultura, 78,* 99–121.

Royce, J. R. (1973). The present situation in theoretical psychology. In B. B. Wolman (Ed.), *Handbook of general psychology* (pp. 8–21). Englewood Cliffs, NJ: Prentice-Hall.

Sasaki, M. (1993). Religious factors and general social attitudes among five industrial nations. *Behaviormetrika, 20,* 187–207.

Schumaker, J. F. (1990). *Wings of illusion: The origin, nature, and future of paranormal beliefs.* Amherst, NY: Prometheus.

Schumaker, J. F. (1992a). Introduction to religion and mental health. In J. F. Schumaker (Ed.), *Religion and mental health* (pp. 3–30). New York: Oxford University Press.

Schumaker, J. F. (1992b). The mental health consequences of irreligion. In J.F. Schumaker (Ed.), *Religion and mental health* (pp. 54–69). New York: Oxford University Press.

Schumaker, J. F. (1995). *The corruption of reality: A unified theory of religion, hypnosis, and psychopathology.* Amherst, NY: Prometheus.

Schumaker, J. F. (1996). Psychopathology across cultures: Lessons from the developing world. In S. C. Carr & J. F. Schumaker (Eds.), *Psychology and the developing world* (pp. 180–190). Westport, CT, and London: Praeger.

Spiro, M. E. (1965). Culturally constituted defense mechanisms. In M. E. Spiro (Ed.), *Context and meaning in cultural anthropology.* New York: Free Press.

Stark, R. (1993). Europe's receptivity to new religious movements: Round two. *Journal for the Scientific Study of Religion, 32,* 389–397.

Steeman, T. M. (1977). Atheism as religious crisis phenomenon. *Social Compass, 24,* 311–321.

Turner, J. (1985). *Without God, without creed: The origins of unbelief in America.* Baltimore and London: Johns Hopkins University Press.

Veevers, J. E., & Cousineau, D. F. (1980). The heathen Canadians: Demographic correlates of nonbelief. *Pacific Sociological Review, 23,* 199–216.

Vernon, G. M. (1968). The religious "nones": A neglected category. *Journal for the Scientific Study of Religion, 2,* 219–229.

Vernon, G. M., & Caldwell, J. D. (1972). Males, females, and religion. In G.M. Vernon (Ed.), *Types and dimensions of religion* (pp. 103–132). Salt Lake City: Association for the Study of Religion.

Wagar, W. W. (1982). *The secular mind.* New York: Holmes & Meier.

Wijeyewardene, G. (1986). *Place and emotion in northern Thai ritual behavior.* Bangkok: Pandora.

Wilson, B. (1971). Unbelief as an object of research. In R. Caporale & A. Grumelli (Eds.), *The culture of unbelief* (pp. 247–269). Berkeley: University of California Press.

Wilson, E.O. (1978). *On human nature.* Cambridge: Harvard University Press.

The Biology and Culture Nexus

Chapter Thirteen

Sexual Motivation Across Cultures

DONA LEE DAVIS

motivation in sexual behavior seems, at the same time, to be both obvious and problematic. Procreation and pleasure, and sometimes romance or love are offered across the ethnographic spectrum as reasons or motivations for people or persons to have sexual intercourse. Yet, there have been so few studies of sexual acts and techniques across cultures that a significant preliminary problem lies in the question of how we can know what motivates people, because we do not know what people actually do (Gregersen, 1994). Moreover, our knowledge of non-Western human sexual behavior has been largely limited to relatively mechanical accounts of the who, what, where, and how of sexual activity (Gregor, 1987), not the why (Davis & Whitten, 1987). It is significant that Marshall and Suggs's (1971) now-classic outline of topics essential to sexual ethnography does not mention motivation. Hatfield and Rapson (1996) also note that the murky waters of intention have been ignored in the cross-cultural sex literature, though I would suggest this is less true for the literature on AIDS and fertility control. Wyatt (1993, July 27) questions why those who do cross-cultural survey research ask, "When did you first have intercourse?" instead of "When did you first choose to have intercourse?"

Ethnographers and survey researchers, however, are beginning to recognize that an individual's sexual activities are based in complex sets of motivations, which in turn are based in numerous external or sociocultural as well as internal or biological and psychological factors (Laumann, Gagnon, Michael, & Michaels, 1994).

Another set of issues concerns what we consider to lie in the domain of "human sexuality." In our 1980s review of cross-cultural studies of human sexuality, Richard Whitten and I (Davis & Whitten, 1987, p. 69) focused on "studies of sexual practice that attempt to deal with human sexual arousal, attraction, and customary means of dealing with sexuality." Herdt's (1987) more detailed explication of what lies in the domain of human sexuality includes (1) sexual behavior, as any sexual act; (2) the erotic or erotics, stimuli that arouse sexual desire; and (3) sexual orientation, or habitualized and enduring preference for male or female, type of sex contact (oral/genital), and emotional quality implied (authoritarian, reciprocal, promiscuous). Clearly, any study of sexual motivations must also be pursued in terms of the wider social contexts of symbol and meaning, emotional and expressive spheres, gender and power relations, and culture and history. It should also be noted that what in some Western cultures is defined as sexual may not be seen as sex-related in other cultures.

Studies of sexual motivation across cultures must also take into account variation among individuals and groups of individuals within a culture and over the life cycle. The nature and structure of interpersonal relations, the roles that cultural, psychological, situational, and individual factors can play in the choices or decisions that a person makes, and the meanings that underlie sexual actions and choices should also be featured in any sexual ethnography. Unfortunately, although there have been enlightening attempts to get into the minds of others, or to delineate the emic perspective, the issue of individual agency as it relates to motivation has been largely neglected in contemporary sexual ethnographies. The current trend is to promote studies that feature human agency, individuals as social actors or as active persons negotiating directly and indirectly within the social and symbolic context of their societies. The interdependence of the subjective and objective (Giddens, 1990; Shweder, 1991) have been very difficult to operationalize, given the intimate nature of sexual behavior and ethical issues involved in its study (Gell, 1993).

For this essay, I have selected a wide-ranging sample of the better-known sexual ethnographies, from the past and present, to illustrate the various ways that the issue of motivation has been addressed and thematically developed. The first section deals with the issue of universal but hidden motives in works characterized by biological or psychoanalytic essentialism. A second section looks at studies from the 1970s. These studies feature a more culturally determinist approach to the identification of motivating factors that underlay the different sociocultural patterning of societies characterized as sexually permissive or restrictive. The third group of studies draws from the cultural constructionist approach, which rejects the notion of biological or psychological givens. The ideal in this approach is to focus on subjective meanings as created or constructed through human agency in specific situations in specific societies. In the final section, I take a more politically minded, cultural activist's approach to the topic of sexual motivation by using these themes to critique the cross-cultural appropriateness of diagnostic categories of sexual dysfunctions in contemporary American psychiatric nosology.

Biological Essentialism

FROM the wide perspective of the discipline, a key issue in the anthropological study of human sexuality concerns the nature and relative roles played by culture and biology in the motivation of sexual activity and behavior.

Kinsey (1948, 1953) viewed sexual behavior in terms of physical and biological factors. He portrayed sex as a biological drive, such as thirst or hunger, endogenous to the individual, likening the drive to a form of sexual energy (also called libido) that is hidden and depicted as a kind of inner wellspring. An individual first experiences a buildup in sexual tension or sexual need, and as sexual activity is experienced, the drive is satiated and the need reduced. Kinsey saw sexual behavior in terms of outlets and orgasms, whose frequency might vary but whose meanings were constant across culture and through history. Individual differences in drive (motivation) were recognized but were assumed to result from the underlying biology or psychology of the individual, not from any cultural influences (Irvine, 1990; Laumann et al., 1994).

Sociobiologists like Symons (1979) also privilege biology in their accounts of the evolution of human sexual behavior. It takes the form of hidden (or yet to be discovered) genetic codes governing complex and different patterns of male and female motivations for sexual behavior and mate choice. These are attributed to the evolutionary forces of natural and sexual selection that are said to operate differently on males and females, and result in a number of cultural universals governing sexual behavior. In the case of the male, this would include preference for polygyny, heightened intrasexual competition, and attraction to young women. Feminist critics note that there is hardly any sexual behavior, activity, or preference that has not been attributed to genes and evolution by the sociobiologists (Hatfield & Rapson, 1996).

Psychoanalytic Reductionism

THE second category of studies features the quest for motivations that, although hidden in the unconscious, are universal and can be discovered or revealed by the psychodynamically informed ethnographer. A classic in this genre is Altschuler's (1971) study of the Cayapa, a tribal group in South America. Cayapa men are described as suffering from feelings of sexual inadequacy and lack of sexual motivation. According to Altschuler, further signs of psychosexual crippling lie in the beliefs that the penis is said to think for itself, at least in terms of sex, and that men lack control over the erogenous zones of their body. This low sex drive is combined with a dependency on alcohol, an anxious and suspicious personality, latent homosexuality, and male fear of the sexual forwardness of women; it was traced by Altschuler to traumas experienced in the earliest stages of child development, particularly harsh sphincter training at the same time that nursing is freely permitted. Alternately rejected and overindulged, the Cayapa child is unable to develop a sense of security, personal worth, or control over his or her behaviors. The situation is worse for men than women, because the frustrated oral incorporative needs of men are resolved through drinking and those of the more sexually aggressive women have become displaced from the mouth to the vagina. It is important to note that the motives were "discovered" by Altschuler, but remain hidden to the Cayapa.

Although also psychoanalytically reductionist, Gregor's (1987) more recent and far more comprehensive portrayal of sexuality among the Mehinaku of Brazil more carefully balances Freudian explanations of sexual behaviors against those of the people themselves. Gregor portrays the pattern of sexuality among the Mehinaku as permissive in that extramarital affairs, especially for men, are a common and tolerated occurrence in village life. Men carry on extensive extramarital relations, in the Mehinaku view, because they like sex. Mehinaku men state that their principal motivation for initiating sexual affairs is desire. Sex is likened to eating as a pleasurable activity. The women's motivations for sexual liaisons appear to be more complex. Although they report pleasure from sexual activity, Mehinaku women do not seem to experience orgasm but value the extended social contacts, support, and food they receive during the course of their affairs. Because sexual initiative lies with men, however, Mehinaku women who do not excite male interest have little opportunity to engage in affairs.

The permissive Mehinaku pattern of sex is, however, tempered by men's anxious feelings, which Gregor (1987) depicts in terms of the themes of castration, fear of women's genitals, and the equation of female sexuality with the images of death, sickness, injury, and failure that permeate Mehinaku myths, dreams, and rituals. These notions of danger, Gregor concludes, although hidden from Mehinaku consciousness, are deep-seated and pervasive among the males, and are rooted in the fears and conflicts that psychoanalysis tells us are at the core of our inner selves. In Gregor's analysis, blame falls on *the mother,* who after two to three years of intense, sensual, intimate contact, rejects and traumatizes her child during the process of weaning. However, although masculinity is characterized by a hostile rejection and anxious separation from the female world, men seek to incorporate the female into themselves symbolically. Gregor refers to practices such as the couvade, dressing and body decoration, and rituals whereby the men continue to identify with women. Although these conflicts are exaggerated in the Mehinaku tribal society, Gregor concludes that they characterize males universally.

Although ultimately reductionist, Gregor's (1987) analysis is thoroughly embedded in a wide-ranging description of Mehinaku society. Not only does he describe emic motives, he explores different ways of thinking about sex. Examples would include the discussion of sex as being analogous with eating, the notion that genitals or body parts have motives and adventures of their own, and the nature of the collective excitement and drama that sexual affairs generate in local life. Gregor also goes to great lengths to root Mehinaku sexuality in the context of a tribal, genderized society in which gender or sex crosscuts the totality of local life and determines the use of public space, the organization of religion, and the politics of village life. Sexual relationships define who a person is in relation to kin, tribe, and the natural world.

Cultural Determinism

A MORE cultural, determinist focus dominates Marshall and Suggs's (1971) dated but frequently cited collection of articles on human sexual behavior. In this collection, human agency and individual psychology take a back seat to vaguely defined cultural and biological forces. By looking at sexual behavior and attitudes in a series of societies that run the gamut from extreme sexual inhibition (Messenger's [1971] puritanical, sex-negative Irish) to extreme permissiveness (Marshall's [1971a] sex-positive, licentious Mangaians), the collection is designed to show the power a society can have to pattern sexual behavior in diverse ways. Yet, underlying all this plasticity is a basic, universalizing, biological imperative, described as a basic source of psychological energy or motivation that gives direction to human behavior and that makes all men kin in sharing many of the same interests, lusts, frustrations, loves, sorrows, and joys that are part of human sexuality. It is, nonetheless, culture that channels, expresses, or represses this energy (Gebhard, 1971a, 1971b; Suggs & Marshall, 1971).

The nature of the role of culture in shaping sexual motivations in the Marshall and Suggs (1971) collection is well illustrated by Marshall's study of the Mangaia of Polynesia. For example, Marshall (1971a) describes Mangaian male sexuality in terms not of seeking pleasure but of extremely competitive cultural standards for sexual performance. These he describes as ever-escalating competitions or races for different sexual partners and the ability to prolong intromission during intercourse so that the woman experiences a number of orgasms. What motivates the male is not the intrinsic rewards of being a skilled sex partner as much as a woman's (and his own) good reports of his performance that are passed on to his male peers. Yet these motivations are also embedded in wider cultural forces. According to Marshall (1971b), the ultimate cause lies in the fact that sexual promiscuity enhances the fertility of a population and was adaptive in the South Seas, where human survival was continually threatened by famine, war, disease, and natural disasters. Thus, population pressures are offered as a key factor underlying sexual permissiveness and restrictiveness in all societies. Moreover, Marshall, by comparing similarities in sexual customs among the Marquesans and Mangaians, argues that these ecologically based phenomena are highly conservative and resistant to change. Once established, they have a life of their own.

Sociocultural Constructionism

IN this section we depart from notions of natural, universal givens and from cross-cultural comparisons based in Western conceptual categories to focus on more emically oriented studies of "The Other." In the cultural constructionist view, sexuality exists in terms of subjective meanings created or constructed in a specific society (Gregersen, 1994). Here, the goal is to understand sexual behaviors and sexuality as they are understood in a particular time and place (Herdt, 1987). In these studies we find both more leeway for individual agency in the more microlevel script, network, and choice theories and a wider variety of sexual motives. These include not only procreation and pleasure but also spiritual transcendence, sin, power, weakness, romantic intimacy, recreation, and economic and social gain.

Small-Scale Societies

With its focus on age-graded, ritualized homosexuality as well as marital heterosexuality among the Sambia of New Guinea, Herdt's large body of work (1987, 1991) challenges the reproductive essentialism of biological-drive theories and provides insight to the meaning of cultural variability in the construction of erotic sexuality and gender identity, although much of his analysis is shaped by a psychoanalytic approach. Herdt (1987) asserts that warfare provides the key for understanding Sambian notions of gender and sexuality. Fear of war's breaking out at any time has conditioned an aggressive masculine ethos, where strength is a central theme and where apprehension and anxiety pervade local life. The sexual antagonism that pervades village life stems from the fact that men marry women from hostile hamlets, and from the belief that women (as wives) and their bodily products such as menstrual blood can be polluting to men and sap their strength. Thus, warfare and body beliefs condition the special way men relate to women in terms of opposition, fear, violence, and aloofness from young children. Sambian males are motivated to dominate them both in war and sexual intercourse.

The Sambia, according to Herdt (1987), are a phallocentric culture in that Sambian men value phallicism and male strength and devalue male weakness. Physical or biological strength (*jerungdu*) is the essence of maleness in body, personality, and spirit. It drives men to be the strongest, bravest, and best. Semen is akin to fundamental life force or *jerungdu*. Although in Sambian folk biology female growth and maturity are innate natural processes, adult masculinity and potency must be fostered. It is nurtured during a complex series of male initiation practices that involve the ingestion of semen and separation from the polluting influences of women. Among the Sambia, men must ingest semen, first as young boys from older boys (through fellatio), and later by symbolic substitutes, to achieve and maintain, in the eyes of other men, their masculinity, warrior prowess, and domination of women.

In the Sambian male's life cycle, he is first sexually excited by boys and then by women. Sex with boys is eroticized but is more casual or promiscuous than sex with a wife, which is also highly erotic but more intense and exclusive. Sambian sexuality is thus based on a capacity to experience more than one kind of desire and sexual excitement, upon which culture builds (Herdt, 1991). Herdt (1987) also comments that it is hard for the outsider to imagine the tremendous power of sexual arousal among the Sambia, which is due in part to their normally prudish, intensely shameful attitudes regarding sexuality and intercourse, by the secrecy of involvement in sexual relations, and by the fact that gender antagonism permeates all levels of this society.

Leavitt's (1991) study of sexual antagonism among the Bumbita of Papua New Guinea also addresses the issue of men's domination in sexual relations with their wives. Leavitt's cultural constructionist analysis draws important distinctions between public and private motivations. Although the ideology of male domination is similar to that of the Sambia, as described by Herdt (1987), Leavitt notes that Bumbita ideology is compromised by both the emotional environment and the changing roles of men and women over the duration of a marriage. Any account of how sex is experienced by males and females as social actors must bridge the gap between cultural ideology and individual experience. Bumbita men characterize themselves as having great prowess as seducers of their wives and lovers, but in actuality it is a wife who comes to control sex by refusing to have sex with her husband over the life of the marriage because she does not want the added work of additional child-bearing. The male public evocation of sexual dominance is further compromised in private by the facts, according to Leavitt, that men and women do develop a level of intimacy over the years of marriage in terms of their exchanges of fluids (because from the male point of view semen comes in part from the milk of the mother, it is not for just anyone) and through the trust, fidelity, and mutual care that evolve over the lifetime of the relationship. Leavitt's analysis shows the importance of considering various permutations and combinations of male/female, public/private, and real/ideal motivational agendas for sexual behavior, as well as how motives and interactions can change over the life cycle.

Large-Scale Societies

The cultural constructionist approach can also be applied to the study of large-scale societies, as in Parker's (1991) discussion of Brazilian sexual culture as the product of a complex set of social and historical processes. Parker is especially interested in the distinctions between legitimate forms of sexual activity such as marriage, monogamy, and procreation, and the illegitimate or sinful forms such as adultery, polygamy, prostitution, sodomy, and incest. It is these forbidden forms that provide Brazilians with their radically different frame of reference for organizing and understanding their sexual universe and for constituting their own sense of self within it. In Parker's account of Brazilian sexual motivations, variety is the spice of life and breaking the rules becomes an end in itself. Across this erotic but hidden and private domain of prohibition and transgression, social actors are able to shape and mold the contours of their sexual universe. Sex becomes an object of knowledge and an issue of free personal choice. In Parker's complicated historical and cultural analysis, desire, potency, passion, and pleasure become ends in themselves among Brazilians, and the sensations produced by corporeal pleasure become more important than the object of desire.

Variations on social constructivist theory also figure in studies of Western society. In their survey of sexual practices in the United States, Laumann and associates (1994) reject the view that there is an inevitable negative conflict between the biological nature of humans and the cultures in which they are reared, and thus reject the notion that social factors function solely to inhibit or constrain people's desires. Instead, they argue that social processes play a fundamental role, along with factors originating in the individual, in determining what is perceived as sexual and how sexual fantasies and thoughts are constructed. Laumann and associates also reject the notion of characterizing societies as sexually permissive or restrictive, and advocate bringing script, choice, and network theory to the task of studying culture and sexual motivations. Script theory focuses on how individuals improvise on the basic cultural scenarios; it addresses culture both as an intrapsychic phenomenon and as a system of interpersonal action and interaction. Choice theory explains how the choices people make are shaped by cost-benefit considerations. Network theory is a way of predicting which individuals will get together to have a relationship. Unfortunately, the nature of their survey data does not permit these types of microlevel analysis, and so this consortium of sociologists ends up reducing their scripts and scenarios to three sexual motivational and attitude complexes—reproductive, relational, and recreational—that crosscut the permissive-restrictive continuum in complex multiple ways.

In their cross-cultural discussion of passionate first loves, Hatfield and Rapson (1996) stress the importance of culture as an effecter of cognition, emotions, and motivations related to notions of romance and intimacy. They relate cultural constructions of self to the way in which people across the ethnographic spectrum are predisposed to seek intimacy in various kinds of social relationships. Those with an independent construction of self, like most middle-class Americans, who believe in the inherent separateness of people and whose culture values individuality, uniqueness, and independence, will seek intimacy in a sexual union with a lover. Those, such as the Chinese, who come from a culture that stresses interdependency, conformity, and tending to the needs of others, and that defines self in relation to ancestors and family, will seek intimacy with parents and kin rather than with mates. Hatfield and Rapson state, however, that as all peoples in all cultures move in the direction of more personal freedom (which they see as inevitable), the emotions and motivations Westerners associate with romantic passionate love will become more and more universal.

It should be said that by focusing on the more exotic sexual ethnographies, I have overlooked many of the sexual motivations of Western culture, such as economic gain or security, need to be vulnerable or invulnerable, need to experience commitment, need for physical or psychological unity with another, need to control or be controlled, and the desire to be liked or loved or attractive to others (see Bleier, 1984).

Medical Models

THE role that biological essentialism and drive theory play in sex research has become an issue of considerable contention among cross-cultural and feminist critics, who have questioned the cultural constructions of Western medical models of sexual dysfunction. In particular, the American Psychiatric Association's Diagnostic and Statistical Manual (DSM-IV; American Psychiatric Association, 1994), despite its stated agenda of cultural sensitivity, is criticized for its focus on desire (or lack of desire) and for its dependence on Masters and Johnson's empirically and conceptually flawed model of the Human Sexual Response Cycle (Davis, 1991; Davis & Herdt, 1995; Irvine, 1990; Reiss, 1990; Tiefer, 1995). In DSM-IV, sex continues to be viewed as an innate natural physiological process, and problems in sexual expression are treated as disease. It is assumed that there is a lusty sexuality hidden inside everyone, and the goal of therapy becomes to restore it. Because sex is reduced to its most biological essentials, it is implied that there can be no substantial cultural variation. Although DSM-IV now concedes that sexual performance standards may vary across cultures, the biological basis of the diagnostic model admits no challenge.

Western feminists have taken issue with the DSM and sexual therapy for their male bias (Irvine, 1990; Tiefer, 1995) and for emphasis on the genitals, masturbation, and orgasm, as well as the trivialization of gender inequality and the assumption that personal happiness and even identity depend on sexual expression. A number of studies in a variety of Western cultural settings have shown that although men seek pleasure, conquest, and release of sexual tension in sexual activity, women seek intimacy, romance, and emotional closeness (Hatfield & Rapson, 1996; Tiefer, 1995). The prevalence of desire disorders or lack of sexual motivation among women (it is estimated that 30 to 35 percent of American women may suffer from desire disorders) is not due to low biological drive, argue feminists, but is more related to issues of fear, anger, boredom, lack of time, inequality in relationships, prior sexual assault, low self-esteem, poor body image, lack of self-confidence, and the different consequences for sexual relations for males and females—all products of historical and cultural constructions of gendered sexuality, not biology.

The Western medical view that sex is a fundamental drive, very individualized and central to personality and intimate relationships but separate from reproduction and life, would be unrecognizable to people living in other cultures (Tiefer, 1995). Based on his experience of working in a sex-therapy clinic in Israel, with its multicultural population, Lavee (1991) asserts that the reasons for having sex and the goals of sexual relationships must be viewed as varying across cultures. The view of sex as good and natural and the basis for exchange of pleasure and intimate communication may characterize the Westernized gender-equal view, but this does not hold for peoples who emphasize male dominance and sexual superiority, for example, Muslims from North Africa. There, men are permitted to engage in bodily centered pleasure but female eroticism is denied, unrecognized, or feared. Not pleasure but the obligations of marriage, satisfying a husband's needs, having children, and proofs of loyalty motivate women in these cultures, and women's sexual inadequacies are not considered a problem unless they interfere with the sexuality of men.

Conclusion

CLEARLY, the cross-cultural study of motivation in sexual behavior is made difficult by the lack of consensus on what actually constitutes sex behavior and the ethical problem inherent in any study of human sexuality. But the predominant view of sexual motivation as stemming from a basic biology or innate drives, or the biological essentialist approach that characterizes sociobiology and biomedicine, are extremely limiting. Comparative studies such as those of Marshall and Suggs (1971) demonstrate the important roles that culture can play in the social patterning of sexual behavior, and the works of anthropologists such as Herdt (1987), Parker (1991), and Gregor (1987) have used ethnographic comparison to challenge Western ways of thinking about erotics, emotion, identity, gender, symbol, meaning, and the very nature of sexuality as culture-bound. Although there has been a move away from looking for hidden causes or origins, from what Shweder (1991) decries as the misguided search for a central processing mechanism and what feminists (Tiefer, 1995) criticize as reductionist thinking (whether psychodynamic or biological), issues of individual agency, action, and intention in relationships remain a rarity in the cross-cultural literature on human sexuality.

References

Altschuler, M. (1971). Cayapa personality and sexual motivation. In D. S. Marshall & R. C. Suggs (Eds.), *Human sexual behavior* (pp. 38–58). New York: Basic Books.

American Psychiatric Association. (1994). *DSM-IV.* Washington, DC: American Psychiatric Press.

Bleier, R. (1984). *Science and gender: A critique of biology and its theories on women.* New York: Pergamon Press.

Davis, D. L. (1991). *Cultural sensitivity and the sexual disorders of DSM III-R.* NIMH Conference on Culture and Diagnosis, Pittsburgh.

Davis, D. L., & Herdt, G. (1995). Cultural sensitivity and the sexual disorders of DSM-IV:

Review and assessment. In J. E. Mezzich, A. Kleinman, H. Fabrega, & D. Parron (Eds.), *DSM-IV Sourcebook: Culture and the psychiatric disorders.* Washington, DC: American Psychiatric Press.

Davis, D. L., & Whitten, R. G. (1987). The cross-cultural study of human sexuality. *Annual Review of Anthropology, 16,* 69–98.

Gebhard, P. H. (1971a). Foreword. In D. S. Marshall & R. C. Suggs (Eds.), *Human sexual behavior,* (pp. xi–xiv). New York: Basic Books.

Gebhard, P. H. (1971b). Human sexual behavior. In D. S. Marshall & R. C. Suggs (Eds.), *Human sexual behavior* (pp. 206–217). New York: Basic Books.

Gell, A. F. (1993). Review of Intimate Communications. *Man, 28,* 838–840.

Giddens, A. (1990). *The consequences of modernity.* Stanford: Stanford University Press.

Gregersen, E. (1994). *The world of human sexuality: Behaviors, customs, and beliefs.* New York: Irvington.

Gregor, T. (1987). *Anxious pleasures: The sexual lives of an Amazonian people.* Chicago: University of Chicago Press.

Hatfield, E., & Rapson, R. L. (1996). *Love and sex: Cross-cultural perspectives.* Boston: Allyn & Bacon.

Herdt, G. (1987). *The Sambia: Ritual and gender in New Guinea.* Fort Worth: Harcourt Brace Jovanovich.

Herdt, G. (1991). Representations of homosexuality. *Journal of the History of Human Sexuality, 1,* 603–633.

Irvine, J. M. (1990). *Disorders of desire: Sex and gender in American sexology.* Philadelphia: Temple University Press.

Kinsey, A. C. (1948). *Sexual behavior in the human male.* Philadelphia: Saunders.

Kinsey, A. C. (1953). *Sexual behavior in the human female.* Philadelphia: Saunders.

Laumann, E. O., Gagnon, J. H., Michael, R. T., & Michaels, S. (1994). *The social organization of sexuality.* Chicago: University of Chicago Press.

Lavee, Y. (1991). Western and non-Western human sexuality: Implications for clinical practice. *Journal of Sex and Marital Therapy, 17* (3), 203–213.

Leavitt, S. C. (1991). Sexual ideology and experience in a Papua New Guinea society. *Social Science and Medicine, 8,* 897–907.

Marshall, D. S. (1971a). Sexual behavior in Mangaia. In D. S. Marshall & R. C. Suggs (Eds.), *Human sexual behavior* (pp. 103–162). New York: Basic Books.

Marshall, D. S. (1971b). Anthropological perspectives. In D. S. Marshall & R. C. Suggs (Eds.), *Human sexual behavior* (pp. 218–243). New York: Basic Books.

Marshall, D. S., & Suggs, R. C. (Eds.), (1971). *Human sexual behavior.* New York: Basic Books.

Messenger, J. C. (1971). Sex and repression in an Irish folk community. In D. S. Marshall & R. C. Suggs (Eds.), *Human sexual behavior* (pp. 3–37). New York: Basic Books.

Parker, R. G. (1991). *Bodies, pleasures and passions: Sexual culture in contemporary Brazil.* Boston: Beacon Press.

Reiss, I. (1990). *An end to shame.* Buffalo: Prometheus Press.

Shweder, R. (1991). Cultural psychology: What is it? In R. Shweder (Ed.), *Thinking through cultures* (pp. 73–112). Cambridge: Cambridge University Press.

Suggs, R. C., & Marshall, D. S. (1971). Anthropological perspectives on human sexual behavior. In D. S. Marshall & R. C. Suggs (Eds.), *Human sexual behavior* (pp. 218–244). New York: Basic Books.

Symons, D. (1979). *The world of sexuality.* New York: Oxford University Press.

Tiefer. L. (1995). *Sex is not a natural act.* Boulder, CO: Westview.

Wyatt, G. (1993, July 27). *Sociocultural influences on sexuality.* Invited address, 19th Annual Meeting of the International Academy of Sex Research, Pacific Grove, CA.

Chapter Fourteen

Aggression, Violence, and Culture

JOHN PAUL SCOTT

When I first wrote about the subject of culture and aggression (Scott, 1958), I attempted to develop a multiple-factor theory of aggression, assuming that there were numerous causes of behavior. I attempted to assemble these systematically on the basis of the various biological and social sciences, assuming that each science would uncover different variable factors, which was indeed the case.

My theory was consistent with the then-popular theory of statistical analysis that assumed multiple causation by factors whose effects were additive. Later I realized that this theory was also based on the assumption of one-way causation. I discovered in the course of my research that in the case of social behavior, both of the assumptions may be false. Social behavior always involves at least two individuals who interact with each other, modifying each other's behavior, and eventually producing a relationship that gradually becomes more stable and predictable. The results of behavioral interaction are rarely additive. Consequently, the analysis of social behavior in an individual, or population of individuals, has little meaning unless the relevant social relationships are considered: the natural unit of analysis of social behavior is that of social relationships.

I therefore developed the theory of polysystemic organization involving multiple levels of organization (Scott, 1975). This theory makes it possible to organize the results of different fields of science in a meaningful fashion. From the viewpoint of polysystemic theory, the human species is different from all other animal species in only one respect: the ability to communicate information verbally and to organize it in the same fashion (Pinker, 1995). That is, humans can organize *verbal* systems of organization, which introduces a new variable into social behavior.

Also, from the viewpoint of polysystemic theory, culture is composed of sets of verbal systems of organized information that can be communicated from one individual to another and from one generation to the next. Such cultural systems not only differ between different populations but may differ between subgroups within a population, and even from individual to individual.

Systems of organization at different levels, whether verbal or nonverbal, affect one another, another instance of two-way causation. As Schneirla (1951) pointed out long ago, the concept of levels of organization has major significance. This means that a complete causal analysis of any sort of behavior is an extraordinarily complex process. Most researchers have simplified the task by concentrating on a single aspect of the causes of social interaction. Most of the research on aggression and violence follows this pattern; researchers have usually selected one probable cause that seems to be most important in a given situation. The danger of this technique is that one can easily overemphasize the importance of the factor in question.

Relationships Based on Agonistic Behavior

ONE of the first discoveries of relationships based on agonistic behavior was of the peck order in chickens, first noted by Schjelderup-Ebbe (1922) and later intensively analyzed by the students of W. C. Allee, particularly A. M. Guhl (Guhl & Allee, 1944). If a flock of hens is set up with a regular supply of food and water and confined to an enclosure, each pair of hens will get into a fight over food. One wins and the other loses. In subsequent meetings the contest is repeated, and one of the pair becomes a consistent loser. The result is a threat-avoidance relationship that is highly predictable and shows a minimum amount of actual fighting. This was the first observational and experimental evidence that one sort of social organization was based on agonistic behavior. Further, if one hen in the flock were removed and replaced by a stranger, the amount of fighting increased, then gradually decreased as its dominance position was established.

Our research with the development of agonistic behavior in dogs (Scott & Fuller, 1965) showed that conflict between litter-mate puppies began about five weeks of age and continued at least until adulthood at one year, the time when our study ceased. The chief instigator of the early conflicts was a single piece of food (a raw bone in this case). When the results were analyzed by the sex of the paired contestants, it turned out that size was the major determinant of the outcome of male-male contests. In male-female pairs, males won over females in the great majority of cases (males are larger than females on the average, and continue to grow several months longer). But in female-female pairs, dominance was established by vocal and gestural threats, without any actual conflict.

Mothers establish dominance over their puppies in the same nonviolent fashion. Thus, every mother and her puppies constitute a subsociety organized on agonistic behavior, but one in which harmful violence is minimized. The same sort of organization ought to exist in wild wolf packs, the ancestors of domestic dogs. Ginsburg (1987) found much the same sort of organization in his captive wolf packs except that a more complex organization resulted from the fact that a wolf pack includes adults of both sexes.

Studies of the social behavior of wolves have been done under two conditions. One is in the wild, where human interference can vary from minimal, as in Adolph Murie's (1944) study of the wolves of Mt. McKinley, where they were protected in a national park, to areas where the wolves have contact with human agricultural activities, as in Mech's (1977) studies of the wolves of Minnesota. A second environment is a zoo or wild animal park, where captive wolf packs are confined by fences and usually are fed artificially. The social behavior of several of these captive packs is described in Frank's (1987) *Man and Wolf*.

Here, I shall summarize what has been discovered about wolf social organization based on agonistic behavior. Wolves occupy the ecological niche of cooperative pack hunters. Their most important prey are large herbivorous herd animals, but they will eat anything that seems edible: insects, rodents, birds, and on up to the large mammals. Their chief hunting weapons are their powerful jaws and large teeth. It is obvious that these same weapons can be employed against their own species in social conflict, but this is normally organized in dominance-subordination relationships that minimize harmful conflict.

A wolf pack consists of adults of both sexes plus immatures ranging from infants to young adults up to two years of age, the normal age of sexual maturity in wolves. Wolves are territorial and defend their borders against intruders from other packs. They regularly patrol their boundaries and deposit urine and feces, "scent marking," which warns any intruding strange wolf that the area is occupied. Near the center of the territory is a den area, where in the breeding season a single female may raise her litter. The hunting pack will usually bring back pieces of bone and meat and bury these near the den, to be retrieved by either adults or young wolves after they emerge from the den. As the young wolves grow up, the litter mates will develop dominance relations among one another. The young are always subordinate to the adults. These relationships have been studied in great detail in captive packs (Schotte & Ginsburg, 1987).

The adults also have a dominance order. As with dogs, there is a tendency for males to dominate females, but there may be exceptions. All the females have dominance relationships with one another, as do the males. One result of this organization is population control. The most dominant female will attempt to keep subordinate females from mating, so that usually only one litter is born in a pack in a single year. Similarly, the most dominant male will attempt to prevent all subordinate males from mating.

One possible organization is a male that dominates all other wolves—the so-called leader, although he never actually leads any group activity. This is not the only form of organization; females have achieved the top ranking in some captive packs, with all males subordinate to them.

Actual fighting and serious injuries or deaths are very rare among wild wolf populations. One of the few that has been described resulted from overpopulation following a year when deer, the major prey animals, were numerous (Mech, 1977). In this case, hungry and semistarving wolves began to invade the territories of their neighbors and were attacked by them, causing serious injuries and a few deaths.

The wolf territories in Minnesota are limited by no geographical barriers. Territories can be extended indefinitely into unoccupied areas. The situation on Isle Royale is different, and there have never been more than three packs on the island at the same time. Peterson (1995) reported that a yearling female from the Middle pack strayed into the East pack's territory and was attacked and killed. Discounting occasional fatalities, wolf packs present a case where social organization based on conflict leads to a minimal expression of harmful violence.

Similar studies of social organization have been done on many species of birds and mammals, including primates, humans' closest biological relatives. In every case, each species has a particular pattern of social organization, presumably produced by its evolutionary history and hence by a combination of genes unique to the species. Although vocalization may be an important part of social organization, as for example in bird songs, no nonhuman species has evolved the capacity for verbal communication and hence the capacity to produce verbally organized cultures and social organization based on them.

Ginsburg (1987) observed that wolf packs have a nonverbal culture consisting of habitual patterns of social interaction that are characteristic of a given pack and are passed along from generation to generation through learning. Similar variations are seen among bird territories and other sorts of social organization developed by mammalian species.

Human Social Organization

THE studies of nonverbal social organization in various animal species bring up the question: Is there any possibility that humans have special nonverbal capacities for social organization that would interact with and limit the verbal-cultural kind of organization? Freud was one of the first to point out that there was what he called unconscious learning and reasoning that might conflict with conscious or verbal thinking, but he was not thinking about social organization per se.

There are several ways to approach this problem. One is to look at the basic physical and anatomical characteristics of humans. A second is to deduce what we can from the fossils and artifacts of prehistoric man. A third is to examine the characteristics of surviving human societies that did not have a written language in the past, the so-called tribal societies.

Most authors now agree that the primitive human society was a group of twenty-five to fifty individuals, including both sexes and all ages from birth to old age. Like us, our ancestors were probably slow developers and relatively long-lived. Above all they were tool users, and it is this last capacity that permitted them to leave their ancestral home in the dry places of semitropical Africa to penetrate every part of the world, in all climates from arctic to tropical, and most ecological habitats, even including deserts. Other than this, there is very little that we can deduce from the bones and artifacts left by our prehistoric ancestors. For evidence on social behavior and organization, we must examine the behavior of our contemporaries. One kind of social behavior that humans develop to a strong degree is that of comfort seeking or shelter seeking. More than any other species we have also become shelter builders, digging caves, building houses, and erecting enormous buildings.

Among other sorts of social behavior, humans have carried sexual behavior to an extreme degree, using it not only for reproduction but also as a sort of social glue that keeps individuals and groups together—that is, a cohesive function. Still another human characteristic is the extension of care-giving behavior to persons who may be only distantly related biologically and also to those who are not biologically related except in the sense of being human. But this behavior is commonly extended even further, to plants and nonhuman animal species, which brings us back to the dog, an animal that has become a stable and important part of human social organization. In respect to aggression and violence, dogs can be used to attack strangers and even for military activities. On the reverse side, a dog, and especially a puppy, can be helpful in establishing friendly relationships between strangers.

Still another sort of nonverbal capacity that humans share with other social animals is that of cooperative behavior. This is what I have called allelomimetic behavior, defined as doing what one or more other individuals do with some degree of mutual imitation. Humans obviously enjoy working in gangs and playing on teams.

We can therefore conclude that there are indeed nonverbal bases for human social behavior and organization. Further, each of these must have motivational-emotional complexes associated with them. Extensive physiological research has been done on some of these, particularly sexual motivation, but the story is far from complete on the others. Why do people like to care for others, and why do we enjoy group activities so much? An obvious answer is evolution, but evolution must work through physiology.

Motivational Bases of Human Violence

It is sometimes argued that violence is a part of human nature and hence that it is impossible to eradicate it. This notion is based on insufficient genetic knowledge. Behavior does not exist in the genes. Like any other characteristic, it must be developed under the influence of a great variety of environmental and experiential processes. What we can say is that humans have genetic capacities to develop a wide variety of behaviors, and that genetic variation among individuals may affect these capacities to some degree. Thus, it is probably easier to teach a little boy to fight than to produce the same effect on a little girl. But these are average differences, not absolute ones.

A peculiarly human problem is that people can invent and use tools for purposes of violence, the extreme example so far being that of the atomic bomb. Humans have long used primitive weapons such as knives, bows and arrows, and spears to attack one another. In any human society, the control of destructive tools of violence is a perpetual problem. One of the obvious bases of the problem is that if some people possess tools for violence, they can always use them for destructive purposes. This dilemma is particularly serious in the case of warfare. A society that has armies, navies, or an air force can always attack and overcome one not so similarly armed. But the possession of these weapons does not necessarily produce their use. Historically, nations have shown that they can either live in peace or in a state of perpetual warfare.

Animal research provides an important answer to the question of whether or not violence occurs in a given society. Gottier (1968), working with a small aquarium fish known as the "Jack Dempsey" because of its tendency to fight, showed that these fish also could develop stable social organization based on dominance-subordination relationships. Under these conditions violence is reduced to a minimum. Following Guhl's lead (Guhl & Allee, 1944), Gottier experimentally demonstrated that if the school of fish was disorganized by removing a member and replacing it with a stranger, the amount of fighting was greatly increased. Subsequently, this phenomenon has been extended to many other species including humans, and has led to an important general principle. Briefly stated, *social disorganization is a major cause of destructive agonistic behavior.* A corollary is that *increasing social organization can be a major method of reducing harmful and destructive violent behavior.*

In the case of humans, it follows that the way to increase social organization, which is so largely based on culture, is to bring about cultural change. Irrespective of conscious effort, cultural evolution takes place spontaneously from one generation to the next, depending on the sort of verbal information that is passed along (Scott & Scott, 1971). This process has been institutionalized in the form of educational systems. It follows that educators and the systems in which they operate play a key role in the control of aggression and the establishment of peaceful behavior.

One of the results of educational systems combined with other social systems, especially economic ones, is to greatly lower the rate of homicide. The rates in most modern industrialized societies are for the most part less than two per 100,000; that of the United States is the highest, nearly five times as much. The rates in nonindustrialized societies, which are rapidly disappearing in the modern world, are much higher, varying upward to over 700 (Kuschel, 1989). Homicide rates can vary within a larger culture. As Paddock (1975) found, two Mexican villages only a few miles apart were markedly different in rates of violence. As far as he could tell, the main cause of the difference was differing cultural traditions passed along from one generation to the next. In the United States, homicide rates vary from state to state; rates in the southern states are uniformly higher than those in the northern ones. The only exceptions are rates for cities like Chicago and Detroit, into which large numbers of southern workers have migrated seeking better employment situations. This pattern may change as northerners in recent years have migrated south, also seeking employment.

We can conclude that cultural information is a major cause of peaceful or violent behavior. If we want to reduce the rate of violence, it is necessary to bring about desirable cultural change (Scott & Scott, 1971).

Although cultural evolution is much more rapid than biological evolution, it is still not instantaneous and may require long periods of time. In past historical times, persons who wished to bring about needed social change worked chiefly within religious institutions. The early Christians, for example, attempted to set up a new religious institution, one of whose major principles was peaceful behavior. The same early Christians in the Roman Empire struggled to replace political institutions based on warfare. Eventually, they were at least partially successful. But the peaceful nature of modern industrial societies is not entirely brought about by religious institutions; the central institutions of these societies are economic ones.

Modern economic institutions require that their members regularly work in some form of peaceful and productive activity, for which each worker is paid. The psychological aspect of this activity is rewarding peaceful behavior, which should bring about strong habits of being peaceful.

Still another institution whose purpose is to discourage violent behavior is the political one, which sets up rules for peaceful and cooperative behavior but attempts to maintain these by force and the threat of punishment. In a modern industrial society, the deviant individuals are usually the result of social disorganization of the more positive institutions, resulting in broken families, lack of education, and unemployment. The forceful methods of political institutions are relatively ineffective remedies for the disorganization of other institutions.

It should not be assumed, moreover, that cultural disorganization is the sole cause of violent behavior. In almost all species of mammals that have been studied (the hamster being an exception) males exhibit a larger amount of overt violence than females. Humans are no exception; rates of female violence are much lower than those in males. This is not entirely a matter of genetics, because most human cultures prescribe male and female social roles that differ with respect to violence. In the light of modern anthropology, the warlike Amazons turned out to be a myth, although as Margaret Mead found years ago in a study of tribal societies, the prescribed male and female social roles may vary widely. Genetics does have some effect, however, in modifying the differences between the sexes and producing variation among individuals within the sexes.

Conclusions

IN the process of cultural change, which may be also called cultural evolution, scientific research plays a role somewhat analogous to gene mutation in biological evolution. That is, research provides a new store of information that may or may not be applied to the problem of desirable cultural change. As I see it, the central problem of research in this area is how to bring about cultural change toward social organization that will minimize violent behavior.

A subproblem is the often observed fact that people react negatively to certain forms of social change. The Plains Indian tribes of North America, for example, welcomed the use of the horse, which was useful in hunting buffalo, but have strongly resisted changes in language, social behavior, and the like. Among the descendants of European immigrants to North America, there are many who strongly resist the sort of cultural change that reduces individual violence. Embodied in their culture is the ideal that violence is a good thing.

The problems involved are not simple ones, and their solution will require research in a large number of social and biological sciences. Furthermore, there may be more than one solution possible. My conclusion is that one of our most urgent problems is how to get people to use the scientific information that is now available. We have the information to create a much more peaceful world, but it is not being effectively used.

References

Frank, H. (Ed.). (1987). *Man and wolf: Advances, issues and problems in captive wolf research.* Dordrecht, The Netherlands: W. Junk.

Ginsburg, B. E. (1987). The wolf pack as a socio-genetic unit. In H. Frank (Ed.), *Man and wolf: Advances, issues and problems in captive wolf research* (pp. 401–413). Dordrecht, The Netherlands: W. Junk.

Gottier, R. F. (1968). *The effects of social disorganization in "Cichlosoma biocellatum."* Ph.D. dissertation, Bowling Green State University, OH.

Guhl, A. M., & Allee, W. C. (1944). Some measurable effects of social disorganization in flocks of hens. *Physiological Zoology, 17,* 320–347.

Kuschel, R. (1989). Honor above all: Generations of blood feuds in Bellona Island. In Proceedings of the 5th European Conference of the International Society for Research on Aggression, Szombathely, Hungary.

Mech, L. D. (1977). Productivity, mortality, and population trends of wolves in Northeastern Minnesota. *Journal of Mammalogy, 58,* 559–574.

Murie, A. (1944). *The wolves of Mount McKinley: Fauna of the national parks,* Series 5. Washington, DC: Government Printing Office.

Paddock, I. (1975). Studies on antiviolent and "normal" communities. *Aggressive Behavior, 1,* 217–233.

Peterson, R. O. (1995). *Ecological studies of wolves on Isle Royale: Annual Report, 1994–95,* Houghton, MI.: Isle Royale Natural History Association.

Pinker, S. (1995). The language instinct. *General Psychologist, 31,* 63–65.

Schjelderup-Ebbe, T. (1922). Beitrage zur Sozial-Psychologie des Haushuhns. *Zeit. Psychologie, 88,* 225-252.

Schneirla, T. C. (1951). The "levels" concept in the study of social organization in animals. In J. H. Rohrer & M. N. Sherif (Eds.), *Social psychology at the crossroads.* New York: Harper & Brothers.

Schotte, C. S., & Ginsburg, B. E. (1987). Development of social organization and mating in a captive wolf pack. In H. Frank (Ed.), *Man and wolf: Advances, issues and problems in captive wolf research* (pp. 349–374). Dordrecht, The Netherlands: W. Junk.

Scott, J. P. (1958). *Aggression.* Chicago: University of Chicago Press.

Scott, J. P. (1975). *Aggression* (2nd ed.). Chicago: University of Chicago Press.

Scott, J. P., & Fuller, J. L. (1965). *Genetics and the social behavior of the dog.* Chicago: University of Chicago Press.

Scott. J. P., & Scott, S. F. (Eds.) (1971). *Social control and social change.* Chicago: University of Chicago Press.

Index